The World Trade System

Some Enquiries into its
Spatial Structure

BELL'S ADVANCED ECONOMIC GEOGRAPHIES

General Editor
PROFESSOR R. O. BUCHANAN
M.A.(N.Z.), B.Sc.(Econ.), Ph.D.(London)
Professor Emeritus, University of London

A. Systematic Studies

GEOGRAPHY AND ECONOMICS
Michael Chisholm, M.A.
AGRICULTURAL GEOGRAPHY
Leslie Symons, B.Sc.(Econ.), Ph.D.
REGIONAL ANALYSIS AND ECONOMIC GEOGRAPHY
John N. H. Britton, M.A., Ph.D.
THE FISHERIES OF EUROPE: AN ECONOMIC GEOGRAPHY
James R. Coull, M.A., Ph.D.
A GEOGRAPHY OF TRADE AND DEVELOPMENT IN MALAYA
P. P. Courtenay, B.A., Ph.D.
R. O. BUCHANAN AND ECONOMIC GEOGRAPHY
(Ed.) M. J. Wise, M.C., B.A., Ph.D. & E. M. Rawstron, M.A.
THE WORLD TRADE SYSTEM
SOME ENQUIRIES INTO ITS SPATIAL STRUCTURE
R. J. Johnston, M.A., Ph.D.

B. Regional Studies

AN ECONOMIC GEOGRAPHY OF EAST AFRICA
A. M. O'Connor, B.A., Ph.D.
AN ECONOMIC GEOGRAPHY OF WEST AFRICA
H. P. White, M.A. & M. B. Gleave, M.A.
AN ECONOMIC GEOGRAPHY OF ROMANIA
David Turnock, M.A., Ph.D.
YUGOSLAVIA: PATTERNS OF ECONOMIC ACTIVITY
F. E. Ian Hamilton, B.Sc.(Econ.), Ph.D.
RUSSIAN AGRICULTURE: A GEOGRAPHIC SURVEY
Leslie Symons, B.Sc.(Econ.), Ph.D.
RUSSIAN TRANSPORT
(Ed.) Leslie Symons, B.Sc.(Econ.), Ph.D. & Colin White, B.A.(Cantab.)
AN AGRICULTURAL GEOGRAPHY OF GREAT BRITAIN
J. T. Coppock, M.A., Ph.D.
AN HISTORICAL INTRODUCTION TO THE ECONOMIC GEOGRAPHY
OF GREAT BRITAIN
Wilfred Smith, M.A.
THE BRITISH IRON & STEEL SHEET INDUSTRY SINCE 1840
Kenneth Warren, M.A., Ph.D.
A GEOGRAPHY OF BRAZILIAN DEVELOPMENT
Janet D. Henshall, M.A., M.Sc., Ph.D. & R. P. Momsen Jr, A.B., M.A., Ph.D.

The World Trade System

Some Enquiries into its Spatial Structure

R. J. JOHNSTON, M.A., Ph.D.

Professor of Geography, University of Sheffield

London

G. BELL & SONS LTD

1976

India
   Orient Longman Ltd, Calcutta, Bombay, Madras and New Delhi
Canada
   Clarke, Irwin & Co. Ltd, Toronto
Australia
   Edward Arnold (Australia) Pty Ltd, Port Melbourne, Vic.
New Zealand
   Book Reps (New Zealand) Ltd, 46 Lake Road, Northcote,
   Auckland
East Africa
   J. E. Budds, P.O. Box 44536, Nairobi
West Africa
   Thos. Nelson (Nigeria) Ltd, P.O. Box 336, Apapa, Lagos
South and Central Africa
   Book Promotions (Pty) Ltd, 311 Sanlam Centre, Main Road,
   Wynberg, Cape Province

ISBN 0 7135 1935 5

*Printed in Great Britain by
The Camelot Press Ltd,
London and Southampton*

TO MY PARENTS

Preface

The origins of this book, by an author most of whose earlier research has been in urban, and especially intra-urban, studies, require some explanation. The work reported here developed as the intersection of two main strands. In the first, there was a perceived need to try to look at a space-economy as a whole. The notion of an integrated spatial system, comprising interacting component places, has become an important one in economic geography and regional science. In trying to piece together such a system at the national scale, however, an immediate problem is almost always an absence of data, particularly for the flows of goods and services, and we have, in fact, no complete descriptions of a space-economy in operation[1]. The world trade system offered a wealth of data (a superfluity, in fact, something which became apparent as the work progressed) and it seemed worth while to take these data and try to define the system in operation.

The first strand, therefore, represents a continuing interest in the handling of large data matrices and the teasing out of their salient features. Indeed, much of the initial empirical work on this project involved experiment with various methods of data handling, with particular reference to factor analytic approaches to matrix simplification and the measurement and interpretation of the distance variable in regression analyses based on the 'gravity model'[2]. Such experiment is far from ended, so the analyses reported here merely represent a stopping-place in the development of methods of portraying a complex pattern in summary form.

A continuing problem in much human geography is the

difficulty of handling the expanding 'data box'. As more and more data are collected and made available, more frequently in machine-readable form, so the researcher is increasingly swamped by interpretable information. He is presented with a choice of increasing specialisation or increasing generalisation: either he can choose to focus on a particular sector within the data box, or he can elect to look at the whole. The latter course involves many pitfalls. It can be argued that analysts have always operated at their limits in terms of the amount of information that they can assimilate and interpret, so that as their data box becomes larger, so they must abstract higher-level generalisations[3]. Nevertheless, this course has been followed here, in an attempt to sketch the major features of the world trade system as a space-economy. The emphasis is thus on the general rather than on particular trade flows; the aim is to portray the salient elements of a complex system.

Data analysis is, to many, an enjoyable, if sometimes tedious, task. It can all too easily become an end in itself, and can result in a sterile exercise with numbers. There has been mounting criticism of such work within geography in the last few years, arguing that the so-called 'quantitative revolution' has in fact provided few real insights into the nature of world problems and their potential solution[4]. This concern forms the second strand which led into the present work. It arose originally from continuing study of the growing problems of inequalities of regional development in New Zealand, and the relevance of the spatial approach in human geography to their analysis and solution[5]. It developed in the present study with the series of reflections on the analytical results, which are presented in the final chapter.

Many people have assisted in the work undertaken for this book. The initial conception, much of the data analysis and all of the writing occurred while I was on the staff of the Department of Geography at the University of Canterbury, Christchurch, New Zealand. I am grateful to Professor Barry Johnston, the head of that department, for his sympathetic attitude to my research activities; to those colleagues who assisted me in the data manipulation — notably Doug

Johnston, who was always so tolerant with my programming troubles — and Alan Wilkinson, without whose successful splicing of ALGOL and FORTRAN I would never have been able to obtain much of the data off the tapes; and to the staff and student colleagues who reacted to my ideas, notably those presented here in Chapter 5. Initial thinking about the problems of interpreting regression coefficients in 'gravity models' was undertaken while I was teaching at the University of Toronto, in 1972, and I am grateful to Geoff Bannister and Greg Stewart, who, in trying to understand my ideas, helped me to understand them too. Finally, most of the experimental work in data analysis, much of the data editing and a lot of reading, took place while I held an Academic Visitor position in the Department of Geography at the London School of Economics and Political Science during 1973. I am grateful to Professor Michael Wise for the privilege of working there, and to the school's computer staff for their tolerance of my inept data handling procedures. For that period I am also grateful to the University of Canterbury for their generous support of my leave programme; the same University also provided the research grant which enabled me to obtain the necessary computer tapes.

Preparation of the data, apart from the material already on tape, was a mammoth task. Grants for this from the University of Canterbury Research Assistants' fund were much appreciated, as were the efforts of Ainslie Lamb and my wife Rita in the preparation of data sheets. Another grant enabled me to employ Tim Jackson to carry out much of the analysis of these data, and I am grateful for his painstaking efforts. In the preparation of the manuscript, my wife Rita has, as always, been of great assistance in many ways, and I am grateful to the editor of this series, Professor R. O. Buchanan, for his sage advice on my unfelicitous phrasing. Judy Robertson and Jan Bedford both worked wonders in typing the text from my handwriting; Noelene Frew, Sue Williams and Joan Dunn have done an excellent task in preparing all the tables: Ann Barham has been a great help with the proof-reading.

Finally, this book is dedicated to my parents, as a very

small token of thanks for all that they did to enable me to drift through my education and eventually find a satisfying career and life.

R. J. JOHNSTON

Sheffield
Christmas 1974

NOTES AND REFERENCES

1. As became very apparent in the writing of R. J. Johnston, *Spatial Structures*, Methuen, London, 1973.
2. Most of this work was done while I was an Academic Visitor in the Department of Geography at the London School of Economics and Political Science, in 1973, using the University of London's computing facilities. Some of it is discussed in R. J. Johnston, Possible extensions to the factorial ecology method: a note, *Environment and Planning*, vol. 5, 1973, 719–34; R. J. Johnston, On frictions of distance and regression coefficients, *Area*, vol. 5, 1973, 187–91.
3. See R. J. Johnston, Mental maps: an assessment, in J. Rees and P. H. Newby (eds), *Behavioural Perspectives in Geography: A Symposium*, Middlesex Polytechnic Monographs in Geography, vol. 1, 1974, 6–34.
4. In particular, see D. W. Harvey, *Social Justice and the City*, Edward Arnold, London, 1973, and S. R. Eyre, The spatial encumbrance, *Area*, vol. 5, 1973, 320–4.
5. R. J. Johnston, Regional development in New Zealand: the problems of a small, yet prosperous, ex-colony, *Regional Studies*, vol. 5, 1971, 321–31; also A decade is too long: observations on regional development in New Zealand, *Canterbury Chamber of Commerce, Economic Bulletin*, vol. 547, 1971; also Regional development and planning: a New Zealand debate, *Town and Country Planning*, vol. 42, 1974, 363–8.

Contents

Tables

Figures

Appendices

example, it may be that the attributes of the places – their supply and demand bundles – are set as the independent variables, and the interactions – the trade – as the dependents. The structure of the system might then be altered by an environmental change in the nature of the attributes of the elements: the failure of the Bangladesh rice harvest and the establishment of a steel industry in Australia both affect the pattern of interactions. If the change is more than an ephemeral attribute variation, the pattern of attributes among the elements may be altered also. Alternatively, however, the environmental impulse may change the interaction patterns, as with the trade boycott of Rhodesia and the formation of common markets, with consequent reordering of the attribute set.

The analysis of causal systems has been widely adopted in geography over recent decades. Most frequently it involves the use of least square regression techniques, either to estimate the influence of a set of causes on a prescribed effect or to identify the interrelationships in a non-causal situation[7]. Such studies normally can display only partial equilibria. Thus Watson and Cant have accounted for the efficiency of dairy farmers in part of New Zealand by five independent variables[8]:

$$Pi = f(Mi \; Ti \; Si \; SDi \; Fi) \qquad (1)$$

where Mi = a measure of the farmer's management ability,
Ti = a measure of the farm's topography,
Si = a measure of the scale of the farm operation,
SDi = a measure of the farm's soil and drainage qualities,
Fi = an index of the fertiliser input, and
Pi = a measure of productivity (butterfat per acre).

Regression methods allow parameters to be estimated for each variable, but these are time-specific. Accepting the system as a complex network of feedback loops, presumably the independent variables, especially Mi, Si and Fi, are not independent of the output. A continuous learning process is in operation, but as yet we are far from incorporating it into most of our causal models[9].

At a more philosophical level, the notion of causal systems

is best represented in geography by the concept of the ecosystem. As Stoddart points out, this represents a monistic approach, one which embraces the totality of man–land interactions as normally conceived by geographers[10]. Ecosystems are structured organic wholes, which function through the interactions among the elements, and which are altered by an environmental change, be it to element or to interaction.

The world trade system can be conceived as an ecosystem. The approach espoused in this book portrays it as a special type of ecosystem — as a *spatial system*. The elements of this system, with their attributes, are characterised by their unique spatial locations; any interaction between two such locations traverses a unique spatial path. The geographical focus on such an ecosystem inquires whether there is order in these patterns of spatial location and interaction, whether there is spatial, functional organisation.

Needed Inputs to the Study of Spatial Systems

Most studies of spatial systems have been empirical, describing patterns at one or more times. Most are but partial descriptions also, since they lack the necessary data on one or more aspect of the elements, the interactions and the environment. The nature of the elements has been most frequently outlined, given the relative plethora of data on this component, from which the other aspects have been inferred.

Even if data are available for investigation of both elements and interactions, such study usually is constrained in its secular coverage to but one temporal cross-section. Such work is of value but, as indicated in the example of dairy-farmer efficiency, the operation of a system which includes human decision-making almost invariably involves a continual process of learning and readjustment, not to mention the occasional 'parametric shocks' which may induce major reorientation[11]. Hence the pattern at any one time may be an amalgam of end-states (the stable results of a learning process), intermediate states (*en route* to the end-states) and transitions between states. The classic geographical solution to this problem has been to take a number of cross-sections to describe patterns at different dates and from these to infer, with supporting narrative, the processes of change[1 2]. If causal models of a quantitative form are being developed, adoption of this approach demands comparable data for a number of dates.

Description of a spatial system and its operation is frequently criticised since it eschews explanation and, at best, may offer only hypotheses concerning cause and effect. The 'understanding' or 'contribution to knowledge' is only inference; the equations of the causal systems are not verified[1 3]. In spatial systems analysis it might be argued that this is mainly a reflection of the underdeveloped state of the field. The studies being reported are operating in what Cattell has called the 'inductive-hypothetico-deductive spiral', in which observation is being used to furnish hypotheses in a continuous feedback process, suggesting relationships which, if properly verified, are worthy of further study aiming at more complete explanation. The present study is certainly at the initial stages of that spiral.

From this discussion, it is possible to specify the requirements for a simple descriptive model of world trade as a spatial system. These are:

1. Data with which the functions of each place in the system can be identified.
2. Data which indicate the volume and type of interactions between the various places.
3. Both of these data sets should be recorded for several years so that changes over time may be charted.
4. Theoretical propositions which account for the patterns so described, and data to test these ideas.

The result of such work would be the specification of what Berry calls a 'spatial field theory', in which there is a 'mutual equilibration of spatial structure and spatial behavior in a state of complex interdependency'[1 4].

The extent to which all of these specifications can be fulfilled is indicated by the contents of this book. The following sections provide the fourth requirement, the theoretical propositions.

A PARADIGM FOR STUDYING WORLD TRADE SPATIAL SYSTEMS

In the vast literature on world trade, few analysts pay attention to the spatial context of the system's operation, and among these it is common to treat the topic only cursorily. Hence, although such works offer many valuable inputs, the main body of stimuli for the spatial investigation must be obtained elsewhere. Fortunately, many analogies can be drawn from studies of other spatial systems, almost entirely within one country, and these are outlined here[15]. In particular, inputs are drawn from urban and regional growth theory and from a wide range of interaction studies. Although there are many conformalities between urban, regional and international systems, however, the analogies can be taken too far — because of the different environments in which they operate. The inter-urban system proceeds often in a *laissez-faire* context; entrepreneurs and individuals determine the patterns of functions and interactions, with a minimum of external interference. In other situations, there is some degree of external control ('planning'), extending to the centralised system, dominated by a single mechanism. Either polar case is easily modelled, *laissez-faire* on concepts of utility, centralised control on power. Operation of the international system, on the other hand, brings together a combination of environments, of competing internal desires and external forces. Nevertheless, there are many useful analogies to be drawn.

The Course of Economic Growth

How do places — towns, regions, countries — attract economic functions to themselves? In some cases there will be control from the physical environment — as with mining towns, for example — although there is still an element of choice since not all sites are selected. In other cases, a location may have many 'natural advantages' for the location of a firm, whereas in others still the result may be the unexpected outcome of a chance decision. Initially, the location of a town or the attraction of an economic function to a place may be the product of chance, or fate, or both, but from then on, it is suggested, development and the attraction of more functions proceeds in an orderly sequence. These are represented by five identifiable stages[16].

1. *Export Specialisation*, in which the place performs one major role in the system only. It is probably a small place and dominated by a single industry, even by a single firm.

2. *Export Complex*, in which the basic role — specialisation — is the same, but the place offers a range of specialisations, perhaps linked to one another. The development of a network of chemical industries is an example of an export complex emerging around an initial specialisation[17].

3. *Economic Maturity*, in which the place has grown to sufficient size, and long-term economic security, to attract to it economic functions aimed largely at its local market. This probably occurs in the first two stages but its volume increases substantially in the third stage.

4. *Metropolitan Status*, in which the place capitalises on its local market and develops a wide ranging set of specialisations for external markets.

Two trends are apparent in the progression through these four stages. The first is *import replacement*. As the economy of a place expands it becomes more self-sufficient in the provision of goods and services[18]. The second is *export diversification*, the widening of the range of functions providing goods and services for consumption elsewhere in the system. Both are clearly relevant to the world trade system: import replacement is a goal of many countries seeking economic independence, often as a by-product of political independence, while, since complete self-sufficiency is rarely possible, export diversification is pursued to ensure economic security[19].

Not all places pass through all of these stages, nor need they progress through the sequence as shown. Thus a fifth stage is suggested:

5. *Professional and Technical Virtuosity*, in which the place develops a wider range of, usually linked, export specialisations typical of the metropolitan stage, without the expected level of internal self-sufficiency. Switzerland is a good example of this stage in the international system.

Although this outline model is phrased in a series of stages, it can perhaps best be represented as a continuum, on which the position of each country can be determined. Classification may then be possible on the basis of a measure of scale position. Development of such continua has been attempted by Michaely, using indices of export and import concentration for forty-four countries over a set of 150 commodities[20]. His results showed considerable variation in degree of export specialisation, from 16·9 (Netherlands) to 99·6 (Mauritius) on a scale ranging from 8·2 to 100·0, but much less so for a similar scale of import concentration — from 15·5 (Belgium–Luxembourg) to only 30·5 (Trinidad and Tobago). What these indices do not indicate, however, is whether countries with similar values trade in similar commodities: in particular, do countries with different levels of export specialisation import similar mixes of commodities?

It is possible to study a spatial system at a certain time and categorise its elements on continuous scales or in 'stages', but why do countries perform different trade functions? How has the current trading system emerged? Most explanations are to some extent based on notions of comparative advantage, differences between places in scale of economy, in tastes, in factor endowments and in technologies[21]. Yet these still beg the question, they assume the existence and exploitation of resources, which are themselves the objects of human appraisal. Some factor endowments may be 'natural', but many, perhaps a majority, are 'man-made'. Other theories suggest that trade results from 'new commodities and the imitation gap', by which the technically most advanced countries practise export diversification while the rest, after a time-lag, mimic them through import replacement. But how did the former countries attain metropolitan status in the first place?

Until recently, the best answer to this question from urban and regional growth theory was the concept of initial advantage[22], but this has now been rephrased by Harvey in terms of the extraction and circulation of a surplus[23]. For one or more of a variety of reasons, a group at a certain location comes to dominate economic activity; by this it organises production and circulation and centralises these processes at its own location. This is best represented in the international system by the 'vent for surplus' theory. Countries develop an unused resource, diverting other resources, such as capital and labour, to this: they then need both to sell the first product and to replace those formerly obtained with the diverted resources. Trade is used for this, to find new markets and new sources for old products. Findlay claims that this is 'an interesting tool for the analysis of the "opening-up" phase in the economic history of the former colonial territories but not for the contemporary problem . . . [which is best accounted for by the] smoothly operating price mechanism and technical flexibility' of the comparative advantage theories[24]. Many would argue, however, that the 'colonialism' of the 'vent for surplus' is a continuing phenomenon[25]. Those able to open the vent are, according to Kuznets, Parsons and others[26], countries that initially had the necessary social and economic environments which were the prerequisites for capitalism. This economic system spread to a few other countries, but the circuit of growth and dependence which is created has been hard to break[27].

The Pattern of Interaction

A complement to an outline of what goods places import and export is the answer to the question, 'which country trades with which others?' Are partners chosen at random; do countries trade with only a few others; is there any spatial order in the trade flows? As a partial answer to such questions, Michaely computed coefficients of geographical concentration for the imports and exports of each of his selection of forty-four countries[28]. The findings were very similar to those for commodity concentration, with a wider range of concentration for exports than for imports. (The extreme values were 95·5 for Panama and 18·7 for the United Kingdom in exports, and 81·2 for Mexico and 19·4 for the United Kingdom with imports: the maximum possible value was 100·0 and the minimum 15·1.) Classification of the countries indicated that larger countries had wider trading contacts than did small ones, and developed countries than did their underdeveloped contemporaries. As similar patterns were discovered in the study of commodity concentration coefficients, the total system of world trade apparently comprises:

(1) Small countries, especially small underdeveloped countries, exporting a few commodities to a few countries and in return importing a wide range of commodities, also from a few partners only.

(2) Large countries, especially large developed countries, both exporting and importing a wide range of commodities and trading with many partners.

From this representation, and other studies, Michaely concluded that[29]:

> a positive relationship exists between the index of size of partner countries and the degree of geographic concentration of trade ... The trade of countries with high geographic concentration of trade usually flows to large countries ...; while large countries, whose trade usually has a large degree of geographic diversification, tend to trade with small countries, although this tendency is rather weak. It thus appears that the two factors which determine the size of the market for the international trade of nations — the degree of geographic concentration of this trade and the size of the trading partners — generally offset rather than augment the operation of each other. As a result, countries are much more alike in the size of the markets for their trade than in either of the two components of this magnitude.

Studies using concentration coefficients do not indicate which countries trade with which, and so cannot be used to infer any pattern of spatial organisation. More complete system description is provided by Russett's analyses, which identified clusters of strongly-linked countries ('choosers and chosen') in a matrix of trade among 115 countries in 1963[30]. Nine overlapping trade blocs were isolated:

1. Northern central America, focused on the U.S.A. and, to a lesser extent, on the industrial nations of western

Europe. This bloc included the member nations of the Central American Common Market.

2. South America, including all of the countries in that sub-continent (Venezuala is in both this and the previous bloc), whose major external links are with Spain and Italy.

3. British Caribbean, linking those countries (none of them of Latin culture) with the U.K. and Canada.

4. Countries of the British Commonwealth and the British sphere of influence, linked to the U.K. and to several other Western European nations.

5. The French Community, again including several other European countries.

6. Western Europe – the Common Market plus several neighbouring countries and Israel.

7. Eastern Europe and proximal nations, plus Cuba.

8. The Arab countries, excluding those of the Mahgreb.

9. Non-communist Asian countries, with external links to the U.S.A., U.K., West Germany, and Australia.

In addition, eighteen countries were not members of any bloc.

In these overlapping blocs, the countries that were members of several clusters were mainly those which could be characterised as metropolitan in the earlier 'stages of growth' model. This strengthens the conclusion drawn from Michaely's work, especially as virtually the same groupings were identified in a separate analysis of the 1954 trade matrix. (The main changes reflected political reorientations, as with the movement of Cuba towards the Soviet bloc.) Russett suggests three bases to the blocs – politics, culture, and distance – though with regard to the latter he concludes[31]:

> it appears ... that the role of proximity can be exaggerated. Distance can be surmounted if the incentives are strong, especially for maritime countries. Much of the cost of marine transport is in loading and unloading, so that the actual mileage to be travelled may be a secondary factor. Nearly half the countries examined are joined to one or more clusters not identified primarily with their geographic neighbors.

Indeed, even where proximity is apparently a factor, it could be culturally determined.

As Russett was concerned only with total trade between pairs of countries, he could not completely categorise the nature of the trade blocs. It is possible to suggest, however, that the pattern is very similar to that of inter-regional trade in India, for which the functions of the component places and the pattern of flows have been described as[32]:

> a set of metropolitan regions within which exchanges of each area are dominantly to and from the metropolitan centers, perhaps via smaller nodes in the urban hierarchy. Each region also has certain specialties that it provides for the nation as a whole — either based upon major resource complexes, or industry in the metropolis and its satellites. Flows of these specialties between regions hold them together in a national economy, although the preponderance of them are routed between the metropolitan centers.

The main difference would be in the role of entrepot centres.

Distance-Decay Patterns

There is a considerable volume of literature in geography and related disciplines concerned with the relationships between distance and interaction patterns, though very little of it relates to international trade. Much of this work is developed from an analogy of interaction with force in Newton's gravity model[33]

$$F = G \, \frac{Pi \, Pj}{d_{ij}^2} \tag{2}$$

where Pi and Pj are measures of the mass at i and j,
$\quad d_{ij}$ is the distance between places i and j,
$\quad G$ is a constant, and
$\quad F$ is the force.

Replacing F by I_{ij}, the amount of interaction between i and j, this states that movement between two places increases as a power function of the product of their masses and decreases as a power function of the square of the distance between

them. In equation (2) the weights for the independent
variables are given; in movement studies they are usually
empirically estimated in regression equations such as:

$$\log I_{ij} = \log a + b_1 \log Pi + b_2 \log Pj + b_3 \log d_{ij} \qquad (3)$$

Since this is an analogue model it is not a full causal
system. Reasons have to be suggested both for the influence
of the variables and for the size of the weights. The mass
variables, Pi and Pj, suggest that larger places trade more,
which is not unexpected. In studying patterns of spatial
organisation it is the distance variable, and its weight, which
is crucial, and this is focused on in the present book.

Why should interaction be related to distance? Movement
costs are an obvious reason, since longer journeys cost more.
The relationship between cost and distance is usually not
constant: the longer the journey, the less is the marginal cost
of an extra mile[34]. This is, first, because the transport costs
include handling costs at the termini, which are invariant
with length of journey, and, secondly, because on longer trips
the 'vessel' is more efficiently used, since it is spending less
time 'in port' between trips.

The preceding argument suggests transport costs as a
power function of distance, which would account for the
observed logarithmic relationship between interaction and
distance. There are many variants to this pattern, however.
Different transport modes have different cost structures:
road is usually cheapest for short trips, rail for those of
intermediate length, and water for the longest, as much
because of variations in terminal as in movement costs. Hence
not only distance but the type of transport influences costs,
and thus movements. Furthermore, each transport sector
enjoys its own economies of larger-scale operation, with in
general the larger its cubic capacity, the lower its unit cost[35].
Finally, contacts between some places may involve changing
the mode of transport, thereby introducing further costs.

Other costs are incurred because of the relationship
between distance and travel time. For example, the longer a
journey the greater the capital investment needed because
more, or larger, vehicles will be needed, assuming a constant
demand at all destinations. Larger stockpiles are probably

necessary at each terminus to avoid shortages. With some goods, rapid movement to the point of demand is necessary because of 'perishability' (both in the usual sense of this word and in the broader sense of a short demand life, as is the case with newspapers). Refrigeration and other technical developments have removed some of this necessity, though they involve extra installation and operation costs and, with some products, although preservation is technically feasible, it is not acceptable to the market.

As well as influencing movement patterns as separate variables, time and cost parameters of distance interact to produce two further influences. The first of these involves information. Decision-makers, including buyers and sellers, must act on limited amounts of information, and any one person's knowledge about spatial patterns of supply and demand is probably constrained by, among other things, his relative location and the time he has to amass data. The search for information, about markets perhaps, is usually constrained by time, and probably by money too, which probably restricts the search to a local area. (This is the main reason suggested for the inter- and intra-urban clustering of many business types.)

For international trade, the constraint of distance on information availability and collection is clear. Exporters need to be aware of market variations, to which they may need to react immediately. This is not so for all products, and a world network of sources (such as trade consulates) is sufficient, but frequently the nearby supplier is at a marked advantage in receiving, processing and reacting to market information. (The same is occasionally true for the reverse situation, with the nearby buyer having the advantage.) In their work on trade within South America, for example, Pederson and Stohr suggested that raw materials are widely exchanged with little distance constraint because they are relatively homogeneous and unchanging[36]. Manufactured goods, on the other hand, are mainly traded between neighbours because of the smaller and more fickle markets.

Finally, time and cost parameters of distance combine to produce a map of spatial opportunities around any particular importing or exporting country. Because of the relative distribution of points of supply and demand, some countries have more favourable locations on the map of spatial opportunities than others. If a country is seeking a market for manufactured products, it probably searches outwards across the map of opportunities, within the constraints of time, space and information. As a result, those with more local opportunities should be better placed for trading, and indeed Michaely's studies indicated that the more favourably located countries on the opportunity surface exported a wider range of products, *ceteris paribus*, to a larger number of destinations, than did the more remote places[37].

Together, these four distance parameters, each in effect a suite of parameters, influence movement patterns. For individual shipments or specialised movements, it is possible to identify the relative strength of each influence, but in looking at a system as a whole, especially one as large as the world trade system, generalisation is necessary. Hence here, as in so many other studies of interaction, one must depend largely on the single surrogate variable d_{ij} (or, more usually, log d_{ij}) to index the distance-decay patterns (see below, p. 74).

Complementarity

The discussion so far has assumed that trade is conducted in a single, homogeneous commodity. Yet adjacent countries, especially adjacent countries all at the same lower levels of the stages of economic growth, may generate very little trade among themselves. Their resource endowments are probably very similar, as are the cultural antecedents influencing their resource development. Each is likely to produce the same commodities as its neighbours, to whom it will not be able to sell them: each will demand the same type of imports, which neighbours cannot provide. Trade between two places requires complementarity in their patterns of supply and demand[38].

In attempting to articulate notions about the spatial structure of world trade, therefore, it seems necessary to fuse the two models, one of the functions of places, the other of distance influences on movement. This will introduce several impediments to the simple notions of the gravity model:

1. The degree of spatial concentration in the production and consumption of various commodities. If a good is exported by several countries, the distance variable should influence its movements, with each producer meeting local demands. Alternatively, if it is exported from one source only, distance will be related to flows only as a function of the location of the source. Results consistent with these notions, with distance exponents in gravity equations varying according to the degree of concentration of production and demand, have been produced in a study of inter-regional trade within the U.S.A.[39].

2. The distribution of supply and demand among countries at various stages of the growth sequence. In general, export specialisation and export complex countries produce raw materials and import partly finished and finished manufactured goods. Mature and metropolitan countries, on the other hand, import raw materials and the manufactured goods which other countries specialise in producing.

3. Institutional barriers. These are in great variety, ranging from particular tariffs to general trade embargoes, the latter usually political. The development of trade blocs, such as those created by the 1932 Ottawa Agreements and by the 1956 Treaty of Rome, are examples of barriers which are both positive, within the bloc, and negative, between the bloc and other countries, in their effects on trade.

4. Intervening opportunities. This is an extension of the gravity model analogy[40]. Countries will tend to trade with their nearest neighbours, but will have to compete with alternative sources or markets. Hence A may have a surplus of x which B wants. C also wants x, however, and is nearer to A so that it can outbid B for it; B then has to buy from D which is further from it than is A, but there are no intervening opportunities between D and B which demand the former's surplus of x. Alternatively A may have a surplus of x which it wishes to sell to C, but D is closer to C than A and its influence prevails in that market. In this case, A's trade pattern is influenced by the pattern of competing opportunities.

A Total Model of Interaction

The pattern of trade is a function of many variables, therefore, but can be summarised by the following model:

$$T_{ij} = f(M_i \ M_j \ d_{ij} \ P_{ij} \ C_{ij} \ IO_{ij} \ CO_{ij}) \qquad (4)$$

where M is a measure of the mass of a country, its supply or
   demand
   d_{ij} is the distance between countries i and j,
   P_{ij} is an index of the preferential trade relationships
   between i and j,
   C_{ij} indexes complementarity between i and j,
   IO_{ij} represents intervening opportunities between i and
   j,
   CO_{ij} represents competing opportunities, and
   T_{ij} is trade between i and j (either uni- or bi-direc-
   tional).

In an operational regression form for this equation it is probably not necessary to index IO_{ij} and CO_{ij}: Haynes *et al.* have suggested that their influence is reflected in the coefficient for d_{ij}[41].

Several researchers have tested a model such as this. Beckermann[42], for example, correlated a standardised volume of trade with ranked distances within Europe, and concluded that there was a

> tendency on the part of the less-developed countries of
> Europe to concentrate their trade more than other
> countries . . . [giving a] possibility of a causal correlation
> between degree of development and distance

which was reflected in trade patterns.

The largest study to date developed out of an appendix to Tinbergen's work on the shaping of the world economy, in which the three variables of G.N.P. of country of origin, G.N.P. of country of destination, and distance between countries accounted for some 65 per cent of the pattern of trade among eighteen countries in 1958[43]. Linnemann expanded on this[44]; from a large number of tests using the 1959 matrix of trade among eighty countries, the following extended equation accounted for 66 per cent of the pattern:

$$\log Xij = 0\cdot91 + 0\cdot78 \log Yi - 0\cdot13 \log Ni + 0\cdot74 \log Yj - 0\cdot06$$
$$\log Nj - 0\cdot82 \log dij + 6\cdot38 \log PBij + 3\cdot68 \log PUij$$
$$+ 3\cdot44 \log PFij + 0\cdot74 \log PUCij + 1\cdot57 \log PFGj$$
$$+ 0\cdot60 \; Cij$$

$$(5)$$

where Xij = exports from i to j,
          $YiYj$ = G.N.P. of i and j,
          $NiNj$ = population of i and j,
          dij = distance between i and j,
          $PBij$ = preferences of Portugal and Belgium for their associated countries,
          $PUij$ = preferences of the U.K. for associated countries,
          $PFij$ = preferences of France for associated countries,
          $PUCij$ = preferences among U.K. associated countries,
          $PFCij$ = preferences among French associated countries, and
          Cij = complementarity between i's exports and j's imports.

This indicates that the greatest trade flows are between complementary large countries that are close to each other and enjoy some preferential agreement. Perhaps slightly unexpected are the negative coefficients for N. Since Y is also included, however, this measure of population size indicates that at any level of G.N.P., larger countries are more self-sufficient, which is in line with the earlier discussion.

As well as fitting the equation to the total trade matrix, Linnemann also submitted it separately to each row and column (i.e. each country's individual import and export flows). Inspection of the pattern of dij coefficients suggested to him that

for countries at the (geographical) periphery of the world economy the distance parameter tends to have a higher absolute value. New Zealand, however, is a clear exception to this rule, and so is Uruguay to a certain extent though the data he presents are far from clear on this[45]. (It is interesting, however, that several other interaction studies have also noted this[46].) In any case, Linnemann was unable to suggest reasons for the observation that[47]

> relatively unfavourably located countries direct a greater part of their exports to their closest neighbours (even if they are rather far away)

and concludes that perhaps

> the assumed log-linear relationship between the variables simply does not fit the facts well enough, so that remote countries and centrally-located countries yield different parameter estimates. Moreover, the individual standard errors of the estimates are so large that the differences are hardly significant.

It could be that this is a technical problem associated with the confusion of distance effects with those of intervening and competing opportunities; this topic is pursued in Chapter 3.

Other of Linnemann's studies, with the whole range of variables, led to the general conclusion that the size and distance variables — the basic gravity model — were the major influences on trade flows, that[48]

> the present analysis does not support the hypothesis of very substantial trade-diverting effects of preferences ... [and] the commodity-composition effect might be of rather limited importance except for a few groups of countries such as the oil countries.

With regard to the conclusion on preferences, however, it should be noted that Linnemann's analyses largely preceded the E.E.C. and excluded the Communist bloc countries.

CHANGING SPATIAL SYSTEMS

The pattern of functional differentiation of countries and of trade flows outlined above suggests a system of trade blocs. These blocs need not be static in their spatial structure, of course, as the stages of economic growth model implies. Indeed, most countries clearly aim to move into the mature if not the metropolitan stage of that model, but to what effect? In recent years a few, notably Japan and, to a lesser extent, Australia and South Africa, have made significant movement, but what is the general pattern of trade reorientation likely to be?

Possible insights on such trends can be gleaned from the incipient theory of spatial convergence. Janelle has suggested that improvements in transport systems, especially in their speed, bring about a relative 'coming together' or time—space convergence[49]; Abler has indicated a similar process of cost—space convergence[50]. If such convergence were universal over the system, all places should be equally advantaged, but improvements are usually unevenly distributed. In the construction of land routes, the selection of which places to join is almost invariably determined by the economics of traffic potential: since large places generate most traffic, they are connected first, creating a continuing spiral of metropolitan advantage. In shipping services, too, the same principle applies. In recent years the trend has been to larger ships, to specialised carrying (such as containers and pallets), and to reduced turn-around time at ports. Such developments favour the heavily-used routes, because of the expense of port installations and the scale economies of large, rapidly-loaded cargoes. As a result, small producers are financially disadvantaged since they must continue to rely on older, more expensive technologies[51].

In all cases, three consequences of transport developments can be suggested, as a paradigm of spatial reorganisation.

1. *Centralisation.* Places benefiting from the transport innovations are able to widen their market areas, because lower overall transport costs allow them to penetrate areas formerly subsidiary to other nodes. They are able to undercut the prices of local producers, or to undercut the prices of nearer but less favourably located producers on the transport net or to inhibit local import replacement trends. As the places with the transport-system-benefit are likely to be larger places, this transport cost advantage is probably

allied to an existing scale of production advantage, which encourages further export diversification there. The result is centralisation of functions at such a node, and probably an increase in the polarisation of countries in the end stages of the economic growth process.

2. *Deconcentration.* As a metropolitan node grows, adjacent countries may obtain a 'spread effect', for one of two possible reasons. First, because of pressure on resources, the metropolitan country may be unable to meet its needs for certain goods so those functions are 'cast-off' to other countries (the import replacement process in reverse). Usually, because of the influence of distance, this transfer of functions is to adjacent countries: it may be a continual rippling-outwards trend, as was the case in the development of horticultural, agricultural, and pastoral zones to serve the British market during and since the Industrial Revolution[52]. Secondly, proximal countries are able to capitalise on their relative location to penetrate the metropolitan market. Michaely's work on this has already been mentioned (p. 15). Work on trade ratios (volume of trade to G.N.P.) has also shown that 'well-located' countries participate more in international exchange, *ceteris paribus*, as shown by the equations[53]:

$$\log M_i/Y_i = -0{\cdot}5 -0{\cdot}26 \log P_i -0{\cdot}12 \log Y_i/P_i +0{\cdot}34$$
$$\log V_i +0{\cdot}06 \log Pr_i \qquad R^2 = 0{\cdot}757 \quad (6)$$

$$\log X_i/Y_i = -1{\cdot}05 -0{\cdot}22 \log P_i +0{\cdot}06 \log Y_i/P_i +0{\cdot}35$$
$$\log V_i +0{\cdot}06 \log Pr_i \qquad R^2 = 0{\cdot}480 \quad (7)$$

where $X_i \, M_i$ = volume of exports and imports respectively in country i,

Y_i = G.N.P. of country i,

P_i = population of country i,

Pr_i = trade preferences of country i, and

V_i = vicinity of country i to all other countries[54].

The measure of *per capita* income (Y_i/P_i) is insignificant in the equations, which also indicate, for variable V_i, that the more accessible countries enjoy higher volumes of trade.

3. *Specialisation.* This is a partial counter to centralisation and is the general situation of which deconcentration is a special case because of the accessibility influence. Most countries possess, or can develop, comparative advantage for the production of some commodities, on which they capitalise and retain a role in the trade system.

In a *laissez-faire* system, the amalgamation of these three trends is likely to result in: (*i*) consolidation of metropolitan status for those possessing it; (*ii*) increased export specialisation for most other countries; and (*iii*) some spread effects around the metropolitan nodes. Thus movement through the various stages of the growth sequence, especially into the mature and metropolitan categories, is likely to be very difficult, especially for small countries away from the main metropolitan markets. As a consequence, trade flows will probably become more intensified also, rather than inter-country links broadening, except among the metropolitan countries as they compete for comparative advantages in sophisticated products.

Institutional Barriers to System Change

Within national economic systems, governments often act to reduce, if not wholly to prevent, the consequences of the above three trends through programmes of regional planning. Somewhat similar actions may be taken in the world system, either by individual component countries or by groups of countries. The former take unilateral action, through trade quotas or tariffs: the latter involve the establishment of economic communities whose ultimate purpose is to accelerate economic growth in the member countries. A typology of such communities has been developed, ranging from the least to the most inclusive in their action[55].

1. Free trade areas, in which tariffs and quotas on flows between member countries are removed.

2. Customs unions, in which the members also erect common tariffs against imports from non-members.

3. Common markets which, in addition to the above two

measures, remove all restrictions on factor movements among member states.

4. Economic unions.

5. Supranational political unions.

Such economic integration policies are supposed to bring both internal and external scale economies to the members. In groupings of mature and metropolitan countries, such as the E.E.C., the policies should be trade creating, generating a greater intensity of flows and higher general living standards. Within the E.E.C., this has not meant greater inter-industry specialisation, however; rather there has been a greater diversification in export patterns because the specialisation has been at a more detailed level than can be identified by the usual trade statistics[56].

Among developing countries at the export specialisation and export complex stages, economic communities are intended to be trade diverting: the volume of world trade does not increase but the proportion handled by the relevant countries does, as they benefit from scale economies. But, as Balassa points out, policies of trade integration often conflict with those of national independence; in Latin America, he claims 'the momentum of integration seems to be slowing down as mutual concessions are more difficult to come by'[57]. Integration could lead to total industrial dominance by one member country, creating new patterns of spatial inequality[58]

> inside the area that may in many respects resemble the present disparities between the developed area and the less developed area inside one country.

Thus the most successful integration schemes would involve countries with industrial sectors of similar size and therefore likely to have few vested interests and greater scope for specialisation. (Indeed, the same is true for developed countries: a full economic union of the U.S.A. and Canada would probably result in the former specialising in about 90 per cent of the industries[59].) Finally, a detailed study of many integration schemes concludes that[60]

Trade between integrational groupings of developing countries remains generally insignificant, and, in any case, shows no upward trend.

THE GEOGRAPHY OF WORLD TRADE

The paradigm presented here for the study of world trade patterns as a set of components of a changing spatial system is based on a wide literature. Other works will be noted in the relevant chapters. Brief mention should be made here, however, of the two main geographical studies of world trade. In the first, Thoman and Conkling concentrate on the broad patterns of commodity specialisation for countries, of trade between various blocs of countries (continents, major trade unions and major political blocs largely), of trade volumes, and of institutional arrangements for trade (the 'logistics and mechanics')[61]. Neither distance nor transport costs rate inclusion in their index, so that although the pattern, composition and value of trade are primary foci of their descriptions, the totality of the system is never outlined.

Freeman's work is in considerable contrast to Thoman and Conkling's, for he presents an ambitious thesis attempting to model mathematically not only the components of the trade system but also the flows of other factors of production, capital and labour, and the interrelationships among these three types of movement[62]. His basic model is that of 'canonical ecology', similar to the one used in Berry's work on interaction within India and Dutt and Pyle's on India's external trade[63]. For a sample of nations he factor analyses, in turn, matrices relating to: (i) the composition of their external trade, migration and capital flows, and (ii) their economic attributes. Canonical analysis synthesises the two basic patterns, stressing the interrelationships between formal and functional regions in the world economy. Inter-country flows are then added to the analysis, with the results suggesting:

1. Strong relationships between pairwise trade and the economic and physical distance between places; the greatest amount of trade is between neighbours at similar economic levels.

2. That labour movements are mainly between countries with the greatest degree of political and economic integration.

3. That capital flows are strongest where disparities in economic development are greatest.

The independence of these three dimensions in the canonical analysis suggests that trade, labour and capital flows are not adequate substitutes for each other in the international system.

This book tends to chart a middle course between these two. A more holistic and quantitative stance than Thoman and Conkling's is adopted, avoiding any detailed repetition of their extensive discussions of the logistics and mechanics of trade and preferring to present statistical tests of a small number of hypotheses and general notions about the trade system. On the other hand, the sophistication of Freeman's modelling is also avoided. In part this reflects a belief that such large-scale matrix analyses so compress their wealth of information as to waste much of its detail, and in part because the methods do not allow detailed testing of the spatial element in the paradigm presented here, the distance variable. Thus succeeding chapters are concerned, in turn, with describing the components of the system and testing for certain regularities in the pattern of functional differentiation; with identifying the patterns of interaction and the apparent influence of distance in these; and with charting the patterns of change during a recent decade. In this way, it is hoped that this book is complementary to the other efforts, suggesting an alternate viewpoint on this most important spatial system. Finally, the last chapter synthesises the conclusions of the analytical chapters and reflects on these and their implications to problems of inequalities in the international system.

NOTES AND REFERENCES

1. Source is International Monetary Fund, *Direction of Trade Annual 1969–1972*, I.M.F., New York, 1973.
2. D. N. Jeans, Competition, momentum and inertia in the location of commercial institutions, *Tijdschrift voor Economische en Sociale Geografie*, vol. 58, 1967, 11–19.
3. J. Chipman, A survey of the theory of international trade, *Econometrica*, vol. 33, 1965, 477–519 and 685–760; and vol. 34, 1966, 1–76.
4. The main exception in geography is D. B. Freeman, *International Trade, Migration, and Capital Flows*, University of Chicago, Department of Geography, Research Paper 146, 1973; and in economics, H. Linnemann, *An Econometric Study of International Trade Flows*, North-Holland, Amsterdam, 1966.
5. D. W. Harvey, *Explanation in Geography*, Edward Arnold, London, 1970, 451.
6. Though there is a continual feedback—observation relationship, as suggested in the 'Inductive-hypothetico-deductive spiral' portrayed in R. B. Cattell, Psychological theory and scientific method, in R. B. Cattell (ed.), *Handbook of Multivariate Experimental Psychology*, Rand McNally, Chicago, 1966, 16.
7. The latter is the result of most factor and principal component analyses in geographic research.
8. M. Watson and G. Cant, Variations in productivity of Waikato dairy farms: an empirical study of multiple causation, *Proceedings, Seventh New Zealand Geography Conference*, New Zealand Geographical Society, Hamilton, 1973, 165–74.
9. R. G. Golledge and L. A. Brown, Search, learning, and the market decision process, *Geografiska Annaler*, vol. 49, 1967, 116–24.
10. D. R. Stoddart, Organism and ecosystem as geographical models, in R. J. Chorley and P. Haggett (eds), *Models in Geography*, Methuen, London, 1967, 511–48.
11. A. Pred, *Behavior and Location*, C. W. K. Gleerup, Lund, 1967 and 1969.
12. This is the classic process of 'sequent occupance'; see D. Whittlesey, Sequent occupance, *Annals, Association of American Geographers*, vol. 19, 1929, 162–5.
13. This is the basis of the argument between advocates of the logical positivist and the phenomenological positions; see D. C. Mercer and J. M. Powell, Phenomenology and related non-positivistic viewpoints in the social sciences, *Monash Publications in Geography*, vol. 1, 1972.
14. B. J. L. Berry, A synthesis of formal and functional regions using a general field theory of spatial behavior, in B. J. L. Berry and D. F. Marble (eds), *Spatial Analysis: A Reader*, Prentice-Hall, Englewood Cliffs, 1968, 420. See also B. Greer-Wootten, Some reflections on systems analysis in geographic research, in H. M. French and J. B.

Racine (eds), *Quantitative and Qualitative Geography: La Necessité d'un Dialogue*, University of Ottawa Press, Ottawa, 1971, 151–74.

15. R. J. Johnston, *Spatial Structures*, Methuen, London, 1973.

16. W. R. Thompson, *A Preface to Urban Economics*, Johns Hopkins, Baltimore, 1965. A. Grotewold, The growth of industrial core areas and patterns of world trade, *Annals, Association of American Geographers*, vol. 61, 1971, 361–70, presents a similar view.

17. W. Isard, E. W. Schooler and T. Vietorisz, *Industrial Complex Analysis and Regional Development*, M.I.T. Press, Cambridge, Mass., 1959.

18. See K. Blechynden, An economic base analysis of Hamilton, *New Zealand Geographer*, vol. 20, 1964, 122–37.

19. See R. J. Johnston, Urban patterns, in R. J. Johnston (ed), *Society and Environment in New Zealand*, Whitcoulls, Christchurch, 1974, 150–169.

20. M. Michaely, *Concentration in World Trade*, North-Holland, Amsterdam, 1962. The formula is $Cjx = 100(Xij/Xj)^2$ where Xij = country j's exports (imports) in commodity i, Xj = country j's total exports (imports).

21. R. Findlay, *Trade and Specialization*, Penguin, Harmondsworth, 1970.

22. A. Pred, Industrialization, initial advantage, and American metropolitan growth, *Geographical Review*, vol. 55, 1965, 158–85; see also M. J. Webber, *The Impact of Uncertainty on Location*, ANU Press, Canberra, 1972.

23. D. W. Harvey; *Social Justice and the City*, Edward Arnold, London, 1973.

24. R. Findlay, *op. cit.*, p. 76.

25. A. G. Frank, *Capitalism and Underdevelopment in Latin America*, Praeger, New York, 1969.

26. S. Kuznets, *Modern Economic Growth*, Yale University Press, New Haven, 1966; T. Parsons, *The System of Modern Societies*, Prentice-Hall, Englewood Cliffs, 1971; E. Casetti, L. J. King and F. Williams, Concerning the spatial spread of economic development, *International Geography*, vol. 2, 1971, 897–9.

27. G. Myrdal, *Rich Lands and Poor*, Harper & Row, New York, 1957, ch. 5.

28. M. Michaely, *op. cit.*

29. *Ibid*, p. 47.

30. B. M. Russett, *International Regions and the International System*, Rand McNally, Chicago, 1967; see also J. E. McConnell, The Middle East: competitive or complementary? *Tijdschrift voor Economische en Sociale Geografie*, vol. 58, 1967, 82–93.

31. B. M. Russett, *op. cit.*, p. 143.

32. B. J. L. Berry, *Essays on Commodity Flows and the Spatial Structure of the Indian Economy*, University of Chicago, Department of Geography, Research Paper 111, 1966, 188.

33. For reviews see G. Olsson, *Distance and Human Interaction*,

Regional Science Research Institute, Philadelphia, 1965, and G. A. P. Carrothers, An historical review of the gravity and potential concepts of human interaction, *Journal of the American Institute of Planners*, vol. 22, 1956, 94—102.

34. R. T. Brown, *Transport and the Economic Integration of South America*, The Brookings Institution, Washington, 1966, 140.
35. A. D. Cooper, *The Geography of Sea Transport*, Hutchinson University Library, London, 1972.
36. P. O. Pederson and W. Stohr, Economic integration and the spatial development of South America, in J. Miller and R. A. Gakenheimer (eds), *Latin American Urban Problems and the Social Sciences*, Sage Publications, Beverley Hills, 1971, 73—103.
37. M. Michaely, *op. cit.*
38. E. L. Ullman, The role of transportation and the bases for interaction, in W. L. Thomas (ed.), *Man's Role in Changing the Face of the Earth*, University of Chicago Press, Chicago, 1956, 862—80.
39. W. R. Black, Inter-regional commodity flows: some experiments with the gravity model, *Journal of Regional Science*, vol. 12, 1972, 107—18; and Substitution and concentration: an examination of the distance exponent in gravity model commodity flow studies, University of Indiana, Dept of Geography, Discussion Paper 1, 1972.
40. S. A. Stouffer, Intervening opportunities and competing migrants, *Journal of Regional Science*, vol. 2, 1960, 1—26.
41. K. E. Haynes *et al.*, Intermetropolitan migration in high and low opportunity areas: indirect tests of the distance and intervening opportunities hypotheses, *Economic Geography*, vol. 49, 1973, 68—73.
42. W. Beckermann, Distance and the pattern of intra-European trade, *Review of Economics and Statistics*, vol. 38, 1956, 31—40.
43. J. Tinbergen, *Shaping the World Economy*, Twentieth Century Fund, New York, 1962.
44. H. Linnemann, *op. cit.*
45. *Ibid*, p. 91.
46. M. Chisholm and P. O'Sullivan, *Freight Flows and Spatial Aspects of the British Economy*, Cambridge University Press, Cambridge, 1973; T. R. Leinbach; Distance, information flows and modernization: some observations from West Malaysia, *The Professional Geographer*, vol. 25, 1973, 7—11.
47. H. Linnemann, *op. cit.*, p. 92
48. *Ibid*, p. 193.
49. D. G. Janelle, Central place development in a time—space framework, *The Professional Geographer*, vol. 20, 1968, 5—10; and Spatial reorganization: a model and concept, *Annals, Association of American Geographers*, vol. 59, 1969, 348—64.
50. R. F. Abler, Distance, intercommunications and geography, *Proceedings, Association of American Geographers*, vol. 3, 1971, 1—5.

51. A. D. Cooper, *op. cit.*
52. M. Chisholm, *Rural Settlement and Land Use*, Hutchinson, London, 1962, 102; and J. R. Peet, The spatial expansion of commercial agriculture in the nineteenth century: A von Thünen interpretation, *Economic Geography*, vol. 45, 1969, 283–301.
53. H. Glejser, An explanation of differences in trade-product ratios among countries, *Cahiers Economiques de Bruxelles*, vol. 37, 1968, 47–58.
54. The measure of vicinity used, $\Sigma Xj/dij$, where Xj = volume of exports of country j, dij = distance from i to j, is the usual measure of population potential; see G. Olsson, *op. cit.*
55. F. Kahnert, P. Richards, E. Stautjesdijk and P. Thomopoulos, *Economic Integration among Developing Countries*, O.E.C.D. Development Centre Studies, Paris, 1969.
56. B. Balassa, Tariff reductions and trade in manufactures among the industrial countries, *American Economic Review*, vol. 56, 1966, 466–73.
57. B. Balassa, *Trade Prospects for Developing Countries*, R. D. Irwin Inc., Homewood, Illinois, 1964, 120.
58. F. Kahnert *et al.*, *op. cit.*, p. 26.
59. B. Balassa, *Studies in Trade Liberalisation*, Johns Hopkins, Baltimore, 1967, 55.
60. R. Cadoni *et al.*, *World Trade Flows — Integrational Structure and Conditional Forecasts*, Centre for Economic Research, Swiss Federal Institute of Technology, Zurich, 1971, 240.
61. R. S. Thoman and E. C. Conkling, *Geography of International Trade*, Prentice-Hall, Englewood Cliffs, 1967.
62. D. B. Freeman, *op. cit.*
63. B. J. L. Berry, *op. cit.*, A. K. Dutt and G. F. Pyle, Dimensions of India's foreign trade, *International Geography*, vol. 1, 1972, 543–6; D. M. Ray, From factorial to canonical ecology: the spatial inter-relationship of economic and cultural differences in Canada, *Economic Geography*, vol. 47, 1971, 344–55.

2

Individual Roles in the Trade System

The role of a place or area in a space-economy has received considerable attention from urban geographers. Attempts have been made to classify towns, for example, according to either or both of their economic functions and their total socio-economic and demographic characteristics. Constraints are usually imposed by the nature of available data.

There are three main approaches to functional town classification. In the first, an index of the town's role, or its degree of specialisation, is obtained, usually from workforce data. This may be a single index, based on one computation[1], or a composite of several indices, as in Harris's study[2]. Such indices are usually unable to separate the town's role as a provider for other parts of the system, as an exporter, from its provision for the needs of its own inhabitants. As a consequence, a second approach has been developed. The economic-base study partitions all production in a town, of goods and services, into that intended for local consumption and that provided for external markets. Detailed analysis requires very full data, and it has usually been applied to small centres only[3]; an exception is the large Philadelphia input—output study[4]. Researchers dealing with whole systems have estimated the proportion of local production by fairly crude empirical methods[5]. The final approach, factor analysis of a large data set, is also empirically based; it makes no assumptions of, or allowances for, local production[6].

For the present study of international trade, function

within the system and interrelationships among the functions could best be displayed through large accounting
matrices. These would be expansions of the usual national
and inter-regional input—output matrices, and would show
the output of each sector of a country's economy according
to its destination, classified by sector and country. Each
sector's inputs would be similarly classified. Not surprisingly,
no such data are available, for a total world view. International trade data provide immense detail concerning the flows
of commodities from country to country, but little or no
information is available on the destination (sectoral rather
than locational) of imports when they reach a country.
Furthermore, no comparable data are available on local
production, on the amount which is retained for local use
rather than exported. It is not possible, therefore, to indicate
the degree to which a country is reliant on others for certain
products, since no detailed production (non-export) data are
available to place alongside the import figures[7].

Data availability strongly influences the approaches undertaken in this chapter. In particular, no analysis comparable to
that of economic-base studies was possible. Each of the other
two approaches to functional role is used here, however;
indices are computed to demonstrate the degree of specialisation for each country, and these are followed by principal
component analyses of commodity imports and exports
designed to suggest types of country by the nature of the
goods that they trade.

THE DATA

World trade data are collected by various agencies, in
addition to the vast data banks amassed by individual
countries for their own transactions. Some of these international collections refer to specific groups of countries —
the E.E.C. and O.E.C.D., for example — whereas a few aim at
total world coverage. The latter are clearly those relevant to
the present task; unfortunately they fail to reach their goal.
All of them deal only with commodity trade (except that
trade in armaments is often not divulged), thus preventing

study of the flows of goods and services and hindering full description of the role of certain countries which dominate trade in currency, insurance, shipping and so on, such as Britain and Switzerland.

The source used is the *Yearbook of International Trade*, collated and published by the United Nations. Although not comprehensive, this offers the best coverage. Initially, attempts were made to expand the coverage from other sources, but this was both time-consuming and of little value and so was abandoned. The United Nations' Standard International Trade Classification (S.I.T.C.) was devised in 1950, with major revision in 1960[8]. Not all countries provide data on the same base, however. Some do not use the S.I.T.C. scheme but use their own, and this is followed in the *Yearbook*. Others did not immediately adopt the 1960 S.I.T.C. revision — some still have not. Consequently, the data base is not strictly comparable for all countries.

The years with which this whole book deals, 1960 and 1969, were largely determined by this data source; 1969 because it was the latest date with available data when the study was initiated, 1960 because of the S.I.T.C. revision then. Ideally, to avoid the problems that might be introduced by a single sample year, notably the possibility of crop failure through climatic vagaries which might seriously distort the reported pattern from the average, it would be desirable to take data for a number of years around the chosen base date and derive an average commodity trade pattern for circa 1960 and circa 1969. Unfortunately, the time that this would involve was too great. This part of the study refers to 1960 and 1969, therefore, with all of the probable sampling errors that this entails.

The S.I.T.C. is a hierarchical classification, with five levels. The finest detail is at the five-digit level, comprising some 1312 separate commodities. These are progressively amalgamated up the hierarchy: at the third level, 177 commodities are recognised; at the second, fifty-six; and at the first, nine. Only the three highest are used here. Unfortunately, because certain countries still, in 1969 as well as 1960, use the 1950 edition of the S.I.T.C., it was not possible to use all commodities at the two- and three-digit levels. To ensure comparability, both at the same date and between dates, all data were transferred to a system which was applicable to the commodities identified in the two schemes. This had no effect on the one-digit classification, which remains at nine categories; the two-digit level now comprises fifty-four categories, and the three-digit, 153. A full list is given in Appendix II.

Use of these data for comparative work is hindered by the nature of the reporting. Countries differ in the amount of detail they provide, especially at the three-digit level. It is usual not to report small volumes of imports and exports (less than 0·5 per cent of the total) at the three- and two-digit levels but the threshold for disclosure clearly varies from country to country. As a result, some data sets appear more complete than others. This introduces obvious bias into the study, both in comparing different countries at the same date and in comparing different countries, and even the same country, at different dates. Such problems are particularly marked at the three-digit level, where variance is obviously greatest, and consequently less weight is given in the analyses to results obtained at that level. Complications need not be as serious at the two higher levels, but it remains possible that some of the differences identified here reflect data deficiencies and are, wholly or partly, not substantive. Where the data are obviously deficient at a certain level, they are not used.

As previously mentioned, some countries whose commodity trade is reported in the *Yearbook* do not employ either edition of the S.I.T.C. It was hoped that their particular commodity classification could be adapted to the S.I.T.C. system. This time-consuming process bore little fruit; it would have been possible to allocate some to the one-digit classification, but the task was abandoned. Consequently the analyses in this chapter refer only to countries using the S.I.T.C. Eighty-nine were employed from the 1960 data set, and 116 from the 1969, although certain deficiencies in some parts of the data mean that the total selection is not used in every analysis. The relevant countries for each analysis are listed in the associated tables in Appendix I.

No common scale is used to measure the intensity of trade

in the *Yearbook*. Several countries employ the U.S. dollar
and several report in British pounds, but most use their own
currencies. For several of the analyses reported here (though
not those in Chapter 4) this was irrelevant, since the focus
was on dimensionless numbers, proportions and percentages.
When conversion was necessary, however, it was achieved by
applying the current exchange rates so that all trade volumes
were converted to millions of U.S. dollars[9].

FUNCTIONAL SPECIALISATION

Many indices have been proposed as measures of functional specialisation, the degree to which a unit concentrates
its activities into certain sectors of a whole. Most indices are
erected on similar criteria, with two major variants according
to the construction of the base. In the first, the norm against
which the structure of a unit is gauged is an even distribution
across all the sectors, and the index measures deviations from
this ideal state. In the other, a norm other than equal
distribution is set, usually one derived from the total system,
and the index measures deviation from that norm. As Duncan
and Duncan have shown, most of such indices are similarly
constructed and represent slightly different ways of making
the same basic computation[10].

Most of these concentration or specialisation indices are
highly intercorrelated[11]. For this study six indices were
initially selected, three based on the norm of equal distribution − relative entropy, the Pelto coefficient, and Michaely's
concentration coefficient[12] − and two − the index of dissimilarity and the index of concentration[13] − which use as their
norm the total distribution of commodity trade over the set
of countries being investigated. The sixth coefficient − a
shares coefficient developed by Michaely[14] − is based on (a)
the percentage of a country's trade (import or export) in a
given commodity, and (b) the percentage of total world trade
in that commodity: the product of these two proportions
gives a measure of the degree to which a country is
dependent on trade in a single commodity for which it is a

major source or destination. Before proceeding with all six, however, their degree of intercorrelation was tested.

Table 2.1 gives the loadings from an unrotated principal components analysis of the six indices, referring to exports for eighty-six countries in 1960, at the one-digit level. The first five are clearly very strongly related, no one being very different from any other in its relative distribution. The sixth, the shares coefficient, does not covary with these five. Its variance is very small, however, indicating that it does not

TABLE 2.1
PRINCIPAL COMPONENTS ANALYSIS: INDICES OF EXPORT SPECIALISATION, 1960

Index	Unrotated solution component		Communality
	1	2	
Michaely	0·97	0·03	0·94
Pelto	−0·92	−0·09	0·85
Relative Entropy	−0·94	−0·02	0·89
Dissimilarity	0·94	−0·12	0·90
Segregation	0·94	−0·07	0·89
Shares	0·04	0·99	0·99
% Variance	0·74	91	

differentiate countries very successfully. On this basis (logically it should not be a good index since few countries are so dependent as a high value would suggest) it was discarded from this portion of the study.

Two indices were selected, although only one is used in this chapter. They are the relative entropy measure — an equality norm — and the index of dissimilarity — a total trade norm. Entropy is a measure of order or certainty in a system. If all of a country's export trade is in one commodity, then one can predict with complete confidence what any one trade bundle will comprise. The more diversified the trade, however, the less confident one can be, until the state of equal proportions in each commodity, at which one's predictive ability is at its lowest. The formula for the entropy measure is

$$H = \sum_{i=1}^{k} \text{Pi log Pi} \qquad (8)$$

where k = the number of categories,
     Pi = the proportion of the total in the ith category, and
     H = the entropy measure: natural logarithms are usually employed.

The range of values available for H varies according to the number of categories, and for comparative work over different category sets it is usually converted to a relative entropy measure.

$$G = \{H/(\log i/k)\} \times 100 \qquad (9)$$

where G has a range from 0 — complete diversity over the k categories — to 100 — complete specialisation.

The index of dissimilarity is the measure of disagreement between two percentage distributions

$$DI = \sum_{i=1}^{k} |Xi - Yi|/2 \qquad (10)$$

where k = the number of categories,
     Xi = the percentage of the total in the ith category for unit (country in this case) X, and
     Yi = the similar percentage for the total population.

The relative entropy measure is used in the analyses in this chapter, it being preferred to DI because in studying the specialisation of a place the equality norm appeared more relevant than the total trade norm. Specialisation is an absolute concept in this context; DI presents it as a relative one only[15]. Table 2.2 illustrates the computation procedure for these two indices.

IMPORT AND EXPORT SPECIALISATION 1960

Data were amassed for eighty-nine countries from the 1960 edition of the *Yearbook of International Trade*, and

TABLE 2.2
INDICES OF SPECIALISATION

Country	1	2	Sector 3	4	5	Total	Relative entropy	Index of dissimilarity
A	10	10	10	10	60	100	76·27	40·00
B	5	86	3	2	4	100	36·76	53·00
C	2	3	2	90	3	100	28·69	69·00
D	0	100	0	0	0	100	0·00	67·00
E	30	20	20	10	20	100	96·75	24·00
F	20	20	20	20	20	100	100·00	14·00
G	5	10	50	15	20	100	82·83	36·00
H	10	40	10	20	20	100	91·39	8·00
I	30	10	10	20	30	100	93·49	28·00

All countries

Total	112	299	125	187	177	900
As a %	12	33	14	21	20	100

Example of Computation — Country G
Relative Entropy

$\{(5/100 \times \log 5/100) + (10/100 \times \log 10/100) + (50/100 \times \log 50/100)$
$+ (15/100 \times \log 15/100) + (20/100 \times \log 20/100)\} \div \log 1/5$
$= \{(0·05 \times 1·61) + (0·10 \times 2·30) + (0·50 \times 3·91) + (0·15 \times 2·71)$
$+ (0·20 \times 2·99)\} / -1·61$
$= -1·33/-1·61$
$= 0·8283$ or $82·83$

Index of Dissimilarity

$(|5 - 12| + |10 - 33| + |50 - 14| + |15 - 21| + |20 - 20|)/2$
$= (7 + 23 + 36 + 6 + 0)/2$
$= 72/2$
$= 36$

indices of import and export specialisation were computed
for each at the one-, two- and three-digit S.I.T.C. levels.
Where data did not allow the computation, a dash is given in
Table A.1,† which lists these indices.

Indices for imports are consistently larger than those for
exports, at all three levels of the classification. They are also

† Long tables, prefixed by A rather than a chapter number, are in a
separate appendix at the back of the book.

less variable, as shown by their coefficients of variation (ratios of standard deviations to means). This is a not unexpected finding, given the model of trade relations outlined in the previous chapter. Although countries may vary considerably in their indices of export specialisation, as a measure of their degree of specialisation within the international system, most should import a wide range of commodities. Hence the high relative entropy measures for imports, very apparent at the one-digit level.

More than three-quarters of the full range of values are displayed in each category for the export specialisation indices. The lowest relative entropies, indicating near-complete, and sometimes complete, specialisation on one commodity alone occur for some small countries, notably Liberia, Mauritius, Netherlands Antilles, Reunion and Surinam, whose functions in the world economy are extremely restricted. At the other extreme are those countries – the United States, United Kingdom, Italy, West Germany and France, for example – with a considerable commodity range in their export bundles, indicative of their metropolitan status according to the model of economic growth previously outlined.

No clear patterns of variation can be discerned in the columns of indices of specialisation for imports. None were anticipated since countries at all levels of economic development are dependent on others for many commodities. It may be that the lesser developed, because of their poverty, are unable to buy a wide range of goods and there is some evidence of this at the three-digit level, for which many of the lower indices refer to small countries commonly categorised as 'underdeveloped' or 'developing'. The only real exceptions to the generally high entropies were two countries – Aden and Netherlands Antilles – whose function in the world economy is to import crude oil, refine it, and export the products[16]. (Sarawak performs a similar function, but petrol is not its only export.)

Table A.1, read across the rows instead of down the columns, shows the indices becoming smaller from the one-digit towards the three-digit level. The extent of the change is an indicator of intra-sector specialisation, the degree to which a country imports or exports only a few of the commodities in a broad category. With imports, the means show a three-digit average about 60 per cent of that for the one-digit level. There is a suggestion of a greater discrepancy for the less 'developed' countries, though there are several exceptions to this among African and South American nations. This is not a surprising finding, however: it fits the earlier expectation that poorer nations might be able to afford only a relatively narrow range of goods. (The narrowness is probably overstated in some cases by the relatively thin reporting at the three-digit level.)

For exports, the variation in size of average indices between one- and three-digit levels is slightly less than it is for imports. There is clearer evidence, however, of greater variation among the smaller countries, those with relatively low one-digit indices in any case. This underlines their very specialised role in the world system, much of their economic security depending on their ability to produce and sell a single commodity (an ability which is often tenuous, dependent on weather, pestilence, non-exhaustion of fixed resources, and buoyancy in distant price markets). Unlike the situation for imports, however, not all countries have a lower export index at two- and three- than at one-digit level. For example, virtually all of Liberia's exports are in category 2 at the one-digit level — inedible crude materials (not fuels) — but within this category, it exports both rubber and iron ore. Hong Kong, too, exports very widely within each of the broad categories, being typical of those countries which provide mainly manufactured goods for the world market. More typical of those concentrating on the supply of foodstuffs and raw materials is Dahomey, which exports mainly oil seeds (category 2 at the one-digit level) and palm oil (category 4), two of the nine categories at the one-digit level, but only three of the fifty-four at the two-digit.

Regression Analyses

The preceding discussion of import and export specialisation indices has been relatively short, because this ground has been covered in other works and because there is little value in subjective interpretation of a large body of figures[17]. It

has, however, suggested several general patterns in the
distribution of indices among the various countries, and
these, plus other hypotheses suggested or developed in other
studies, have been used in the formulation of a descriptive
model of functional specialisation.

Multiple linear regression analysis is used to develop this
model[18]. The dependent variables are the six vectors of
indices of specialisation (Table A.1); the independents are the
following (a complete list is in Table 2.3: only those referring
to 1960 are listed here).

1. Measures of trade volume (variables 1 and 2): the larger
the volume of trade emanating from or converging on a
country, the wider the range of commodities that should be

TABLE 2.3
REGRESSION ANALYSES: IMPORT AND EXPORT
SPECIALISATION, KEY TO INDEPENDENT VARIABLES

Stage 1

1. Total Imports, 1960	2. Total Exports, 1960
3. Total Imports, 1969	4. Total Exports, 1969
5. Import Potential, 1960	6. Export Potential, 1960
7. Import Potential, 1969	8. Export Potential, 1969

Stage 2
A. 9. G.N.P. *per capita*, 1963
B.10. Population, 1960   11. Population, 1969
C.12. G.N.P. x Import/Export Potential 1960/69

Stage 3
   13. Member, 'British Trading Group'
   14. Member, 'French Trading Group'
   15. Member, 'Portuguese Trading Group'
   16. Member, L.A.F.T.A.
   17. Member, C.A.C.M.
   18. Member, E.E.C.
   19. Member, E.F.T.A.
   20. Member, O.E.C.D.

Stage 4
Variables 21—28
      Variables 13—20 respectively multiplied by variable 9

involved. There may be exceptions to this, such as the Netherlands Antilles which imports and exports large volumes of oil
and oil products. Nevertheless, strong positive correlations
between these variables and the dependents are anticipated.

2. Measures of the country's location in the trade system
(variables 5 and 6): the discussion in Chapter 1 suggested
that, holding size constant, countries relatively close to the
main trading nations should be able to benefit from this
proximity, especially in the range of exports they are able to
place on those markets. Accessibility to markets was
measured by an index of import–export potential:

$$POTi = \sum_{i \neq j}^{k} Tj/dij \tag{11}$$

where Tj = the trade of country j (imports or exports),
dij = distance between those countries[19], and
$POTi$ = the trade potential for country i.

Export indices should be positively correlated with import
potentials (proximity to markets) and import indices with
export potentials (proximity to sources).

3. Measures of the country's size (variables 9 and 10):
holding the volume of trade constant, rich countries might
trade more widely in commodities because of scale
economies, suggesting a positive relationship with G.N.P. *per
capita*[20]. Large countries, however, may be more self-
sufficient and less dependent on a wide range of imports,
suggesting a negative correlation with population. Rich,
accessible countries may be particularly advantaged, since
their scale economies would allow them to develop large
nearby markets, justifying the introduction of the interaction
variable (12).

4. Membership of trade blocs (variables 13–20): the
various forms of economic union are organised to stimulate
trade, and so members of such unions, including 'colonial'
groups, should have larger relative entropies, *ceteris paribus*.
Eight of the major unions have been selected.

5. Size within trade groups (variables 21–28): as pointed
out in Chapter 1, trade agreements are often most beneficial
to their larger members.

Variables 1—11 are all logarithmically transformed to counter positive skewness.

The procedure followed in the regression analyses is outlined in Table 2.3. For each dependent variable, six regressions were run, adding to the list of independents at each stage. The results (Table 2.4) indicate: (*a*) the goodness of fit of the equation, its multiple correlation coefficient; and (*b*) the 'significant' independent variables. Since the analyses were not dealing with samples and forming the bases for inductive generalisations, traditional significance tests are irrelevant. By significant here is implied the accuracy of the 'explanation' provided by the independent variables. This is indexed by the *t* value, the ratio of the regression coefficient (the slope of the *ceteris paribus* relationship between it and

TABLE 2.4
REGRESSION ANALYSES: IMPORT AND EXPORT
SPECIALISATION, 1960

			Significant variables at stage[a]			
	1	2A	2B	2C	3	4
Imports						
One-digit	6	6	6	6	−1,(6),13,(14), (−16),(17)	as 3
R	0·33	0·36	0·37	0·39	0·58	0·63
Two-digit	6	6	6	6	(6),(14),(17)	6,−10,12
R	0·42	0·44	0·45	0·45	0·56	0·59
Three-digit	(1),6	(1),6	6,(9),10	6,(9),10	(6),(9),10,14, (17)	as 3
R	0·52	0·52	0·60	0·60	0·69	0·70
Exports						
One-digit	2,5	2,5	5,(10)	5,(10)	(10),(13),(14), 20	(5),(10), (−12),(14), 20,(27)
R	0·64	0·64	0·66	0·66	0·76	0·78
Two-digit	2,5	2,5	2,5,10	(2),5,10	(5),10,20,(16)	(2),20,(27)
R	0·63	0·74	0·77	0·77	0·81	0·83
Three-digit	2,5	2,5	2,5,10	2,5,10	(5),10,(14), (16),20	as 3
R	0·75	0·76	0·79	0·79	0·84	0·86

[a] See text, p. 43.

the dependent) to its standard error (the standard deviation of values around the regression)[21]. Two critical values of t were selected: 1·65 and 2·30. The latter suggests much more accurate predictions. In the table, the variables providing less accurate, or significant, predictions are shown in parentheses: minus signs indicate negative relationships.

The method adopted here introduces problems of multi-collinearity among the independent variables, notably 1, 2, 9, 10 and 12, and to a lesser extent 18, 19 and 20. This can result in a high multiple R but few, or even no, significant independent variables[22]. No attempt has been made to correct for this. The stagewise procedure enters variables according to their expected importance, and collinearity problems can be seen from changes in the t values. The main aim is to test for the importance of the variables, particularly those entered at the first stage, as predictors. Analysis of the residuals from the stage 6 regression suggests the countries for which the 'predictions' are least accurate: for this aim, the collinearity problem is not particularly relevant.

For the import specialisation indices, the conclusions from the first three regressions (stages 1, 2A and 2B) are that size is unimportant but that accessibility is a significant predictor. Countries close to the world's main exporters on average import a wider range of commodities; presumably such purchases are relatively cheap because of low transport costs. (Other suggestions could be made, such as dumping by the main producers.) At stage 2C at the three-digit level, variables 9 and 10 suggest that it is the largest and richest as well as the most accessible which import most widely; this could well be a function of the data, however, since larger countries will report a wider range of imports in volumes greater than 0·05 per cent of their total. Finally at stages 3 and 4, members of the French community and of the C.A.C.M. clearly benefit from their bonds with those blocks; L.A.F.T.A. members, on the other hand, apparently import less widely than do their peers, at least at the one-digit level. The main residuals from these regressions suggest no dominant patterns of under- and overprediction, nor independent variables that should be included (Table 2.5). (In this and similar tables absolute residuals, marking deviations above and below the stated

TABLE 2.5
REGRESSION ANALYSES: IMPORT AND EXPORT
SPECIALISATION, 1960: MAIN RESIDUALS
(countries ordered by size of absolute residual)

Imports

One-digit — threshold ±7·0
    positive: Sabah, Spain, Guatemala, Israel, Malaya, South Africa
    negative: Netherlands Antilles, Aden, Afghanistan, Sarawak, United
    Kingdom

Two-digit — threshold ±10·0
    positive: Hong Kong, Cyprus, Jamaica, Sabah, Israel, Malaya, Papua,
    South Africa, Cuba, Ceylon
    negative: Netherlands Antilles, Sarawak, Aden, W. Samoa, Zanzibar

Three-digit — threshold ±11·0
    positive: Israel, South Africa, Cuba, Sabah, Congo, Malaya,
    Morocco, Sudan, Ghana, Egypt, Rhodesia, Pakistan,
    British E. Africa
    negative: Cyprus, Hong Kong, Netherlands Antilles, Sarawak, United
    Kingdom, El Salvador

Exports[a]

One-digit — threshold ±20·0
    positive: Singapore, S. Africa, Madagascar, Mexico, India, Israel,
    Cameroons, Senegal, New Guinea, S. Korea, Mauritius
    negative: Iceland, Panama, Liberia, Netherlands Antilles, Papua,
    Gambia, Ecuador, Costa Rica, New Zealand, Sudan

Two-digit — threshold ±16·0
    positive: S. Africa, Morocco, Hong Kong, Israel, Madagascar,
    Singapore, Niger, Senegal, British E. Africa, Libya, Mexico
    negative: Gambia, Netherlands Antilles, Mauritius, Surinam,
    Reunion, Trinidad

Three-digit — threshold ±13·0
    positive: S. Africa, Hong Kong, Morocco, Israel, British E. Africa,
    Yugoslavia, Madagascar, Singapore
    negative: Mauritius, United Kingdom, Netherlands Antilles, Iceland,
    Trinidad, Belgium, Egypt, Sudan

[a] The higher thresholds for exports reflect the wider range of values
involved and not the higher correlations.

threshold, are listed in order of size to indicate the main areas of failure for the regression[2][3].) Among the overpredictions, those more concentrated than predicted (negative residuals) in their import range, the 'oil countries' of Netherlands Antilles and Aden stand out, as do several other very small countries (but also the U.K.); among the positive residuals (wider range of imports than expected) Israel, South Africa and Cuba are noteworthy, the first two being relatively rich, relatively isolated countries.

Not surprisingly, the equations for the export indices were more successful in predicting inter-country variations than were those for imports. (At stage 4, the average 'explanation' $-R^2$ — was 0·41 for imports and 0·66 for exports.) In these equations problems of collinearity arise. The first stages support the main hypothesis that well-located nations with large export volumes trade in the widest ranges of commodities. Stages 2B, 2C and 3 suggest that size can be measured in several ways, though trade volume and population are generally additive. At stages 3 and 4, variable 20 tends to replace 5, suggesting that O.E.C.D. membership is more significant than general access (but inspection of residuals from stages 1 and 3 suggests that both variables are necessary). L.A.F.T.A. countries are apparently somewhat more catholic in their export bundle than their counterparts (variable 16), as are the richer countries in E.F.T.A. (variable 27). The positive residuals from these regressions (Table 2.5) emphasise the better-than-expected export performance for a number of countries; some of this pattern may reflect the depth of the data source, but clearly of relevance are the 'isolated' yet relatively industrialised countries of Hong Kong, Mexico, Israel, South Africa, Singapore and, perhaps, Morocco. The negative residuals highlight the narrow specialisms of some very small countries — Gambia, Liberia, Costa Rica, Mauritius, Reunion, the specialised economies of Netherlands Antilles, Trinidad, Surinam and Iceland, and the relative specialisation of the U.K. The regression analyses suggest few differences between the various levels of the commodity classification. These were confirmed by regressions between the various pairs (Table 2.6), with the

TABLE 2.6
IMPORT AND EXPORT SPECIALISATION, 1960:
INTERRELATIONSHIPS

Key to variables

I_1 – Import concentration,
one-digit

I_2 – Import concentration,
two-digit

I_3 – Import concentration,
three-digit

X_1 – Export concentration,
one-digit

X_2 – Export concentration,
two-digit

X_3 – Export concentration,
three-digit

Within group		*Between group*	
$I_1 = 45 \cdot 16 + 0 \cdot 52\,I_2$	$r = 0 \cdot 72$	$I_1 = 76 \cdot 37 + 0 \cdot 09\,X_1$	$r = 0 \cdot 24$
$I_1 = 73 \cdot 46 - 0 \cdot 13\,I_3$	$r = 0 \cdot 28$	$I_2 = 59 \cdot 11 + 0 \cdot 23\,X_2$	$r = 0 \cdot 40$
$I_2 = 52 \cdot 16 + 0 \cdot 30\,I_3$	$r = 0 \cdot 47$	$I_3 = 37 \cdot 88 + 0 \cdot 44\,X_3$	$r = 0 \cdot 46$
$X_1 = 8 \cdot 85 + 0 \cdot 95\,X_2$	$r = 0 \cdot 83$		
$X_1 = 14 \cdot 11 + 0 \cdot 97\,X_3$	$r = 0 \cdot 78$		
$X_2 = 5 \cdot 99 + 1 \cdot 02\,X_3$	$r = 0 \cdot 93$		

only 'wayward' variable that for three-digit imports. Levels of import and export specialisation were only weakly related to each other, however.

SIMILARITIES IN TRADE COMPOSITION 1960

The indices discussed so far in this chapter provide a broad statement of the degree of functional specialisation by country within the world system. But they conceal differences between countries in the commodity composition of their trade. Two countries with similar specialisation indices may be trading in very different commodities.

During the last decade, geographers have commonly sought for general patterns in a large data matrix through a principal components or a factor analysis. In its most usual form, this method takes a data matrix of n variables and m observations — in this case the variables would be commodities in the S.I.T.C. scheme, and observations the countries — from which it derives the $n \times n$ matrix of inter-variable product moment correlations. Extraction of the eigenvectors from this matrix produces hybrid variables which account for successively decreasing proportions of the total variance described by the correlations. The most substantial of these are then usually rotated to obtain 'simple structure', which aids in the identification of groups of intercorrelated variables. Group identification is achieved by interpretation of the loadings, the correlations between the original variables and the hybrids; the original observations are arranged along the hybrid variables as weighted sums of the products of the loadings and the values for the observations on the original variables — these are termed the factor or component scores[24].

Application of this method to commodity trade matrices encounters several problems. First, use of the product-moment correlation coefficient reduces the original values to dimensionless numbers — Z deviates — thereby removing some of the variation between countries. Secondly, if raw trade data were employed, the total volume of trade by country would dominate the results, but if trade in each commodity is expressed as a proportion of the country's total, non-orthogonal (related) variables are introduced. Thirdly, the method of 'grouping' variables suggests redundancy among them, when in fact all variables (commodities) are of equal value in determining the similarity between countries[25].

These problems can be surmounted by using a Q-mode, cross-product input. In this, the countries form the variables, and the commodities the observations. Each trade value is expressed as a proportion of the country (column) total, with no consequent non-orthogonality. Factoring, via the principal components method, is on the cross-products rather than the correlation matrix; the former measures the degree of overall similarity between pairs of countries in their trade patterns (profile height as well as profile shape). The result is a matrix of loadings indicating the degree of agreement between individual countries and hybrid countries; the first vector of loadings shows the average pattern, with subsequent vectors identifying groups of countries with common patterns of deviations from that average. The scores vectors indicate the average values of trade in the commodities for each 'group' — in relative not absolute numbers.

Cross-product principal component analyses were performed on the one-digit and the two-digit import and export matrices (imports and exports were analysed separately and jointly at the one-digit level). The three-digit matrices were not analysed, partly because of the more variable data and partly because of their great demands on computer space and time. In the results, the loadings are expressed as percentages of the total variance for each country, to allow standardised representation[26].

Four components extracted from the analysis of imports at the one-digit level accounted for 88 per cent of all of the inter-country variance. The first component's scores (Table A.2) show an average import composition dominated by foodstuffs (category 1), manufactured goods (7 and 8), and, to a lesser extent, fuels (4). For most countries, this average pattern was similar to their own, as shown by the loading percentages (Table A.3). The second, third and fourth components identify groups of countries with common deviations from the average. Thus positive loadings on the second component pick out countries which import more foodstuffs and machinery than is usual — a pattern displayed, for example, by Greece and several central American countries — whereas negative loadings designate large imports of fuel and manufactured goods, notably by many West European nations plus the U.S. Positive loadings on the third component further emphasise countries for whom fuels form above-average proportions of their imports, along with chemicals, and negative loadings delineate the relatively large importers of manufactured goods. Finally, the last component identifies, by its positive loadings, countries very dependent on fuel imports (see the scores, Table A.2), notably Japan among the industrialised nations and the 'oil entrepôts' of Aden, Netherlands Antilles and Sarawak.

Analysis of the exports matrix also produced four interpretable components (89 per cent of total variance). The average pattern of the first emphasises exports of food and raw materials (commodities 1 and 3), which the loadings identify as the dominant pattern for non-European countries.

The second component differentiates between dominantly food (negative) and dominantly raw material (positive) exporters, which spatially tends to separate American (food exporters) from Asian and African countries. The positive pole of the third component isolates equipment and oil exporters; the fourth emphasises the manufactured goods' exports of European countries plus a few others, such as Israel and Hong Kong, as well as Sierra Leone (industrial diamonds).

Combination of the two matrices, giving eighteen observations (nine import and nine export commodities), re-emphasises the earlier findings. The average pattern — the tables are not reproduced here — is characterised by food/raw materials exports and manufactured imports, although the average country also imports considerable volumes of food. Successive components: (2) differentiate food from raw material exporters; (3) isolate importers of fuels and exporters of manufactured goods plus foods; (4) contrast the oil entrepôts with the main sources of manufactured goods; (5) contrast raw material importers with those importing finished goods; and (6) stress those countries which import large foodstuff volumes.

Not surprisingly, the greater detail of the two-digit classification produced more complex patterns (Tables A.4 and A.5), though these largely restate the findings from the aggregate level. Greater differentiation of particular specialisations is possible, however, and the scores indicate which commodities dominate the different pattern of trade — cereals, sugar, textile fibres, petroleum, textile yarns, metals, machinery and transport equipment among the imports, cereals, fruit, sugar, oil seeds, rubber, textile fibres, ores, petrol and metals among the exports (Table A.4). The loadings identify groups of countries with similar detailed supplies and demands in the world market, such as the machinery importers in South America (component 4, Table A.5), the meat exporters of the 'New World' (component 6) and the rubber exporters of Asia (component 8).

The initial purpose of these analyses was to produce a typology of countries according to the nature of their world trade participation, as an application of Thompson's model

(pp. 7–9) and as a possible input to later investigations of
trade flows; but the results suggested otherwise. At the
two-digit level, the detail was such that any valid classification – in which the 'within-group' similarities were considerable – would produce a multitude of small groups and
emphasise the unique role of each country. At the one-digit
level, preliminary classifications suggested the irrelevance of
the exercise. The tables of loadings indicate a clear
dichotomy between the industrial nations, mainly of Europe,
and the export specialists. This simple typology, along with
the clear relationships between country size and location and
its degree of export specialisation, was deemed sufficient for
the further analyses.

TRADE PATTERNS IN 1969

The processes of change in trade patterns during the 1960s
are the concern of Chapter 4, and at this stage the aim is
merely to present a brief discussion of analyses of the 1969
trade matrices which paralleled those just reported. For
these, 116 separate countries were studied. The vectors of
import and export specialisation indices (Table A.6) differ
from their 1960 counterparts (Table A.1) mainly in their
larger means and lesser relative variance. On average, countries apparently have developed a wider range of exports –
following along the paths of the Thompson model – from
the fruits of which they can obtain a wider range of imports.
In part, this conclusion could result from a greater level of
detail in the 1969 data, but as the additional countries to
those on the 1960 list are mainly non-European and one of
the largest changes in indices is at the one-digit level for
exports, part of the interpretation seems valid. Similarly,
there was a considerable reduction in the coefficient of
variation for one-digit exports.

That some slight change occurred in the functional pattern
is indicated by a comparison of the two sets of regression
analyses (Tables 2.4 and 2.7); the correlations are substantially lower at the second date. The content of the regression
equations, and their relative accuracy, is similar, however.
For the import indices, accessibility to exporters remains the

TABLE 2.7
REGRESSION ANALYSES: IMPORT AND EXPORT
SPECIALISATION, 1969

			Significant variables at stage[a]			
	1	2A	2B	2C	3	4
Imports						
One-digit	8	8,(9)	8	8	none	(13),(−22)
R	0·30	0·34	0·34	0·34	0·39	0·46
Two-digit	8	(8),(9)	(8),(9)	(8),(9)	none	13,(−22)
R	0·31	0·33	0·33	0·34	0·40	0·46
Three-digit	3,(8)	(3),(8)	(8),(11)	(8),11	11,13,(17)	(13)
R	0·29	0·32	0·39	0·39	0·48	0·40
Exports						
One-digit	4,7	4,(7),9	(7),9	(7),9	9,(11),−12, 20,16	9,(−12), 20,16
R	0·54	0·56	0·58	0·58	0·58	0·60
Two-digit	4,7	4,7,(9)	4,7,(9)	4,7,(9)	(4),9,−12, (17),20	9,(−12),20
R	0·64	0·65	0·65	0·65	0·69	0·69
Three-digit	4,7	4,7,9	4,7,9	4,(7),9	9,−12,20	(4),9,−12, 20,(27)
R	0·67	0·69	0·69	0·69	0·74	0·73

[a] See text, p. 43.

most accurate predictor of inter-country variations, with only a little evidence that other variables, notably those relating to country size, contribute significantly to the equations' power. Both location and size clearly influence the distribution of export indices, on the other hand, although the effect of relative location is again confounded by the O.E.C.D. membership variable.

Principal components analyses of the 1969 trade matrices indicate little change from the 1960 patterns. The component score profiles (Tables A.7 and A.9) indicate the same dominant flows, though there are some changes in the relative size of some values; the only main alteration is with the need for a fifth component at the two-digit level to stress the relative importance of machinery and chemicals in some industrialised countries' export manifests. (The positive scores; only a few countries had negative loadings, and these

were small — Table A.10.) The same groups of countries with
similar trade vectors are suggested by the loading patterns
(Tables A.8 and A.10), such as the American food exporters
and the greater specialisation in industrial raw materials from
Asia and Africa. At the two-digit level, the large scores for
petroleum in the average pattern for 1969 probably reflect
the enlarged list of countries — especially in the Middle
East — compared to 1960, rather than any particular widespread development of oil exports.

CONCLUSIONS

Extension of these analyses is possible, with perhaps more
quantitative expression of the similarities and dissimilarities
between the 1960 and 1969 matrices, for example, and more
detailed discussion of the output. Much of this, however,
would involve over-documentation of the relationships
already outlined, and could easily labour the obvious. The
aim of the chapter has been fulfilled by the work already
discussed.

The indices used in the first part of the chapter have
indicated, not surprisingly, that countries vary in their role
within the world trade system, especially in their basic
contribution to it through export activities. In analysing
possible relationships between these specialisation patterns
and other characteristics, several major findings stand out.
First, larger countries are able to trade more widely in
commodities, and especially are able to export more widely.
Secondly, and perhaps most importantly for these studies of
the spatial structure of world trade, the relative location of a
country within the system of trading nations is apparently a
major determinant of the commodity composition of its
trade. This is especially so for imports. Countries with high
export potentials — i.e. countries relatively near to those
exporting in large volumes — tend to import a wider range of
products than do their more isolated counterparts. Accessibility is undoubtedly important in this relationship, with the
high potential countries in a favourable buying position
because of low transport costs; possibly the market-searching

activities of exporters are also spatially biased, so that entrepreneurs seeking to sell products look first at neighbouring countries. For exports, too, countries located close to major importers – i.e. countries with high import potentials – are able to export a wider range of commodities, *ceteris paribus*, than their more distant competitors. Again, relatively low transports costs and relatively easy access to market information probably account for this although, because of collinearity with the O.E.C.D. variable, this phenomenon may be particularly relevant to countries on the periphery of Europe's core area, such as Spain, Turkey and Yugoslavia[27]. (Note, however, from the residuals that it also applies to other 'well-located' countries such as Morocco, Mexico and Israel.) And thirdly, some of the economic unions designed to stimulate trade have apparently benefited their members, in contrast to similar countries not in unions. This is particularly the case for four of the five members of the Central American Common Market, the exception being the poorest member, Honduras[28]; L.A.F.T.A., the E.E.C., O.E.C.D., and the British and French colonial and ex-colonial trade groups all show through in some analyses as significant trade catalysts.

The cross-product principal component analyses reported later in the chapter use more of the information in the country by commodity trade matrices. Their results are very clear and have not been pursued in any great detail. The major pattern shown is a dichotomy between what may be termed the industrialised and the material-source countries. The export trade of the former is dominated by manufactured goods, including chemicals, transport equipment and machinery, whereas the main role of the latter is to provide foodstuffs and raw materials. Among the former, at the one-digit level similarities in this role dominated; at the two-digit level, the almost unique composition of each country's export manifest is indicated by the low loadings obtained by most of the general patterns. Among the latter group of countries – the suppliers of food and raw materials – concentration on one or the other suggests a further basic dichotomy, and outstanding as specialists in a single function alone are the oil exporters. At the two-digit level, these broad groupings are further subdivided into sets of countries based on trade in a particular commodity, such as rubber or sugar, but the basic pattern remains.

Analysis of the import matrices indicated much more similarity between countries in the make-up of their trade. This pattern is the obverse of export specialisation. The majority of countries concentrate on providing only one or a few commodities for the world market. In return, they import a wide range of other goods necessary for a high material standard of living. Differences between countries reflect varying levels of internal self-sufficiency for certain goods and relative priorities in those which they choose to buy, but the majority are clearly dependent on other producers for a wide range of manufactured goods plus some foodstuffs and, in several cases, fuel. This pattern applies to many of the industrialised nations also, indicating the complex industrial division of labour that has developed within that group, several of whose members depend on outside sources for large volumes of their food and raw material requirements also.

Thus the findings reported here, dealing only with the commodity composition of trade, and not with its origins and destinations also, are in line with the general model proposed in Chapter 1. The world trade system comprises a group of industrialised nations, most of them in Europe or North America, which are supplied with needed goods by an aureole of specialist exporters. Among the latter, those favourably located relative to the first group are able to trade in a wider range of commodities, to sell more commodities than is usual, and to purchase more in return; in this way they benefit from their proximity, with economies which perhaps are more stable because of their broader base. Among the specialist exporters, also, are a few countries apparently moving through the stages of economic growth towards the metropolitan status of the industrialised nations. This is indexed in particular by the component loadings for exports, especially in 1969. Japan is clearly a country involved in this process, as is South Africa; to a lesser extent Hong Kong, Singapore, Israel and India are also involved, but further movement for the first three may be constrained by their small size, as suggested by the earlier regression analyses.

In general, although total world trade increased from U.S. $127 500 m. in 1960 to U.S. $244 759 m. only nine years later, the general structure of the system appears to have been very stable. Some changes in detail have occurred, such as Libya's discovery of, and growing dependence on, oil. Patterns of change, however, are the focus of Chapter 4, in which attempts will be made to analyse the alterations to the system, both in commodity trade composition as discussed here, and in the origin-destination pattern which is discussed in the next chapter.

NOTES AND REFERENCES

1. A review of some of these is given in A. G. Ferguson and P. C. Forer, Aspects of measuring employment specialization in Great Britain, *Area*, vol. 5, 1973, 121—38.
2. C. D. Harris, A functional classification of cities in the United States, *Geographical Review*, vol. 33, 1943, 86—99. A full review of city classifications is R. H. T. Smith, Method and purpose in functional town classification, *Annals, Association of American Geographers*, vol. 55, 1965, 539—48.
3. J. W. Alexander, The basic—nonbasic concept of urban functions, *Economic Geography*, vol. 30, 1954, 246—61.
4. See G. J. Karaska, Interindustry relations in the Philadelphia economy, *East Lakes Geographer*, vol. 2, 1966, 80—96.
5. G. Alexanderson, *The Industrial Structure of American Cities*, University of Nebraska Press, Lincoln, 1956; E. L. Ullman and M. F. Dacey, The minimum requirements approach to the urban economic base, *Lund Studies in Geography*, B24, 1962, 121—43.
6. B. J. L. Berry, Latent structure of the American urban system, with international comparisons, in B. J. L. Berry (ed.), *City Classification Handbook*, John Wiley, New York, 1972, 11—60.
7. Labour data are available from various agencies (U.N., I.L.O.), but not in sufficient detail for the present purposes.
8. United Nations, *Standard International Trade Classification, Revised*, United Nations Statistical Papers, Series M, Number 34, 1960.
9. Data given in United Nations, *Yearbook of International Trade Statistics, 1969*, United Nations, New York, 1971, table 1 for each country, were used in the conversions.

10. O. D. Duncan and B. Duncan, An alternative to ecological correlation, *American Sociological Review*, vol. 18, 1953, 665–6.
11. A. G. Ferguson and P. C. Forer, *op. cit.*; P. E. Hart, Entropy and other measures of concentration, *Journal, Royal Statistical Society*, vol. 134, 1971, 73–85.
12. C. R. Pelto, Mapping of multicomponent systems, *Journal of Geology*, vol. 62, 1954, 501–11; W. R. Tobler, *Selected Computer Programs*, Department of Geography, University of Michigan, Ann Arbor, 1970, 25–30; M. Michaely, *Concentration in World Trade*, North-Holland, Amsterdam, 1962, 8.
13. O. D. Duncan and B. Duncan, Occupational stratification and residential distribution, *American Journal of Sociology*, vol. 50, 1955, 493–503.
14. M. Michaely, *op. cit.*, p. 27.
15. In any case, the analyses of Table 2.1 show there is no need to use both. The utility of the entropy measure is shown by its use in three papers in the October 1973 issue of *Economic Geography*.
16. Only countries for which data were available are listed.
17. R. S. Thoman and E. C. Conkling, *Geography of International Trade*, Prentice-Hall, Englewood Cliffs, 1967.
18. There are many texts on this method: see, for example, F. N. Kerlinger and E. J. Pedhazur, *Multiple Regression in Behavioral Research*, Holt, Rinehart and Winston, New York, 1973. In the present analyses, the various indices are all normally distributed but the intervally-scaled independents (population, trade volume, p.c. G.N.P., potentials) are all positively skewed, and are logarithmically transformed. It could be argued that usual regression methods do not apply because the dependent variable has a range of 0 to 100 only. This is the domain of the regression, therefore, an approach preferred to transforming the entropy measure to logits; N. Wrigley; The use of percentages in geographical research, *Area*, vol. 5, 1973, 183–6.
19. The method of obtaining distances is explained in the next chapter.
20. G.N.P. data could be obtained for 1963 only on a broadly comparable basis.
21. The t test is introduced in Kerlinger and Pedhazur, *op. cit.*, pp. 68–9. The chosen t values approximate to the 0·05 and 0·01 significance levels, were strict statistical tests being applied.
22. This problem of overlapping variables is not considered especially important here. The method adopted suggested (a) the dominant role of size and relative location and (b) the extra contribution of the G.N.P. and membership variables. Part (a) is fully accounted for in the first stage regression. Part (b) is not concerned with the relative importance of individual variables, but with improvement of the goodness-of-fit prior to identification of major residuals: if any membership variable were significant, independent of the other, it should stand out. It was not necessary, therefore, to orthogonalise the variables, as suggested in J. B. Riddell, On

structuring a migration model, *Geographical Analysis*, vol. 2, 1970, 403—10. For a fuller discussion of this topic, see R. L. Gorsuch, Data analysis of correlated independent variables, *Multivariate Behavioral Research*, vol. 8, 1973, 89—108.

23. The thresholds for listing the residuals are arbitrary; an attempt was made to have about 20—25 per cent of the major residuals listed. Absolute rather than relative or standardised residuals were used to emphasise deviations in terms of index size.

24. R. J. Rummel, Introducing factor analysis, *Journal of Conflict Resolution*, vol. 11, 1968, 444—80, is the best general introduction to factor analysis, and his *Applied Factor Analysis*, Northwestern University Press, Evanston, 1970, provides a full and lucid treatment.

25. R. J. Johnston, Possible extensions to the factorial ecology methodology: a note, *Environment and Planning*, vol. 5, 1973, 719—34, discusses these approaches.

26. J. N. Sheth, Using factor analysis to estimate parameters, *Journal of the American Statistical Association*, vol. 64, 1969, 808—23.

27. M. J. Webber, *The Impact of Uncertainty on Location*, A.N.U. Press, Canberra, 1973, 194—6, makes some interesting observations on this.

28. J. E. McConnell and E. C. Conkling, Trade specialization and regional integration in central America. Paper presented to an I.G.U. Colloquium on Regional Inequalities of Development, Victoria, ES, Brazil, April 1971. (The authors are in the Department of Geography, State University of New York at Buffalo.)

3

Patterns of Interaction

This chapter complements the preceding one, looking at the other component of the world trade system, the flow of goods between countries. For this, precedents from analyses of other spatial scales are not nearly so numerous, since data on intra-country flows of goods are relatively scarce[1]; indeed, Berry has pointed out the anomaly that one of the richest data sources comes from a relatively undeveloped country[2]. There is a great volume of completed research on various other aspects of spatial interaction, however, notably of migration, from which stimuli were drawn for the present work.

The basic question posed here regarding international trade is 'who trades with whom?' For convenience, this is broken into two separate questions. The first asks to what extent each country trades with all of the others, or, alternatively, how much each specialises in its choice of partners. As in the study of commodity specialisation, this can be answered by using concentration indices which, in turn, become the focus of analyses seeking underlying regularities in patterns of trading partner specialisation. The second question is, assuming that trading partner specialisation exists, with which other countries does any one country exchange commodities? Again, this is similar to the analysis of the preceding chapter, which sought regularities in which commodities were traded[3].

As noted in the first chapter, analogies have been drawn between patterns and processes of spatial interaction and the Newtonian gravity model[4]. Yeates, drawing on the work of Linnemann, has suggested that this body of empirical analysis

58

provides a valid basis for a theoretical approach to international trade flows[5]. Its generalised form has already been noted (equation (4), p. 17); its use suggests a set of causal influences on trade flows, rather than a remapping of the basic flow patterns, which is provided by factor and component analyses.

There are two main sections to this chapter, therefore. The first, following a description of the data, and using the relative entropy index described earlier (equation (9), p. 36), describes the degree of trade-partner specialisation within the various elements of the world trade system; the second uses regression models to account for trade-partner choice. They are followed by a discussion of similar patterns for the flows of individual commodities.

THE DATA

The *Yearbook of International Trade* provides information on the origin and destination of each country's trade manifests, comparable with that on their composition employed in the preceding chapter. Logistic considerations, which involved avoiding excessive data coding and punching, led, however, to the use of an alternative source. Comprehensive trade data, by partner but not by commodity, are collected and published by the International Monetary Fund (I.M.F.) as part of its work in the co-ordination of international exchange. These are published in its monthly bulletin *Direction of Trade* and in its five-yearly supplements. They are also stored and made available for purchase on magnetic tape, which allows direct machine-reading of the information. Relevant tapes were obtained, which is why this alternative source was used[6].

The I.M.F. tape provides annual trade data between each pair of reporting countries for the years since 1948, quarterly data for the most recent years, and monthly data for the current year. If a flow is not reported by one country, it may be estimated from the trade data of another. A common currency, United States dollars, is employed, which avoids the problems of conversion alluded to previously. Only the annual data are employed here. In all analyses, export values were used, since these are given as f.o.b. values; c.i.f. values for imports impede the study of distance effects on trade flows, so each country's import vector was assembled from the export vector of each of its partners.

Coverage of world trade in the I.M.F. file is extensive, but not complete. The main gap is for trade among the Communist bloc countries[7], although data are given for trade between these and all other countries. Thus a complete, square matrix of flows between all pairs of countries could not be compiled; the investigations reported here cover all trade except that among the Communist bloc countries. The number of countries for which records are available varies from year to year, as of course does the number of separate sovereign states involved in the trade system. As this set of inquiries, like that in the previous chapter, looks at two separate years – 1960 and 1969 – the number of countries for which analyses are reported, and between which trade was possible, varies also.

In the discussion of the commodity trade data, the desirability of analysing information for the average of a series of adjacent years was pointed out. Availability of data for each calendar year since 1948 on the I.M.F. tape allowed such averaging in the study of interactions. Thus the data for 1960 analysed here are the average for 1959, 1960 and 1961 and those for 1969 are the average for 1968, 1969 and 1970. This procedure further reduces any direct comparability between the present data set and that used in Chapter 2; it is intended to overcome the possible problem of acute anomalies caused by unusual trading conditions in any particular year. If data were not available for one or two of the relevant years, an average was taken for those for which records were provided.

TRADING PARTNER SPECIALISATION

The relative entropy measure of concentration, termed this time an index of trading partner specialisation, was again employed. As in the study of commodity specialisation, it was necessary to decide between an equality and a total trade norm. The former was adjudged more apt, since it allowed focus on the degree to which countries were dependent on a small number of partners, irrespective of the extent of those partners' participation in the world trade system. Thus for Canada, for example, it is more relevant that 71 per cent of its exports in 1969 went to the United States[8], than that this percentage of its exports went to a country which was responsible for 16 per cent of all imports within the system during that year. The latter aspect, the total trade norm, is employed in the second part of this chapter, dealing with trade-partner choice; here attention is directed to degree of absolute dependence.

Indices of trading partner specialisation were computed, for both imports and exports, in 1960 (where relevant) and in 1969, for each country for which a separate record was given in the I.M.F. publications for the latter date[9]. These indices are recorded in Table A.11: an index of 100·0 indicates a similar proportion of a country's trade originating from, or destined for, each of the others; an index of 0·0 indicates complete reliance on a single partner.

The analyses of commodity trade specialisation found that, on average, countries imported widely, but exported over a much narrower range. The mean indices of trading partner specialisation, on the other hand, indicate a wider dispersal of export than of import trade, though the differences between the two are but slight (Table A.11). There appears to be a general, though far from universal, pattern that the larger and more industrialised the country, the more likely that its export index is greater than its import index. Thus the smaller countries, those which earlier analyses have shown to be the most dependent on exports of but a few commodities, are the most dependent on a few overseas markets for the sale of their products; they use the income from those sources in a wider market place, presumably because of the intra-industry specialisation of the industrial countries. The latter group, on the other hand, export more widely than they import, though the difference in range is usually not great. Their exports are spread more widely because most of the many smaller countries are dependent on the few larger, industrialised ones for supplies of many manufactured goods.

As suggested by the standard deviation for each vector of indices, the range of specialisation is not as great in trading partners as in commodities, particularly in export trade. At both dates, the country with the greatest dispersion of its exports was the United Kingdom (70·58 and 69·43 in 1960 and 1969 respectively); the most specialised in 1960 was Martinique (1·98) and in 1969, S.W. Africa (4·95), though for the latter the completeness of the data is in doubt. Extreme values are relatively rare, however, and mostly represent either a special situation, such as Brunei's export of crude oil to the refineries in Sarawak, or extremely small countries such as Martinique. The United Kingdom also imports in more nearly equal proportions from the wide range of possible sources than any other country; again, Martinique is the most specialised in its trade relations.

Regression Analyses

Despite the relatively narrow scatter of index values displayed in Table A.11, some relationships between their magnitudes and other characteristics of the countries suggest themselves, such as the greater range of trading partners for the larger countries. Regression analyses are used to test these notions, relating the four separate vectors of indices to selected independent variables.

As in the similar analyses of commodity specialisation, three major characteristics of the countries were chosen as representative of the possible determinants of the dispersion of their trade flows — measures of their size, of their relative location, and of their membership of various trade blocs. However, because of difficulties in assembling a complete data matrix for the greater number of countries for which data were available by trading partner, relative to commodity, the G.N.P. variable was excluded from the regressions reported here. Following from this, the interaction variables employed in Chapter 2 (Table 2.3) were also omitted. Thus, for any one dependent variable, eleven independents were employed.

1. Measures of the trade volume of the countries (variables 1–4, Table 3.1), for which it was hypothesised that the greater the volume of trade, the greater its dispersion among trading partners.

2. Measures of the countries' location within the trade system (variables 5–8), indexed by the potential values calculated according to equation (11) on p. 41. The hypothesis is that, holding size constant, favourably located countries relative to the world's largest trading nations should benefit by a wider dispersion of their own trade.

3. The countries' populations (variables 9 and 10), which were included on the hypothesis that larger populations should demand a wider range of goods, requiring more suppliers, and should also produce a wider range, that can be sold more widely. Population size is also taken as an index of economic strength, of potential trade, which other partners would wish to develop.

4. Membership of trade agreements (variables 11–18). Although these blocs are intended to increase the total

TABLE 3.1
REGRESSION ANALYSES: INDICES OF TRADING
PARTNER SPECIALISATION

Key to variables

Stage 1

1.	Total imports	1960	3.	Total imports	1969
2.	Total exports	1960	4.	Total exports	1969
5.	Import potential	1960	7.	Import potential	1969
6.	Export potential	1960	8.	Export potential	1969

Stage 2

9.	Population	1960	10.	Population	1969

Stage 3

11.	Member 'British trading group'	15.	Member C.A.C.M.
12.	Member 'French trading group'	16.	Member E.E.C.
13.	Member 'Portuguese trading group'	17.	Member E.F.T.A.
14.	Member L.A.F.T.A.	18.	Member O.E.C.D.

volume of trade, their intention is to narrow this to the members as much as possible, so a negative relationship between specialisation and membership was anticipated.

The approach used in the regression analyses was the same as in Chapter 2. It was expected that the independent variables in groups (1) and (2) would be the major influences on the degree of specialisation and that the others would perhaps add slightly to the statistical explanation. Consequently, each regression was run in three, incremental stages. In the first, the trade volume and relative location independents were included; in the second, the population variable was added; and in the third, the trade bloc memberships were also included. Collinearity problems are likely in the latter stages, especially involving the measures of trade volume and population. In these, however, the main interest was the total 'goodness-of-fit' rather than the relative strength and independence of the various predictors. As in the previous analyses, also, the measure of whether an independent variable was 'significant' was its t ratio — between the regression coefficient and its standard error — and the intervally-scaled independent variables (1–10) were transformed to base ten logarithms.

Overall, the regressions were probably more successful in accounting for variations in trading partner specialisation (Table 3.2) than for variations in commodity specialisation (Tables 2.4 and 2.7). In the former, however, the single variable of trade volume size loomed large in the total 'explanation'. The relative location variable (5–8) was 'significant' only in the regression for export partner specialisation in 1960, and then apparently only marginally, indicating that favourably located countries were able to spread their products more widely. In 1969, this relationship did not appear. Basically, therefore, the simple finding of these regressions was that large countries trade more widely; a secondary finding was that the O.E.C.D. countries — the industrialised nations — trade slightly less widely than their size might otherwise suggest.

The main residuals from the regressions reported in Table 3.2, those countries whose indices of trading partner special-

TABLE 3.2
REGRESSION ANALYSES: INDICES OF TRADING
PARTNER SPECIALISATION

| | | *Significant variables at stage*[a] | |
	1	2	3
1960			
Imports	1	1	9,−18,16
R	0·61	0·62	0·69
Exports	2,(5)	2,5,9	9,−18
R	0·67	0·71	0·74
1969			
Imports	3	3,10	−(8),10,−18
R	0·55	0·63	0·67
Exports	4	4,10	4,10,(17)
R	0·62	0·69	0·71

Import—export index relationships

1960	*1969*
$I60 = 13·64 + 0·62E60$	$I69 = 17·39 + 0·59E69$
$r = 0·75$	$r = 0·74$

[a]See text, p. 64.

isation deviated most from the values predicted by the
equations, throw further light on the failure of the relative
location variables in the analyses. For example, among the
countries with high positive residuals for imports in 1960,
those with a wider range of sources than predicted, are
several which are very favourably located, such as Gibraltar,
Malta and Iceland. But other, relatively favourably located
nations — most notably Canada and Mexico — are in the list
as having large negative residuals, a narrower spatial spread of
trade than predicted. Clearly it is not only accessibility to a
large market but also the number of countries into which
that market is divided, which is relevant.

At both dates, about 55 per cent of the variation in indices
of trading partner specialisation by imports could be
accounted for by the variation in the comparable indices for
exports (Table 3.2). (The import indices were set as the
dependent variable on the argument that a wider export field
would provide the basis, notably in information, for a wide

range of import sources.) The two regression equations both indicate that countries with export indices below 30·0 have higher import than export indices, with the converse for countries with export indices exceeding 30·0. Nations whose export trade is spatially very concentrated thus draw on a greater range of import sources; those whose exports are widely spread draw their supplies from a more restricted range. Such a finding is in line with the model presented in Chapter 1. The specialised exporters must draw from a larger number of sources because of the high degree of specialisation — at the three- and four-digit level of the commodity classification — in the most industrialised countries which take most of the exports (see below); the industrialised nations export their specialised products very widely but, as manufacturing products come to dominate world trade, get most of their imports from their few counterparts. There are no particular common characteristics among the countries whose import indices are badly under- or over-predicted by these relationships.

Commodity Specialisation and Trading Partner Specialisation

The preceding discussion suggests clear relationships between levels of commodity specialisation and of trading partner specialisation. Those countries importing/exporting a wide range of products should be less dependent on a few trade partners than those whose trade is dominated by but a few commodities. The validity of this proposition was tested by regressing the commodity specialisation indices on those for trading partner specialisation. The former were selected as the independent variables since the notions being tested propose that breadth of commodity trade determines range of partners. Two regressions were run for each dependent variable. In the first, the one-digit commodity specialisation indices were the only independent; in the second, the two-digit indices were added. Collinearity problems are likely to be severe in the second stage analyses, in which the focus is clearly on the correlation coefficients.

The clearest result of these equations is their poor performance, particularly for the study of trading partner specialisation in imports (Table 3.3). For exports, the general

TABLE 3.3
COMMODITY TRADE SPECIALISATION AND
TRADING PARTNER SPECIALISATION

Dependent Variable	Stage 1		Stage 2[a]		
	Correlation	$t(X_1)$	Correlation	$t(X_1)$	$t(X_2)$
Imports 1960	0·15	1·28	0·17	0·37	0·68
Exports 1960	0·52	5·32	0·57	0·25	2·22
Imports 1969	0·14	1·21	0·14	0·32	0·20
Exports 1969	0·41	3·92	0·43	0·44	1·24

[a] See text, p. 66.

nature of the hypothesis is clearly confirmed; the greater the range of commodities traded, the less dependent the exporting country is on a few markets. Nevertheless, this is but a partial finding, as suggested by the low correlation coefficients, the largest of which indicates a statistical explanation of only 32 per cent. Reasons for this are suggested by the patterns of residuals, which are very similar for each of the two dates. The countries whose trading partner specialisation is much less than their commodity specialisation would suggest comprise two groups: (1) those located close to very large trading nations (Canada, Mexico and Ireland); and (2) small ex-colonies, especially African ex-colonies, whose trade is still dominantly with the 'mother country' (Mauritius, Senegal, Sierra Leone and Reunion). Among those whose trading partner specialisation is less than predicted (i.e. which trade widely), the most notable are the oil states, including the 'oil entrepôts' (Aden and the Netherlands Antilles). Also in this group are the United Kingdom and Argentina.

From the analyses of import specialisation, it is clear that the range of commodities brought in has very little influence on the extent of trade-partner linkages. This is not particularly surprising, given the relatively small scatter of values for import commodity specialisation (Table A.1); most countries import a considerable variety of commodities, but whether they get these from a few or from many countries depends on, among other things, such factors as the exact nature of those commodities and the historical pattern of trade links for the relevant countries. Inspection of the residuals from the 1960 and 1969 regressions does suggest two general patterns, however. First, as in the export flows, there are a few countries (notably Canada, Mexico and Ireland) whose imports are dominated by a few partners, and, secondly, with those exceptions, countries of the 'developed' world tend to trade with a wider spread of partners than do their 'developing' contemporaries, especially those in Africa.

THE CHOICE OF TRADE PARTNERS

Although indices of specialisation provide a valid measure of a country's participation in the international economy, they do not specify its nature. Thus the variation in import and export indices just described could represent a number of different flow patterns, being some combination of the two polar types of discrete 'metropolitan' regions and a single interacting whole. (In the former, sets of export specialisation countries would each serve a clearly defined metropolitan group; in the latter all countries would, to some extent, be trading with all others, with no apparent clusters of countries more closely tied to each other than to the rest.) Detailed portrayal of the interaction patterns, therefore, requires depiction of who trades with whom.

Components analysis was used in the previous chapter to indicate groups of countries trading in similar commodities; it can also be used to isolate groups trading with the same partners[10]. Four matrices were constructed, two each for 1960 and for 1969, containing (1) the percentage distribution of exports from each country, and (2) the percentage distribution of imports, and these were submitted to cross-products principal components analyses. The results of each were dominated by the first components, indicating a general world-wide pattern of trade orientation towards the major industrialised countries of Western Europe, North America and Japan. Minor components picked out more specialised flows focusing on individual countries, such as that between France and its 'trading group' and an Asian group orientated on Japan, but these detailed patterns were submerged in the general picture, which the loadings and scores together indicated was a composite of two elements: (1) trade among the metropolitan countries; and (2) trade between the metropolitan countries and the specialised exporters.

An alternative data input to the components analysis would be to standardise the trade flows in some way in order to partial out the obvious metropolitan focus. This has been done, for example, by Russett who factor analysed a matrix of inter-country trade volumes, expressed as a ratio of the relevant countries' G.N.P.s. From this he identified nine clusters of countries which traded more among themselves than was predicted (p. 10). A similar approach was used with the present data sets, with a predicted trade flow for each being computed by

$$\widehat{I_{ij}} = \{(E_i/\Sigma E) \times (H_j/\Sigma H)\} \times \Sigma E \qquad (12)$$

where E_i = total exports from country i,
        ΣE = total exports from all countries,
        H_j = total imports to country j,
        ΣH = total imports to all countries, and
        $\widehat{I_{ij}}$ = predicted exports from i to j.

According to this, the exports from any country to another are proportional to the country of origin's proportion of all exports and the destination's proportion of all imports; each country trades equally with all others in ratio to their proportion of the total trade[11]. Deviations from these predictions can be represented as

$$L_{ij} = I_{ij}/\widehat{I_{ij}} \qquad (13)$$

where I_{ij} = observed exports from i to j,
        $\widehat{I_{ij}}$ = as defined for formula (12), and
        L_{ij} = the deviation ratio for export trade from i to j.

If L_{ij} exceeds 1·0, more of i's exports go to j than would be the case if no variable other than the volume of trading activity at origin and destination influenced trade flows.

If within the general pattern of metropolitan dominance in trade flows there are groups of countries which trade more with each other than predicted, this should be demonstrated by components analyses of the L_{ij} values. Results of such analyses were of little value, however. The main reason for this was the large number of zero, or near-zero, values of L in the matrices, representing pairs of countries between which there was no trade. These dominated the solutions and apparently precluded the output of more interesting findings relating to the other deviations. Some manipulations of the matrix were attempted, omitting certain countries, but it was decided that other analytical approaches would be more fruitful.

Interaction Equations

Models of interaction were reviewed in Chapter 1, with special reference to those based on an analogy with Newton's gravity equation (pp. 12–19). These have been widely used in studies of flows to measure the influence of different variables on interaction volumes. In their 'purest' form, they include only the 'Newtonian' variables – a measure of 'mass' at origin and at destination – as indices of propensity to interact, and a measure of distance between origin and destination, as an index of the frictional effects of distance on location. In many studies, however, extra variables are introduced to index other influences, such as institutional constraints and intervening opportunities.

Two model equations have been applied to the present data sets. The first – termed the Indifference Model – assumes that the only independent variables influencing flows between two places are mass and distance, and it further assumes that the coefficients for mass are unity, not varying by country. It is expressed as

$$\log I_{ij}/O_i D_j = \log a + b \log d_{ij} \qquad (14)$$

where I_{ij} = the trade from i to j (imports or exports),
       O_i = the total trade from i,
       D_j = the total imports to j, and
       d_{ij} = the distance between i and j.

If mass were the only influence on interaction, the values of $\log I_{ij}/O_i D_j$ should not vary between pairs of origins and destinations; the size of the flow would be the proportion of all trade in the system as indexed by the product of O_i and D_j[12]. The nature of the equation suggests that deviations from this 'indifference' pattern of trade are a function of the relative location of the partners: the value of b should be negative, so that the greater the intervening distance, the smaller the trade volume.

The indifference model ignores the many 'imperfections' of the international trade system which impede the free flow of goods according to its criteria of mass and distance influences. To account for these, a second model — termed the Total Interaction Model — was developed, with the form

$$\log I_{ij} = \log a + b_1 \log D_j + b_2 \log P_j + b_3 \log d_{ij}$$
$$+ b_{4-10} M_{1-7} \qquad (15)$$

where I_{ij} = the trade from i to j (imports or exports)
$\quad\quad D_j$ = the exports of j, if imports are I; the imports of j if exports are I,
$\quad\quad P_j$ = the population of j,
$\quad\quad d_{ij}$ = the distance separating i and j,
$\quad\quad M_1$ = membership of the 'British trading group' (variable 4)
$\quad\quad M_2$ = membership of the 'French trading group' (5)
$\quad\quad M_3$ = membership of the 'Portuguese trading group' (6),
$\quad\quad M_4$ = membership of L.A.F.T.A. (7),
$\quad\quad M_5$ = membership of the C.A.C.M. (8),
$\quad\quad M_6$ = membership of the E.E.C. (9), and
$\quad\quad M_7$ = membership of the E.F.T.A. (10).

This equation was reached after a number of trials with a wider range of independent variables. It was hoped, for example, to include some measure of trade-partner function, based on the analyses reported in the previous chapter, to examine the role of G.N.P. *per capita* rather than population as an added indicator of size, and to look at the interactions among variables, such as distance and trade group membership[13]. Several factors mitigated against such analyses. First, there was the problem of data availability, notably G.N.P. volumes for many smaller countries. Secondly, there was the problem of multicollinearity, of variables confounding each other, and in some cases producing singular matrices. Thirdly,

the larger the number of variables, the greater the proportion
of the trade vectors which had too few non-zero values, and
so could not be analysed. And finally, since the focus here
was on individual countries and not on the total pattern of
interaction[14], use of a larger data set would involve many
hours of experimentation and computer time to find the best
combination and fit for each of the four trade vectors for the
large number of countries being studied. As it was, the results
using this model were in general encouraging; detailed study
of individual countries is clearly desirable as a follow-up, but
the set of variables adopted here was successful in accounting
for large proportions of the trade flows[15].

As already indicated, each of these models was fitted to
the separate import and export trade vectors, for 1960 and
for 1969, for each country with sufficient available data. For
the indifference model, non-zero trade flows with at least ten
other countries were required, for the total interaction
model, twenty. Use of only non-zero flows follows the
tradition of other trade studies. It avoids certain technical
problems, such as taking the logarithm of zero and the
heteroscedascity that would be introduced with a large
number of zero flows (pairs of countries between which there
was no trade). On the other hand, it also introduces
interpretative difficulties. The coefficients in the equations
indicate only the influence of the independent variables
within the set of countries *with which a nation chooses to
trade*: nothing is indicated concerning those with which it
does not trade. For many countries which trade with most
others, this is not serious, but for some it is, particularly the
smaller ones. For these latter, therefore, the regression
coefficient for, say, distance could be misleading.

All the data for trade flows, and the I_{ij}, O_i and D_j values,
were derived from the I.M.F. tape; population data were
obtained from the *United Nations Demographic Yearbook*
for the relevant years, and group memberships from available
sources[16]. (For the British, French and Portuguese trading
groups recent as well as present colonial areas were included.)
Major difficulty was experienced in the measurement of
inter-country distances, however. For many countries, notably small ex-colonies with primate urban systems[17], the
choice of a single point to measure from was easy — the main

town. But for a few large countries with a dispersed market — such as Canada and the United States — no easy choice was available; in these cases an arbitrary decision was made based on accessibility within that country, such as maps of population potential. (For Canada the choice was Toronto; for the United States, New York.) Clearly this introduces 'noise' into the model; if, for example, most New Zealand—Canada trade involves British Columbia at the latter end, use of the Auckland—Toronto distance should considerably underpredict the volume. Unfortunately, no data were readily available for testing such an assumption, so no attempts were made to change the distance base-points according to partner.

The distances were computed using a program devised by Tobler for deriving spherical distances; the inputs were the latitudinal and longitudinal coordinates of the selected base-points[18]. Again, this procedure introduces 'noise'. The great circle distances on the globe may differ quite considerably from those used in the interaction between two points: journey-length from East Africa to Europe would be underestimated relative to journey-length from West Africa, especially for 1969, when the Suez Canal was closed. Changes in transport mode, with consequent effects on time and cost, are also ignored. Use of what is closer to an 'airline' distance than a 'freight' distance can clearly make predictions from the models in equations (14) and (15) invalid in the 'real world'. Several experiments were undertaken to introduce weightings for different routes, such as the East and West Africa to Europe example, but no satisfactory set was found which performed better in the equations than the spherical distance measure.

In the context of the present enquiries, use of a single measure of the distance between two countries, omitting considerations such as mode(s) of transport used, probable locations of journey end-points, and probable route, has other advantages. Most of the analyses reported here, particularly those relating to total trade between pairs of countries, treat bundles of widely differing commodities rather than a single homogeneous product. Different commodities may be carried by different transport modes, and along different routes; different rates may be charged, because of those two factors and also variations in such aspects as the volume, bulk and regularity of a flow. Any investigation of total trade, which is either unable to subdivide that trade into homogeneous commodities or has no information on the rates charged to move different items, must adopt some average structure. As travel costs in most cases increase at a decreasing rate with increasing distance, then if trade volume is negatively related to costs, the volume of trade should decline at a decreasing rate as distance increases. Such a pattern is represented by the 'gravity model' formulations adopted here, in which the logarithm of trade is related to the logarithm of distance. In the lack of any superior information, and given the need for a measure which can be universally applied in a large number of analyses, therefore, the use of such an 'average' surrogate for the costs of movement is justified.

Major attention in this study of the trade system is clearly being focused on its spatial parameters, the coefficients for distance in equations (14) and (15). One problem in their interpretation has already been indicated. Another follows from the finite nature of the system, and the logarithmic transformation of distances to fit the 'gravity' analogy. Several interaction studies, including Linnemann's of world trade, have indicated a relationship between a place's location in a system and the parameter for distance in a regression model[19]. It has been suggested, however, that this is at least partly because of the influence of location, or map pattern[20]. Analyses show that the more remote places tend to have steeper distance-decay coefficients (the b values), which suggests that such places tend to trade more with their near neighbours. Yet this is counter-intuitive, since near neighbours are further away for remote places within a spatial system.

It can be demonstrated that in a spatial system with no self-trade, as in the world trade system, where all other variables except map pattern are held constant, the more remote the location within the system, the steeper its regression coefficient for distance[21]. Figure 3.1 illustrates this point. Places A and B each send the same amount of trade to their nearest neighbour, each sends the same amount to its second nearest, and so on. But A is more remote than B, and on a logarithmic scale, the extra distance to D relative to C is less

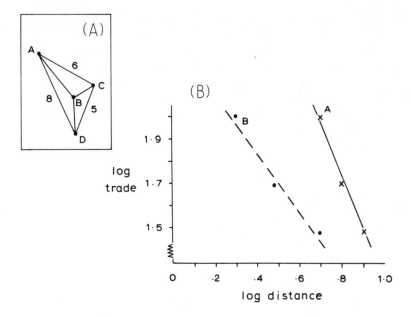

Fig. 3.1. The effects of location on regression coefficients for distance in gravity-type models. Diagram *A* shows a system of four countries and the distance between each. Every country sends 100 units to its nearest neighbour, fifty to the second nearest, and thirty-three to the third. In Diagram *B*, the distance/trade regressions for A and for B are shown: A has the steepest distance-decay function, as a consequence of its position in the system.

for A than is the extra distance to A relative to D for B. The result is a steeper distance-decay curve. To standardise for this effect all distances within each trade vector are expressed as a percentage of the range of distances in that vector (plus one, to avoid taking the logarithm of zero), so that

$$sd_{ij} = (d_{ij}/(R_{di} + 1)) \times 100 \qquad (16)$$

where d_{ij} = the distance from i to j,
         R_{di} = the range of distances from i, and
         sd_{ij} = the standardised distance.

Each regression equation was run twice; once using d_{ij} and the other using sd_{ij}. The coefficients for each distance variable have interpretative value. That for d_{ij} indicates the degree of distance-decay, but it cannot be compared with that for another country, since the map pattern influence is unique to each. The sd_{ij} values are directly comparable, since they measure the strength of the distance-decay effect in an interaction field of standard radius. Variations in sd_{ij} values indicate the degree of favouring nearer neighbours. Differences between d_{ij} and sd_{ij} suggest the penalty which a remote country must pay for its remoteness; the sd_{ij} value should be less steep, with the greater the difference between it and d_{ij} the greater the isolation penalty.

As with the analyses of commodity trade specialisation and trading partner specialisation, this section of the work aims not only to describe variations in the parameters of the interaction models, but also to account for these by other variables. Thus regression analyses, arranged in stages, are employed as before.

The Indifference Model

Three major parameters of these equations have been selected for consideration:

1. the b_d coefficient, for log d_{ij};
2. the r coefficient, the goodness-of-fit of the equation; and
3. the b_s coefficient, for log sd_{ij}.

These are given, for import and export trade vectors at each date, in Table A.12.

Although the indifference model is a very simplistic one, assigning all variation in trade flows not accounted for by the 'mass' of the origin and destination (which itself is considered as a constant) to distance, a salient feature of the results is its relative success as a predictive equation. The frequency distributions for r are

r	Imports		Exports	
	1960	*1969*	*1960*	*1969*
< 0·3	20	29	26	30
0·3—0·4	47	70	41	47
0·5—0·6	50	39	42	50
0·7—0·8	19	14	19	20
0·9 <	1	0	1	2

In very few cases was a majority of the variation in flows accounted for by the distance variable (this would need a correlation coefficient of just over 0·7), but in only about one-fifth to one-sixth was distance of hardly any relevance. (One point not brought out in this tabulation is that in a few cases, such as Greenland's imports, the sign of the coefficient was positive, indicating increasing trade with increasing distance.) For the prediction of imports, the validity of distance declined over time, whereas for exports there was a general upward shift; for 1960, the distributions for imports and exports differ only slightly, but for 1969, distance clearly is a better predictor of export than of import flows. Together these results suggest a less constrained search for import than for export markets.

The regression coefficients indicate considerable variation among countries in the distance-decay effect. As anticipated from other studies, remoter countries tended to have the highest coefficients (note New Zealand, for example), a relationship which was constant over the b and b_s coefficients. Remoter countries tended to have the highest location 'penalties' also: for New Zealand the ratio $b_d:b_s$ for exports 1969 was 3·8; for Belgium it was 1·2.

The independent variables employed to account for variations in the parameter of the model were those used in the earlier analyses of trading partner specialisation (Table 3.1). Their influence was slight; in no case did the multiple correlation exceed 0.5 (Tables 3.4 and 3.5). Prediction was slightly more successful for imports in 1969, for exports in 1960. With both, the major predictor of the size of the b_d coefficient was relative location in the system; the positive signs indicate that those countries with higher potentials had less steep distance-decay curves. With the b_s coefficients, however, this relationship had largely disappeared, suggesting that the differences in b_d coefficients by location were mainly a function of the map pattern influence. Inspection of the residuals from the stage 3 regressions suggested no other obvious relationships; the only point to be gleaned is that the Middle East oil states trade more widely than the distance variable suggests, on the basis of countries of similar size and location.

The Total Interaction Model

The output from these regressions is voluminous; much of it could be assimilated in only general terms and a small proportion is summarised in Table A.13. For each trade vector (imports 1960, etc.) the values tabulated are:

1. R — the multiple correlation coefficient;
2. b_d;
3. b_s;
4. b_1 — the regression coefficient for variable D_j; and
5. the 'significant' M variables — p. 71 — being those with t values exceeding 2·0.

Probably the most outstanding feature within these results is the highly successful performance of the equation. In all but nine, the multiple correlation coefficient was 0·7 or

TABLE 3.4
REGRESSION ANALYSES: PARAMETERS OF THE
INDIFFERENCE MODEL, 1960

		Significant variables at stage[a]	
	1	2	3
b_a *coefficient*			
Imports	6	(6),(1),(−9)	6,(−9)
R	0·28	0·32	0·40
Exports	2,5	2,5,−9	2,5,−9
R	0·41	0·49	0·53
r *coefficient*			
Imports	(6)	none	−15
R	0·22	0·23	0·38
Exports	2,(5)	2,−9	2,5,−9,13,−15
R	0·33	0·43	0·50
b_s *coefficient*			
Imports	none	none	(14), (−15)
R	0·12	0·15	0·31
Exports	5	(5),−9	(5),−9,(−15)
R	0·20	0·31	0·38

[a] See text, p. 64.

greater. The success rate was greatest with the prediction of imports,

	Imports		Exports	
R	1960	1969	1960	1969
< 0·5			1	1
0·5		1	1	1
0·6			1	3
0·7	2	5	11	19
0·8	45	57	46	53
0·9<	33	40	26	25

suggesting a greater tendency to import from nearby large sources — especially if there was some kind of preferential agreement — than there was to export to local large markets. Most of the regression coefficients for the distance variables were 'statistically significant' (t greater than 1·65; those

TABLE 3.5
REGRESSION ANALYSES: PARAMETERS OF THE
INDIFFERENCE MODEL, 1969

	Significant variables at stage[a]		
	1	2	3
b_d coefficient			
Imports	8	8	8,−12,13,(14)
R	0·30	0·30	0·53
Exports	7	7,4,−10	7,(4),−10,−12,−18
R	0·29	0·34	0·48
r coefficient			
Imports	(3)	none	(3),13,(14),−15
R	0·21	0·21	0·50
Exports	none	(4),(−10)	4,−10,13,−18
R	0·09	0·21	0·40
b_s coefficient			
Imports	none	none	13,−15
R	0·12	0·12	0·47
Exports	(7)	−10	−10,(−15),(16)
R	0·15	0·25	0·36

[a] See text, p. 64.

lower than that value are indicated by brackets around the coefficient in Table A.13), whereas those for trade partner size suggest that since more, and especially those for imports, exceed 1·0, there is a tendency to 'over-trade' with the larger suppliers or purchasers. The number of times each of the other variables was significant was

	Imports		*Exports*	
	1960	*1969*	*1960*	*1969*
P_j	28	40	28	34
M_1	41	36	29	43
M_2	21	31	24	36
M_3	10	17	15	18
M_4	25	37	26	37
M_5	15	30	9	18
M_6	19	15	25	36
M_7	15	23	28	38

and the number of times that D_j was not significant was

7	9	12	15
(4)	(3)	(6)	(9)

(The figures in parentheses indicate the number of times when D_j was insignificant but P_j was significant.)

The frequency of significant coefficients for some of the trading group variables, notably M_4 and M_5 (L.A.F.T.A. and C.A.C.M.), is perhaps surprising. A considerable proportion of the coefficients were negative, however, indicating relatively low volumes of trade between those countries and many others, particularly countries in other hemispheres[22]. Within the various trading groups, however, each member should have displayed a significant regression coefficient for the relevant group. The proportions that did were:

Group	Imports		Exports	
	1960	1969	1960	1969
British	15/21	16/24	13/16	17/26
French	8/8	12/15	8/8	14/15
Portuguese	3/3	3/3	3/3	3/3
L.A.F.T.A.	1/7	4/7	2/7	4/7
C.A.C.M.	3/3	5/5	1/3	4/5
E.E.C.	1/5	0/5	1/5	1/5
E.F.T.A.	4/7	3/7	3/7	3/7

(Note that in this tabulation, not every country in a group traded with sufficient partners for a regression equation to be fitted.)

Each of the colonial and ex-colonial groups remains a significant distributor of trade volumes, less so in the British case from which some have broken ties (e.g. South Africa), some have developed relatively independent trade ties (e.g. Singapore), and others, because of the commodity specialisation, are less dependent on Britain (e.g. Nigeria and Zambia). Of the two Latin American groupings, the C.A.C.M. has clearly been more successful as a trade generator; in 1969 only Honduras did not have a significant regression coefficient for exports as well as imports: L.A.F.T.A., on the other hand, has proved much less able to generate intra-group trade[2 3]. Neither of the two European groups, especially the E.E.C., appears to have been particularly successful as trade generator or director. (Note that the Belgian and Luxembourg trade figures are combined in all of the statistical sources, to give only five E.E.C. countries in both 1960 and 1969.)

Four of the parameters of the total interaction equations were used as dependent variables in regression analyses; the independents were those listed in Table 3.1. As with the similar analyses of the parameters of the indifference model, predictive success was limited, although slightly less so in the present case (Tables 3.6 and 3.7). Three of the sets of equations for the b_d coefficients underlined the map pattern influence on this parameter by placing the relevant potential variable as the major explanans: the exception was for the

TABLE 3.6
REGRESSION ANALYSES: PARAMETERS OF THE
TOTAL INTERACTION MODEL, 1960

	Significant variables at stage[a]		
	1	2	3
b_d coefficient			
Imports	6	6	6,−13
R	0·45	0·46	0·58
Exports	5	5	5
R	0·41	0·43	0·51
t ratio for b_d coefficient			
Imports	1,(−6)	1,(−6)	(1),
R	0·30	0·32	0·39
Exports	2	(9)	(9), 18
R	0·27	0·34	0·46
R coefficient			
Imports	(6)	none	15,
R	0·17	0·17	0·53
Exports	2	2	none
R	0·41	0·42	0·53
b_s coefficient			
Imports	(6)	(6)	(6),(14)
R	0·27	0·28	0·44
Exports	none	2	(2),(−12)
R	0·27	0·33	0·45

[a]See text, p. 64.

1969 export flows, which produced a low multiple correlation of only 0·38. For import flows in 1969 there is the suggestion that the larger importing countries had steeper distance-decay curves for their flows (a not easily interpreted finding), but no other obvious regularity showed through. After the distance variable was standardised for the map pattern influence, even fewer regularities in b_s could be discerned, notably for export flows. In 1960 there was a slight relationship between larger exporters and a wider distribution, and also a suggestion that French group countries traded less widely; the former finding was absent from the 1969 analyses, while the latter was reversed. For imports there was still an indication, however, that despite the

TABLE 3.7
REGRESSION ANALYSES: PARAMETERS OF THE
TOTAL INTERACTION MODEL, 1969

	Significant Variables at Stage[a]		
	1	2	3
b_d coefficient			
Imports	−3,8	−3,8	−3,8,12,13
R	0·41	0·42	0·59
Exports	none	none	12
R	0·03	0·03	0·38
t ratio for b_d coefficient			
Imports	3	3,−8	3,−12,−13,15,−18
R	0·31	0·34	0·59
Exports	4	4	4,(−16),18
R	0·42	0·42	0·52
R coefficient			
Imports	none	none	15
R	0·13	0·15	0·40
Exports	4,7	4,7	18
R	0·43	0·44	0·51
b_s coefficient			
Imports	(−3),8	(−3),8	8,12,13
R	0·25	0·26	0·44
Exports	none	none	12
R	0·07	0·08	0·39

[a] See text, p. 64.

standardisation for the map pattern influence, countries with high potentials relative to exporters tended to trade more widely.

The extremely poor results from these regression analyses suggest either that the spatial distribution of the b_d and b_s coefficients is to a considerable degree random or that the underlying influences to the pattern were not being tested by the models employed here. Inspection of the regression residuals throws some light on the failure, especially for the export flows, where it is clear that the oil producers are not constrained by distance in their range of trading partners. For the import flows, however, there is no such apparent relationship, and the conclusion must be that variations in these distance parameters are extremely difficult to predict over a population of seventy or more countries.

The other two parameters examined related to goodness-of-fit, the first (the R coefficient) of the whole equation, and the second (the t ratio for the b coefficient — see p. 43) of the distance variable. Only 20—30 per cent of the variation in each could be accounted for by the selected variables. There is a clear suggestion of closer fits for the larger countries (the collinearity of the size and trade volumes impedes display of this relationship in some instances) and also, for exports 1969 R coefficient, that there are better fits for the more favourably located countries. With the t ratios for imports, on the other hand, the inference is that the countries relatively close to large export markets are more variable in the strength of the distance measure as an independent influence on trade flows.

Distance and Interaction: Some Conclusions

These tests of the indifference and total interaction models have confirmed the basic tenet of much research in geography and regional science, that the amount of movement between one place and a range of others is conditioned by the distances involved. International trade is constrained by many variables, yet still it seems clear that distance — as a surrogate for cost, time, information and opportunities — influences decisions on where goods should be obtained from or sent to. As was suggested in the model of economic growth discussed in Chapter 1, and confirmed by the factor analyses of the trade matrices (p. 68), there is an obvious pattern of metropolitan dominance in trade flows, of orientation towards a few countries which together account for a very large proportion of the world's trade[24]. Despite this, the two models tested here indicate that, within the group of countries with which they trade, for most nations distance influences trade volumes. Thus the indifference model showed that countries directed more exports towards, and obtained more imports from, their neighbours than those partners might have expected on the basis of their total trade. The total interaction model introduced several other variables, but still for most countries distance remained a significant predictor of trade volume; there was a strong tendency in almost every case to direct most trade towards the world's major trading nations, but even so, of that group, the closest would be most favoured. For many countries, trade agreements or preferences were important, but, within such groups, it was the largest and the nearest which were apparently favoured.

Even where the influence of distance on trade is constant among countries, its intensity may vary. In some cases, nearby partners may receive most of a country's exports; in others, there may be a wider distribution, while still reflecting a distance-decay pattern. In line with other studies, the present tests have indicated that the intensity of the distance influence was greatest for those countries which were, on average, furthest from the main trading nations, though there were some notable exceptions, such as the oil-exporting states. This suggests that such peripherally-located countries must trade more with their neighbours, because of the greater trade costs involved in movement of their goods, but this finding is a function of the method rather than of the trade flows. Countries on the edge of a map are likely to show this relationship merely because of their location; standardisation of the distance variable removes such an influence and analysis of the revised results indicated no such pattern. Within the group with which they choose to trade, there is no indication that the peripheral countries experience a greater intensity of the distance influence. But, because virtually all countries trade with the European—American metropolitan core, those on the edge of the map of trade potential — those furthest from the core — must pay a location penalty. To achieve a similar distance-decay pattern (the b_s coefficient) they must move their goods further on average (as indicated by the b_d/b_s ratio[25]).

INDIVIDUAL COMMODITY FLOWS

The analyses reported thus far in the present chapter have been of total trade between pairs of countries. Do the various results hold for the flows of different commodities? Investigations at other scales and of other movement patterns have often indicated that interaction models provide better fits to total flow than to disaggregated flow patterns[26]. This suggests some kind of regression to a mean pattern when flows are summed; a possible reason for the differences is the degree to which either or both of the production and consumption of a commodity is spatially concentrated[27].

Investigation of whether any such differences occur in international commodity movements requires relevant data. For many countries, trade data are the most detailed and perhaps also the most effectively collected; there is certainly a great volume available. Their collection, collation and preparation for analysis, at a world as against an individual country scale[28], is immensely demanding of time and effort, however. For this reason, a compromise was necessary: only one source was used, and only the one-digit commodity classification was employed.

The source used here is the United Nations publication, *Commodity Trade Statistics*, which appears several times each year and which publishes data at each level of the commodity classification and for all partners, where reported by the relevant country. These data refer to the January—March, January—June, January—September and January—December periods[29]. For 1960 (again, no three-year averaging could be undertaken) the publication covered thirty-two countries, but three of these (El Salvador, Malaya and Nigeria) were not included in the 1969 series; to allow comparability over the two dates, only the twenty-nine countries in both lists were used (Table 3.8), despite the availability of a much larger list for 1969. Unfortunately this leads to an over-concentration on (*a*) 'developed' and (*b*) European countries; only Ghana and Trinidad and Tobago can be considered examples of relatively remote, export specialisation countries, since Netherlands Antilles is a special case[30]. The decision to use only the one-digit level of the commodity classification was largely imposed by the effort needed to prepare data at other levels; in any case, coverage at even the two-digit level is far from universal, which would impede the types of analysis undertaken here.

Given the restraints of commodity classification and the set of countries, complete replication of the analyses

TABLE 3.8
KEY TO COUNTRIES USED IN STUDIES OF
INDIVIDUAL COMMODITY FLOWS

1. U.S.A.	11. Sweden	21. Israel
2. Canada	12. Austria	22. Australia
3. Belgium-Luxembourg	13. Portugal	23. New Zealand
4. France	14. Switzerland	24. Ghana
5. West Germany	15. Iceland	25. Japan
6. Italy	16. Ireland	26. Singapore
7. Netherlands	17. Greece	27. Hong Kong
8. United Kingdom	18. Turkey	28. Trinidad and Tobago
9. Denmark	19. Finland	29. Netherlands Antilles
10. Norway	20. Yugoslavia	

reported in this and the preceding chapter of total interaction patterns was neither necessary nor possible. Full presentation of results of all the analyses conducted would require much space. As an alternative, the data have been used to test a series of simple hypotheses[31].

Trading Partner Concentration and
Commodity Concentration

Trading partner specialisation in the movements to and from each of the twenty-nine countries in each of the nine commodities is shown by the relative entropy indices. Variations in these should correlate with the commodity specialisation, measured here as the percentage of the relevant commodity flow involving the twenty-nine countries going either to or from the particular country. For example, the greater the proportion of the total exports of commodity X (i.e. the total for the twenty-nine countries) which flows from country A, the more widespread that nation's trade in X should be. Similarly, the greater the proportion of all imports of Y which goes to A, the more countries it should have to draw on. To test such notions, the proportion of trade, by commodity, either emanating from or destined for each country was computed and this vector of proportions was correlated with the vector of relative entropy indices (equation (9)) for that commodity flow. It is hypothesised that the correlation should be positive.

TABLE 3.9
TRADING PARTNER SPECIALISATION AND
COMMODITY SPECIALISATION[a]

Analysis by commodity

| | 1960 | | | | 1969 | | | |
| | Imports | | Exports | | Imports | | Exports | |
Commodity	$\overline{G}$	r	$\overline{G}$	r	$\overline{G}$	r	$\overline{G}$	r
1	52·2	0·36	44·1	0·30	55·7	0·42	46·2	0·27
2	34·5	−0·51	37·6	0·45	40·8	0·27	35·3	0·54
3	51·7	−0·25	44·6	−0·66	56·9	0·17	49·2	−0·20
4	35·6	0·27	35·2	0·60	40·3	0·27	31·9	0·41
5	39·6	0·44	40·2	0·38	38·8	0·66	36·5	0·49
6	39·3	0·23	53·2	0·13	42·2	0·17	53·5	0·55
7	43·6	−0·18	51·1	0·48	48·1	0·29	50·3	0·38
8	33·7	−0·22	54·6	0·45	37·2	−0·30	52·5	0·29
9	37·9	−0·69	43·2	0·19	43·2	0·18	46·3	0·48

Analysis by country

Country	$\overline{G}$	r	Country	$\overline{G}$	r	Country	$\overline{G}$	r
1	53·4	0·29	11	49·1	0·18	21	41·8	−0·04
2	27·5	−0·17	12	43·9	0·12	22	41·9	−0·32
3	42·5	−0·43	13	43·6	0·27	23	37·7	−0·21
4	51·4	0·08	14	46·5	0·39	24	38·6	0·27
5	54·6	0·38	15	31·8	−0·53	25	44·6	0·31
6	50·9	0·07	16	29·2	−0·08	26	38·0	0·35
7	49·1	−0·18	17	44·5	0·01	27	39·6	−0·57
8	59·0	0·03	18	40·4	−0·57	28	32·5	0·06
9	47·8	−0·20	19	41·5	0·34	29	33·3	0·23
10	46·2	0·05	20	45·3	−0·50			

[a] $\overline{G}$ = mean relative entropy.

Most of the correlation coefficients support the hypothesis, but not strongly (Table 3.9). Only seven of the thirty-six coefficients (six of them for 1960) are negative, but the highest positive value is 0·66 and the average for the twenty-nine is only 0·28. The most consistent relationships over both dates and imports and exports are for commodity 5, animal and vegetable oils and fats; in general, correlations appear unstable. Most of the negative relationships are either for manufactured goods' imports — indicating that the larger importers are dependent on a few origins, which means that most trade in manufactures is within the metropolitan core, while importers of small volumes draw on more sources —

and for the movement of inedible crude materials (commodity 3).

The mean values for the relative entropy index $(\overline{G})$ over the twenty-nine countries all fall between 30 and 60 (Table 3.9). Most widely dispersed across countries is the movement of food (commodity 1), especially its import, and of inedible crude materials (3), and the export of manufactures (6—9). This is in line with the general notions of trade fields developed in this book, especially with regard to the more 'developed' nations which dominate the present data set. Needed raw materials, except those (2, 4 and 5) which are produced in relatively few countries, are sought widely, and world-wide markets are established for manufactured exports. Manufactured imports, on the other hand, are obtained from relatively few producers.

Similar analyses are applied to the commodity flows from each country. Over the nine commodities, the larger the proportion of the total imports going to the particular country, for example, the wider should be its trade field and therefore the larger its relative entropy index. Thus there should be a positive correlation between the proportions (commodity specialisation) and the relative entropies (trading partner specialisation): this was tested using the data for the two years combined, giving thirty-six observations. Again the hypothesis is generally but not strongly supported.

Two types of country stand out in Table 3.9 as having strongly concentrated trading patterns averaged over the imports and exports in each commodity at both dates; those which have much larger neighbours (Canada, Ireland), and the relatively 'underdeveloped' (notably Trinidad and Tobago and the Netherlands Antilles). Conversely, the United States, West Germany, the Netherlands and the United Kingdom have, on average, the most diversified trade in terms of range and intensity of partners. Most of the other countries have very similar mean values for G, though these could conceal very different frequency distributions. In the relationships with commodity specialisation, twelve of the twenty-nine countries produced negative correlations, but these have no apparent common characteristics; the clearest conclusion to be drawn from the table is the overall low value for the correlation coefficients.

*Commodity Specialisation and the Parameters of
Interaction Models*

The analyses of total trade flows reported earlier in this chapter have suggested that distance is a significant influence on the interaction patterns to and from most countries. The present section inquires whether this is so with disaggregated flows, and whether there are any relationships between the parameters of the interaction models and the degree of commodity specialisation as shown by the proportions discussed earlier. It is hypothesised that:

1. The greater the proportion of a given trade flow focused on a particular country, the smaller the regression coefficient for distance (in both indifference and total interaction models), because of the wider range of countries which will be involved. Standardisation of the distance variable (see p. 74) should demonstrate this correlation more clearly.

2. The greater the proportion of a given trade flow focused on a particular country, the more important the role of distance (in both models), because in the wider search transport costs will assume greater significance. There should be a positive correlation between these measures (r coefficients in the indifference model, t and R coefficients in the total interaction model) and the measure of commodity specialisation.

These hypotheses were tested for the indifference model, in which distance is the only independent variable and size of trading partner assumed to have a constant effect, for the 1960 data only. The average correlations are small (Table 3.10), similar to those for the same set of countries when total trade flows were investigated (Table A.12), for both each commodity and each country. According to the mean values of r, distance was relatively unimportant in explaining the spatial patterns of standardised commodity flows, and the correlations between the r values and the measures of commodity specialisation provide no strong evidence that distance is a stronger constraint on the larger flows. The export flows of manufactured goods show the strongest constraints. Export of foodstuffs (commodity 1), on the other hand, shows that the greater the proportion of the flows which originates in one of the twenty-nine countries, the weaker is the influence of distance on the interaction pattern. Among the countries, there are several negative correlations, suggesting that the goods they trade relatively small proportions of, in world terms, are those whose movements are most constrained by distance, but none of the coefficients in that part of the table is large.

Because most of the values of the b_d and b_s coefficients are negative, affirmation of the first hypothesis is shown by positive correlations between these and the proportions; the greater the proportion of a given trade flow that involves a particular country, the closer its negative regression coefficient should be to zero. This proves to be the case, particularly in the export of manufactured goods and both import and export of foods and fuels, but again most correlations are only small and the hypothesis gets only lukewarm support. Among the individual countries, the lower section of Table 3.10 indicates few clear patterns, although those with negative correlations for r also tend to have the same sign for b_d and b_s, indicating that those countries for whose trade distance is apparently little of a constraint are also those which tend to trade most widely in small volumes. Strongest confirmation of the hypothesis is for the United Kingdom and the United States.

Distance also proves to be a relatively unimportant predictor of commodity trade flows in the total interaction model, once the influence of size of trading partner and membership of various trade blocs is held constant[32]. This is indicated by the mean t coefficients for b_d, for both 1960 and 1969, in Table 3.11 (results for t coefficients for b_s were virtually the same and so are not reproduced here). In general, the distance influence appears greatest on export flows, and seems to have become slightly more important during the decade.

Despite the relatively minor significance of the distance variable, the total interaction model is very successful in predicting the pattern of commodity trade for the twenty-nine countries. In every case, the mean value of R indicates a

TABLE 3.10
COMMODITY SPECIALISATION AND PARAMETERS OF THE INDIFFERENCE MODEL

Analysis by Commodity

	1	2	3	4	5	6	7	8	9
					Commodity				
b_d *coefficient*				*Correlation with proportions*					
Imports	0·43	0·20	−0·05	0·43	0·45	0·52	0·16	0·27	−0·06
Exports	0·29	0·07	−0·09	0·51	0·30	0·47	0·66	0·61	0·26
b_s *coefficient*				*Correlation with proportions*					
Imports	0·46	0·28	−0·26	0·45	0·27	0·35	0·17	0·18	0·02
Exports	0·34	−0·03	−0·05	0·28	0·12	0·55	0·67	0·60	0·09
r *coefficient*				*Mean value*					
Imports	−0·35	−0·29	−0·35	−0·44	−0·32	−0·42	−0·38	−0·34	−0·36
Exports	−0·35	−0·34	−0·31	−0·24	−0·20	−0·36	−0·37	−0·39	−0·42
				Correlation with proportions					
Imports	0·49	0·23	0·17	0·49	0·55	0·53	0·26	0·08	0·10
Exports	−0·35	0·09	−0·04	0·49	0·24	0·47	0·66	0·60	0·28

Analysis by Country[a]

Country	b_d	b_s	r	$\bar{r}$	Country	b_d	b_s	r	$\bar{r}$	Country	b_d	b_s	r	$\bar{r}$
1	0·28	0·47	-0·31	-0·10	11	0·19	0·30	0·07	-0·47	21	-0·01	0·23	0·07	-0·34
2	0·25	0·35	0·32	-0·32	12	-0·29	-0·25	-0·49	-0·59	22	0·08	0·13	0·02	-0·33
3	-0·26	-0·17	-0·15	-0·37	13	0·02	0·14	0·13	-0·11	23	-0·15	0·02	-0·02	-0·38
4	-0·25	-0·21	-0·17	-0·20	14	-0·09	-0·03	-0·34	-0·39	24	-0·65	-0·32	-0·27	-0·43
5	-0·49	-0·54	-0·34	-0·33	15	-0·42	-0·51	-0·30	-0·11	25	-0·05	0·03	0·02	-0·35
6	0·43	0·44	0·54	-0·41	16	-0·09	-0·04	0·03	-0·35	26	0·20	0·23	0·35	-0·52
7	0·21	0·17	0·28	-0·27	17	0·55	0·24	0·45	-0·39	27	0·23	0·27	0·30	-0·50
8	0·52	0·53	0·49	0·05	18	-0·39	-0·68	-0·24	-0·33	28	0·11	-0·03	0·09	-0·17
9	0·26	0·22	0·28	-0·38	19	0·29	0·32	0·35	-0·47	29	0·68	0·31	0·69	-0·29
10	0·53	0·48	0·37	-0·39	20	0·20	0·19	0·16	-0·51					

[a]Imports and exports combined.

TABLE 3.11
COMMODITY SPECIALISATION AND PARAMETERS OF THE TOTAL INTERACTION MODEL

				Commodity					
	1	2	3	4	5	6	7	8	9
b_a coefficient				*Correlation with proportions*					
1960									
Imports	0·13	0·00	0·46	-0·26	0·79	0·20	-0·03	-0·08	-0·32
Exports	0·10	0·24	-0·34	0·15	0·04	0·20	0·09	0·36	0·28
1969									
Imports	-0·07	0·21	0·00	-0·73	0·91	0·74	0·25	-0·29	-0·16
Exports	-0·23	0·37	0·17	-0·35		0·38	0·12	0·12	
t coefficient for b_a coefficient				*Mean value*					
1960									
Imports	1·63	1·90	1·65	0·97	1·53	2·21	2·72	24·1	1·94
Exports	2·10	1·22	1·50	2·16	1·84	1·42	1·94	2·03	1·98
1969									
Imports	1·78	1·41	1·72	1·19	1·09	2·64	2·93	3·02	3·43
Exports	2·18	1·44	2·74	2·83		3·18	3·53	3·32	
				Correlation with proportions					
1960									
Imports	-0·10	-0·39	-0·16	-0·30	-0·44	-0·10	-0·09	0·25	0·05
Exports	0·36	0·22	0·23	-0·46	-0·44	0·04	-0·12	-0·13	-0·04
1969									
Imports	0·20	-0·42	0·17	0·60	-0·82	-0·46	-0·08	0·08	-0·03
Exports	0·24	-0·08	0·03	0·36		-0·02	0·27	0·31	

Correlation with proportions

b_s coefficient

1960									
Imports	0·13	0·02	0·37	-0·32	0·68	0·28	-0·19	0·12	-0·38
Exports	0·17	0·42	-0·41	0·26	-0·08	0·40	0·20	0·38	0·45
1969									
Imports	-0·07	0·53	-0·06	-0·27	0·91	0·65	0·25	-0·27	-0·14
Exports	-0·22	0·33	0·18	-0·26		0·29	0·26	0·21	

R coefficient

Mean value   *Correlation with proportions*

1960									
Imports	0·74	0·89	0·78	0·84	0·82	0·83	0·85	0·81	0·84
Exports	0·82	0·88	0·85	0·87	0·84	0·92	0·87	0·95	0·78
1969									
Imports	0·80	0·92	0·85	0·86	0·86	0·95	0·92	0·97	0·96
Exports	0·88	0·92	0·92	0·87		0·91	0·91	0·87	

Correlation with proportions

1960									
Imports	0·33	-0·10	0·47	-0·02	-0·31	0·27	0·08	0·40	-0·36
Exports	-0·14	-0·30	0·01	-0·37	-0·14	-0·10	-0·58	-0·10	0·22
1969									
Imports	0·37	0·30	0·25	0·34	-0·30	-0·02	0·08	0·53	0·14
Exports	-0·09	-0·32	0·09	0·24		0·47	0·32	0·44	

predictive power exceeding 50 per cent, and in most cases for 1969 it exceeds 80 per cent; the relative weakness is in forecasting the flows of foodstuffs. Scrutiny of the detailed results indicated that trading partner size was by far the major independent variable in the regressions. Commodities move from the major supply areas to the major demand points — an expected relationship more clearly brought out in the study of particular commodities than of total trade — with but a relatively minor constraint introduced by the distance factor.

The correlations between the distance parameters and the commodity specialisation proportions display no general relationships, thereby underlining the conclusions reached concerning the unimportance of distance as a variable influencing individual commodity movements. And not only are the correlations low — with the exceptions of imports in commodities 5 and 6 — but their signs often vary between 1960 and 1969. Very clearly, therefore, the two hypotheses are not substantiated by the results of the total interaction model. Similar analyses by individual countries (not reported here) also fail to offer any support. In every case the model provided good fits, with mean R coefficients always exceeding 0·8, but correlations between its distance parameters and the commodity specialisation indices were uniformly negative, except for Turkey.

Distance and Commodity Flows

The analyses reported here do not substantiate the findings of other studies that interaction models are better predictors of total than of disaggregated flow patterns. The movements of nine separate commodities to and from twenty-nine countries — involving all other countries with which they trade — are very predictable, mainly through the use of a variable indicating the demand for the commodity at each destination or the supply at each source. But there is little predictability in other aspects of the flows. The distribution of a country's trade over the available partners is not strongly related to the relative amount of the total trade involving that country, and neither are the strength and slope of the relationship of this distribution strongly related to distance nor the strength of the total interaction model. As the world trade system is disaggregated into its commodity components so, it seems, the uniqueness of each flow pattern comes to dominate the general parameters which have been uncovered earlier in this work.

Some of the hypotheses tested in this book relate a country's spatial location in the world trade system to the slope of its regression coefficients for distance, though the subsequent analyses have barely substantiated such propositions. It could be that, in the present set of analyses, this locational effect has confounded the expected relationships, with the poorly-located among the twenty-nine countries having steeper regression coefficients (for b_s as well as b_d) because of their location as well as their proportion of the total flow. This was not suggested by the analyses for the individual countries, however, in which the location effect was held constant, nor was it indicated by the residuals from the many regressions summarised in Tables 3.9, 3.10 and 3.11.

TRADE-PARTNER CHOICE: SOME CONCLUSIONS

The general model of a space-economy outlined in Chapter 1 has as a salient feature a system of metropolitan dominance. The extent of such dominance has been illustrated by the analyses reported here. Although there are no cases where one country is totally reliant upon another, there are many members of the world trade system whose prosperity in the international market is based on but a few buyers of their exports. And, for almost all of those exporters, who specialise in a few commodities for a few markets, the buyers are the same — the industrialised nations who are grouped together in the O.E.C.D. Yet the reverse is not true; although the industrial countries may rely for certain of their imports and for some export markets on those small countries whose trade relations they dominate, much of their own trade is with their peers; international trade is dominated by intra-metropolitan exchange.

At both an aggregate and an individual (one-digit) commodity level, it is possible to predict the direction of trade to and from individual countries with considerable accuracy. (Although, as noted earlier, such predictions, because the interaction models exclude zero flows, avoid the important question of why there is no trade at all between many pairs of countries.) To a large extent, such predictive success reflects the metropolitan focus of trade flows; much of the trade of metropolitan countries is among themselves, and small countries trade with the metropoli. The size of a country's trade manifest is thus a major determinant of the amount of exchange between it and another. Other variables add to the predictive success; trade preference agreements or 'blocs' tend to direct the flows to and from some countries in certain directions, and, all other things being equal, the distance between two potential partners is an influence on their trade volume.

The precepts of this study of the international economy as a spatial system involve notions of spatial order and the role of location as an influence on system performance. The already noted influence of distance on the amount of trade is one example of such spatial order; the ability of countries located close to major market areas to trade with a wider range of partners, relative to their less-favourably located counterparts, is another. But many of the findings in this chapter do not strongly support the hypothesised nature of the spatial order. In particular, the inter-country variations in the parameters of the interaction models, and especially those related to distance, are not easily accounted for by other variables representing the structure of the spatial system. It is clear that the countries on the 'periphery' of the system pay locational penalties in order to be able to trade widely; since they do not restrict their trade fields relative to those of the better-located, they must presumably pay higher prices for their imports and produce their exports more cheaply (in order to sustain higher transport costs).

NOTES AND REFERENCES

1. A major exception is the American inter-state data analysed by, *inter alia*, E. L. Ullman, *American Commodity Flow*, University of Washington Press, Seattle, 1957.

2. B. J. L. Berry, *Essays on Commodity Flows and the Spatial Structure of the Indian Economy*, University of Chicago, Department of Geography, Research Paper 111, 1966. But see B. H. Farmer, Geography, area studies, and the study of area, *Transactions, Institute of British Geographers*, vol. 60, 1973, 11. International trade data are also very suspect in many cases, of course, but probably less so because of countries' needs to maintain trade and payments balances.

3. Different methods of analysis are possible, such as those in D. B. Freeman, *International Trade, Migration, and Capital Flows*, University of Chicago, Department of Geography, Research Paper 146, 1973, and B. M. Russett, *International Regions and the International System*, Rand McNally, Chicago, 1967.

4. See pp. 12–19.

5. M. H. Yeates, A note concerning the development of a geographic model of international trade, *Geographical Analysis*, vol. 1, 1969, 399–404; and: *An Introduction to Quantitative Analysis in Economic Geography*, McGraw-Hill, New York, 1968, 134–41.

6. Purchase of these tapes was made possible by a grant from the University of Canterbury Research Fund, which is gratefully acknowledged. Using the data from the tapes would probably have proved impossible without the considerable computing expertise freely shared with me by Alan Wilkinson, the tolerance of the staff of the University of Canterbury Computer Centre, and the readiness of Doug. Johnston to assist in the debugging problems which my Fortran so frequently produced.

7. These countries are Albania, Bulgaria, China, Cuba, Czechoslovakia, E. Germany, Hungary, Mongolian Republic, N. Korea, N. Vietnam, Poland, Romania and U.S.S.R.

8. The average value of this trade in 1968–70 was $U.S.9634m.

9. These countries are listed at the back of each volume of *Direction of Trade*. Some countries not so listed were on the tape, and although several of them could be identified, they were not included in the analyses.

10. W. R. Black, Towards a factorial ecology of flows, *Economic Geography*, vol. 49, 1973, 59–67.

11. The basis for such work is S. J. Brams, Transaction flows in the international system, *American Political Science Review*, vol. 60, 1966, 880–98; see also R. J. Rummel, *Applied Factor Analysis*, Northwestern U.P., Evanston, 1970.

12. This formulation has as its dependent variable a measure analogous to the deviations produced in Brams' transaction flow method.

13. As in J. E. McConnell, A flow algorithm for the trade of small developing nations, *The Pennsylvania Geographer*, vol. 9, 1971, 10–15.

14. This was largely the case in H. Linnemann, *An Econometric Study of International Trade Flows*, North-Holland, Amsterdam, 1966.

15. Other models, such as those based on entropy-maximisation developed by Wilson (A. G. Wilson, *Entropy in Urban and Regional Modelling*, Pion, London, 1970) were not applied, nor were those which add constraints to ensure that the total volume of trade was not under- or over-predicted. The latter may be desirable in many circumstances, because of problems of interpretation which may arise (though see R. J. Johnston, *On Regression Coefficients in Comparative Studies of the 'Frictions of Distance'. I. Simulated Data* (forthcoming paper)) but it proved sufficient for the present purpose, with its focus on (1) the goodness-of-fit of the equations, and (2) the relative size of the distance parameters, to rely on the traditional multiple regression representation of the gravity analogue. A full discussion is given in M. Batty and S. Mackie, The calibration of gravity, entropy, and related models of spatial interaction, *Environment and Planning*, vol. 4, 1972, 205–34.

16. The latest issue of the *Oxford Economic Atlas* was a major source.

17. A. S. Linsky, Some generalizations concerning primate cities, *Annals, Association of American Geographers*, vol. 55, 1965, 506–13.

18. W. R. Tobler, *Selected Computer Programs*, Department of Geography, University of Michigan, Ann Arbor, 1970. The program is SDIS, pp. 35–8.

19. For example, H. Linnemann, *op. cit.*

20. L. Curry, A spatial analysis of gravity flows, *Regional Studies*, vol. 6, 1972, 131–47; G. O. Ewing, Gravity and linear regression models of spatial interaction: a cautionary note, *Economic Geography*, vol. 50, 1974, 83–8.

21. R. J. Johnston, *op. cit.*, and R. J. Johnston, On distance-decay and regression coefficients, *Area*, vol. 5, 1973, 187–91.

22. It may be that these coefficients represent some collinearity between trade groups' membership and distance, but experiments suggested no particular distortion of the parameters for the distance variable.

23. E. S. Milenky, *The Politics of Regional Organization in Latin America*, Praeger Publishers, New York, 1973.

24. The developed countries accounted for 76 per cent of all exports in 1969, and 75 per cent of all imports. (Developed countries are those so defined by the I.M.F.)

25. This suggests that the 'peripheral' countries should have higher $b_d:b_s$ ratios, a proposition indicated, though not strongly supported, by correlations between those ratios and the potential variables.

26. R. E. Alcaly, Aggregation and gravity models: some empirical evidence, *Journal of Regional Science*, vol. 7, 1967, 61—73.
27. The basic notions for this section were developed from the stimulus of W. R. Black, *Substitution and Concentration: An Examination of the Distance Exponent in Gravity Model Commodity Flow Studies*, University of Indiana, Department of Geography, Discussion Paper 1, 1972.
28. See A. K. Dutt and G. F. Pyle, Dimensions of India's foreign trade, *International Geography*, vol. 1, 1972, 543—6.
29. To be completely accurate, different time periods should be used for different hemispheres (January—December for the northern, and July—June for the southern) to provide data for single years in terms of primary production, but the January—December convention was used for all.
30. Data are available in the E.E.C. trade figures for associate members for several countries of 'French Africa'. These were not used because for most flows there were insufficient partners to allow fitting the interaction models.
31. Where no trade was reported, or, in the case of the interaction models, there were too few partners listed, analyses were amended. In some cases, this precluded full analysis, which accounts for the gaps in Tables 3.10 and 3.11.
32. The variables were those employed in the analyses of total trade flows (p. 71), except that D_j was the total trade of partner j in the relevant commodity.

4

The Changing System

Although various aspects of the world trade system at two dates have been described in the preceding chapters, the analyses have been static in their approach. From them it is possible to identify major changes in the structure between those two dates but few inferences can be made about the processes of change, since temporal progressions are not defined. Thus the present chapter focuses on the changes between 1960 and 1969, by looking at the trade patterns of the individual countries and how they altered.

THE MEASUREMENT OF CHANGE

Change can be indexed in a number of ways, each of which highlights certain aspects of the alterations. Duncan *et al.*, in their book *Statistical Geography*, have suggested four different methods of indicating change over a set of areal units[1].

1. Absolute change — the difference in the value of variable X in area i between the two dates t and v (where v is the later date):

$$AC = X_{iv} - X_{it} \qquad (17)$$

2. Relative change — the difference expressed as a ratio of the value of variable X at time t:

$$RC = (X_{iv} - X_{it})/X_{it} \qquad (18)$$

Very often RC is multiplied by 100 to give an index of percentage change (PC).

3. Positional change — which is the changing location of area i on variable X in the normal distribution of X between dates t and v:

where
$$Z_t = \frac{X_{it} - \bar{X}_t}{SX_t} \tag{19}$$

and
$$Z_v = \frac{X_{iv} - \bar{X}_v}{SX_v} \tag{20}$$

$$PosC = Z_v - Z_t \tag{21}$$

A number of variants of this measure can be devised[2].

4. Deviational change — which is the difference between the value for X_i in area i at time v and that predicted for on the basis of its value at time t:

where
$$\hat{X}_{iv} = a + bX_{it} \tag{22}$$

$$DC = X_{iv} - \hat{X}_{iv} \tag{23}$$

The measures of relative (RC) and percentage (PC) change are probably the most frequently used, but the rates that are displayed are in part a function of the size of the initial value, X_{it}. These may be valid measures, but they may conceal certain patterns and, where areal units are of unequal size, as in the present study, over-emphasise changes in the smaller units relative to those of the larger. They also require data measured on a ratio scale with an absolute zero. The measure of absolute change (AC), on the other hand, is likely to provide a converse distribution, over-emphasising growth (or decline) in the larger units. Measures based on $PosC$ and DC introduced fewer complications, though the latter is clearly dependent on the data meeting the requirements of the linear regression model[3]. Analyses based on these last two are preferred in the present chapter.

So far, only measures of change on individual variables have been discussed, which are relevant to the analyses of the preceding chapters, which used indices of concentration. In a multivariate population, involving several variables measured to each observation unit, methods which simultaneously consider all of the variables are required. Factor analysis can be applied to such matrices in a variety of ways, for example:

1. Factoring indices of change between two dates over the set of variables – the incremental R technique[4]. In most applications using this approach, the variables have been either AC, RC or PC measures, with the consequent problems[5]: $PosC$ or DC measures could be introduced[6].

2. Factoring the matrices for the two dates separately, and then 'objectively' comparing their output using a technique such as Veldman's RELATE[7]. This requires the same set of variables in each matrix, clearly a drawback in the present study which has a different population of countries at the two dates.

In matrices whose variables form a 'closed system' it is possible to derive measures of deviational change for the multivariate situation. This applies, for example, where the variables are additive to a population total, as in the commodity structure of a country's exports. In the data used here, two matrices of one-digit export commodity structures can be assembled for a population of countries (all countries must be in both matrices, thereby slightly limiting the approach because of data limitations). The commodities form the matrix columns and the countries the rows. The sum of each row signifies the dollar trade of that country in the relevant year; the column sums indicate the dollar trade in each commodity, and the sum of these sums is the total trade during that year. Comparison of the latter sums for the two years can produce a PC measure of the total growth in world trade during the period; comparison of the column sums produces PC measures of trade growth in each commodity. Has the growth of exports by country X in commodity a been as fast as the growth of world trade as a whole, or of exports of that commodity as a whole? By how much does it deviate from those rates?

Shift and share analysis is a method of measuring deviational changes in such a system, using predictions based on the column and total sums[8]. It divides change into three components: (1) that accounted for by total change in the system; (2) that accounted for by change in the relevant commodity; and (3) that which is not accounted for by either of the preceding two components. The formulae are:

$$D_{ijg} = G_{ij} + K_{ij} + C_{ij} \qquad (24)$$

where D_{ijg} = growth of category i in place j between two dates

$$G_{ij} = D_{ijt} \times R_{t,t+1} \text{ Total Growth Component} \qquad (25)$$

where D_{ijt} = value for category i in place j at time t
R = total growth rate for all categories in time period t to $t + 1$

$$K_{ij} = D_{ijt} \times (r_i - R_{t,t+1}) \text{ Category Growth Component} \qquad (26)$$

where r_i = growth rate for category i in time period t to $t + 1$

and $C_{ij} = D_{ijt} \times (r_{ij} - r_i) \text{ Regional Advantage Growth Component} \qquad (27)$

where r_{ij} = the growth rate for category i in place j between t and $t + 1$.

G_{ij} predicts the rate of growth for a given category (e.g. commodity in the export trade) if all categories in all places grew at the same rate; K_{ij} predicts the additional growth or decline from the growth rate of that category relative to all categories; and C_{ij} shows the further growth or decline which is place-particular and cannot be related to system-wide growth rates.

Finally, change can be measured by the analysis of time series for a number of dates. Where this applies to one variable and one area, the usual measures of time series analysis can be applied. With many areas, a number of techniques are available, including factor analytic approaches[9]. Either the time periods or the areas may be used as the variables. In the former case, the components or factors pick out common time paths or temporal trends, with the scores indicating the areas which conform to those trends; in the latter case, the loadings index areas with common trends. Most of the data used in this book apply only to the two dates, 1960 and 1969, but it is possible to obtain longer time series from the I.M.F. tapes, and these are analysed in the manner suggested here.

CHANGING TRADE SPECIALISATION

Positional (*PosC*) and deviational (*DC*) indices have not been separately derived for these studies; instead a modified *DC* approach has been developed which focuses on (1) the relative stability of the structure, and (2) the main deviations from the predicted pattern. This involves regressing the 1960 indices on those for 1969, identifying the strength — indexed by the correlation coefficient r — and slope of the relationship, and then noting the major residuals from that regression, those whose position in the structure has altered most during the nine-year period. Unfortunately, this approach allows analysis only of those countries for which indices of trade specialisation (the relative entropy indices) could be calculated at both dates[10].

Commodity Specialisation

There was much greater stability in export than import commodity structures during the 1960s, with the initial value accounting for an average of 63 per cent (over the three classifications) of the 1969 indices for exports, but only 33 per cent for imports (Table 4.1). The comparisons involved eighty countries. The two sets of regressions also differ in their slope coefficients, these being much greater for exports. For imports, this indicates that on average absolute increases were greater for the smaller indices (not surprising given the relatively small increases possible for those countries with indices in 1960 already exceeding 80·0), since the intercept values add more in relative terms to the small 1960 indices. For exports, however, the slope coefficients are closer to unity and the intercept values are relatively small, indicating that change has been relatively constant across the whole range of indices in 1960, though with some greater movement for the countries whose trade was most specialised by commodity.

TABLE 4.1
IMPORT AND EXPORT SPECIALISATION, 1960 and 1969:
INTERRELATIONSHIPS

Key to Variables

One-digit	Imports 1960 IO_1	1969 IT_1	Exports 1960 EO_1	1969 ET_1
Two-digit	Imports 1960 IO_2	1969 IT_2	Exports 1960 EO_2	1969 ET_2
Three-digit	Imports 1960 IO_3	1969 IT_3	Exports 1960 EO_3	1969 ET_3

Imports		*Exports*	
$IT_1 = 37.91 + 0.52\ IO_1$	$r = 0.60$	$ET_1 = 23.69 + 0.67\ EO_1$	$r = 0.71$
$IT_2 = 37.90 + 0.52\ IO_2$	$r = 0.52$	$ET_2 = 15.55 + 0.83\ EO_2$	$r = 0.81$
$IT_3 = 45.03 + 0.35\ IO_3$	$r = 0.59$	$ET_3 = 10.80 + 0.89\ EO_3$	$r = 0.86$

During the decade under review, therefore, there has been
a general tendency towards less commodity specialisation of
trade, especially among the more specialised countries and in
their import manifests. Although most, it would seem, have
been able to broaden their export base somewhat, this has
been slight compared to their demands for a wider range of
imports. Of those countries which deviated most from this
general pattern, several groups stand out in their export
trade. The members of the C.A.C.M. (except Honduras) have
all been able to diversify their sales considerably, as have a
number of countries on the 'periphery' of Europe (Austria,
Denmark, Finland, Greece, Ireland and Spain), as well as
Belgium. Of those whose exports were not diversified as
much as predicted, the most notable are the specialist
producers of sugar — British Honduras, Cuba, Guadeloupe,
Mauritius and Reunion. Oil developments in Libya and
Nigeria led to a narrowing of the trade base there. With the
import indices, on the other hand, no such clear groupings
are apparent.

Trading Partner Specialisation

Both regression equations produced high correlations,
accounting for 71–72 per cent of the variance in the 1969
trade partner specialisation indices by the variance in the
same indices for 1960 (Table 4.2). As with the commodity
indices, there was a greater tendency towards diversification
in importing than exporting among the more specialised

TABLE 4.2
IMPORT AND EXPORT SPECIALISATION
BY ORIGIN–DESTINATION:
REGRESSION OF 1969 ON 1960 INDICES

Regression equations		
Imports	$I69 = 13 \cdot 35 + 0 \cdot 75 I60$	$r = 0 \cdot 84$
Exports	$E69 = 10 \cdot 73 + 0 \cdot 85 E60$	$r = 0 \cdot 85$

traders, though here this difference between the two activities was much less marked. Overall the system showed
considerable stability in the proportional distribution of
countries' trade contracts, and the residuals from the two
regressions indicate no groups of nations which deviated from
the general trend and which had other characteristics in
common.

Individual Commodity Flows

Between 1960 and 1969, the relative importance of each
of the twenty-nine countries studied, in the import and
export movements of the nine separate commodities identified at the one-digit level, varied very little. Correlations
between the relevant pairs of vectors of proportions (Table
4.3) indicated that only in the movements of inedible raw
materials, plus the imports of beverages and tobacco, was
there any obvious alteration to the pattern. Several countries
(listed in Table 3.8) changed quite notably in their proportions of the various commodity flows, particularly several
of those located on Europe's 'periphery' (Portugal, Iceland,
Turkey and Yugoslavia), plus Hong Kong, Australia (through
the developing mineral trade) and two E.E.C. countries,
France and Belgium–Luxembourg.

Comparison of the indices of trading partner specialisation
(the relative entropies) in 1960 and 1969 indicates also that
stability was the main feature of the decade (Table 4.4). Only
one commodity flow — imports of beverages and tobacco —
and three countries — Turkey, Hong Kong, and Trinidad and
Tobago — deviate from the generally high correlations. These
findings do not necessarily indicate that the countries traded
in similar proportions with each partner at both dates, only
that the relative distributions over the available sets of

TABLE 4.3

COMMODITY TRADE FLOWS: SPECIALISATION CHANGES

Analysis by commodity

Commodity	Correlation Imports	Exports	Commodity	Correlation Imports	Exports	Commodity	Correlation Imports	Exports
1	0·89	0·95	4	0·89	0·87	7	0·78	0·96
2	0·46	0·98	5	0·98	0·97	8	0·85	0·94
3	0·56	0·37	6	0·95	0·85	9	0·85	0·95

Analysis by country

Country	Correlation	Country	Correlation	Country	Correlation
1	0·65	11	0·75	21	0·64
2	0·54	12	0·58	22	0·46
3	0·15	13	0·13	23	0·94
4	0·16	14	0·80	24	0·81
5	0·83	15	−0·06	25	0·83
6	0·63	16	0·88	26	0·80
7	0·83	17	0·48	27	0·12
8	0·64	18	−0·20	28	0·99
9	0·90	19	0·86	29	0·99
10	0·89	20	0·01		

[a] For list of countries see Table 3.8.

TABLE 4.4
COMMODITY TRADE FLOWS: CHANGES IN TRADING PARTNER SPECIALISATION

Analysis by commodity

Commodity	Correlation		Commodity	Correlation		Commodity	Correlation	
	Imports	Exports		Imports	Exports		Imports	Exports
1	0·88	0·89	4	0·84	0·76	7	0·76	0·85
2	0·11	0·83	5	0·72	0·80	8	0·88	0·77
3	0·74	0·66	6	0·89	0·84	9	0·65	0·84

Analysis by country

Country	Correlation	Country	Correlation	Country	Correlation
1	0·83	11	0·74	21	0·83
2	0·73	12	0·94	22	0·48
3	0·45	13	0·64	23	0·60
4	0·84	14	0·96	24	0·64
5	0·90	15	0·88	25	0·87
6	0·91	16	0·86	26	0·79
7	0·81	17	0·91	27	0·09
8	0·95	18	0·27	28	0·35
9	0·82	19	0·84	29	0·64
10	0·76	20	0·55		

partners have not changed. It can be strongly inferred, along with other evidence presented in this chapter, that the results do suggest such stability, however.

SHIFT AND SHARE ANALYSIS

Shift and share analyses produce a considerable output. In addition to the three change coefficients, for each variable for each observation, other variables can be derived, such as an index of dissimilarity, or redistribution, for either variables over observations or observations over variables. (Indices of dissimilarity are introduced on p. 36.) Summarising procedures are necessary to handle all of this information. One such method uses factor analysis to identify areas with similar profiles on the various change coefficients, but this was not particularly relevant to the present task[11].

In the general model of a trade system outlined in Chapter 1, the concept of time–space convergence was used to suggest major trends of intensification of existing patterns of concentration. Each country should develop its export trade in those commodities in which it currently had a comparative advantage; as a consequence, it would not undertake import replacement but would import in ever greater volumes those commodities which it traditionally obtained from elsewhere. These changes in commodity composition should induce parallel changes in trade partner composition, with an intensification of the major flow patterns.

In operational terms, the hypothesis outlined in the preceding paragraph suggests a positive correlation between the initial state of the system at time t and the regional advantage coefficients between then and time $t + 1$. Thus in a three-commodity system, if country X specialises in commodity a, and exports only small amounts of b and c, it should build on its comparative advantage in a. The growth rate in exports of a from this country should be greater than either the growth rate for b and c or the growth rate for a over the whole system; it should have a larger regional advantage coefficient for a than for b and c.

An alternative to this hypothesis, derived from the urban and regional growth theory discussed in Chapter 1, suggests

that the major policy aims of countries will be import
replacement and export diversification. If such a policy were
effective, existing patterns would not be intensified but
rather countries would seek new markets for new products
and reduction of dependence on certain suppliers for other
products. The result would be a negative rather than a
positive correlation between initial size and regional advantage coefficients. A large negative coefficient would indicate
most regional advantage (or the smallest negative regional
advantage) going to commodities/routes in which there was
no previous trade.

Shift and share analysis divides variables (commodities)
according to whether their growth rate over the prescribed
period exceeds that for the sum of all the variables. This is
indicated by the sign of the structural coefficients: above-
average growth variables have positive signs, and below-
average have negative. The size of the structural coefficient
for each country is a function of the size of that variable at
the original date so that, for any variable, the trade
intensification hypothesis suggests a clear correlation between the structural and regional advantage coefficients. If
the variable is a slow-growth one (S in Table 4.6), this correlation should be negative; if it is fast-growth (F in Table 4.6), the
correlation should be positive (see Figure 4.1). Alternatively,
a reversal of the coefficients would indicate an import replace-
ment/export diversification pattern of trade change.

Commodity Trade

Shift and share analyses were conducted at both the one-
and two-digit levels of the commodity classification; the third
digit was omitted, partly because of the large number of
categories and partly because of the problems inherent in the
data at that level (p. 000). Eighty countries for which
comparable trade data were available for 1960 and 1969 were
included in the analyses.

The bulk of the evidence from the correlations of initial
size with regional advantage coefficients supports the import
replacement/export diversification hypothesis since the
majority of the coefficients are negative (Table A.14). At the

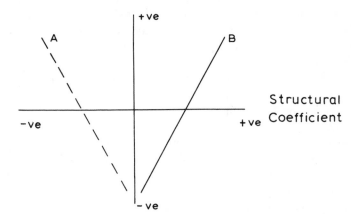

Fig. 4.1. Hypothesised relationships between structural and regional advantage coefficients, according to the trade intensification hypothesis. If the structural coefficient is negative (indicating a slow growth component) the regression slope should also be negative (line A), with the greatest regional advantage in those places already concentrating on that component: if the structural coefficient is positive, the regression slope (B) should be also.

one-digit level, the same general commodity mix of exports prevails and has been intensified in about one-third of the countries; the same is so for imports. Australia is typical of this group at the one-digit level for exports; about 80 per cent of its exports in 1960 were in categories 0 and 2 and, although it had positive regional advantage coefficients for every category, those for these two were at least twice as large as that for any other. Yet at the two-digit level, there was much more variation; for example, with the rapid growth of exports in metal ores within category 3, inedible crude materials (previously most of Australia's exports in this group had been category 18, textile fibres). Trinidad and Tobago's export trade exemplifies the export diversification process. At the one-digit level, the correlation of -0.97 indicates most regional advantage in commodities formerly very un-important in the country's exports. Its main specialisation in 1960 was in commodity 3 (inedible crude materials), and exports increased by only U.S.$137m. to 1969, against an expected 271; exports of commodity 5, on the other hand, increased from U.S.$6m. to U.S.$45m., compared to a predicted 1969 total of 15.

Tabulation of the spatial distribution of positive and negative correlations in this analysis points up clear differ-ences in the locations of the two processes (Table 4.5). The centralisation trend, characterised by positive correlations, is most marked among the twenty-four 'developed' countries, where it is especially strong at the one-digit level. Many of these countries are continuing to concentrate their trade in established fields, therefore, but are, according to the signs of the correlations at the two-digit level, diversifying within those general areas. Latin America, Middle East and Asian countries are very much following the other process, the main exceptions (by size of coefficient, as well as sign) in the export field being Honduras, Surinam and Sabah. In Africa, on the other hand, several countries have maintained and accentuated their existing specialisations, Liberia in particu-lar, and also Ghana and Sierra Leone in exports.

For the individual commodities, the results almost entirely favour the import replacement/export diversification hypoth-esis (Table 4.6). As already indicated, the sign of the correlation between the structural and regional advantage coefficients should be positive for commodities in which trade was expanding faster than average, and negative for others. The proportions with the correct signs to support the concentration hypothesis were:

	One-digit	Two-digit
Imports	4/9	3/54
Exports	0/9	1/54

giving only eight of the 126 in total. For virtually every item of commodity trade, therefore, there has been some spatial diversification. The countries which specialised in certain export lines are finding their hegemony being challenged;

TABLE 4.5
CONCENTRATION OR DIVERSIFICATION IN COMMODITY TRADE:
INITIAL SIZE—REGIONAL ADVANTAGE CORRELATIONS

	Sign			*Sign*	
	Positive	*Negative*		*Positive*	*Negative*
Developed			Latin America		
Countries			Caribbean		
Imports:			Imports:		
one-digit	10	14	one-digit	4	14
two-digit	5	19	two-digit	2	15
Exports:			Exports:		
one-digit	11	13	one-digit	5	12
two-digit	5	19	two-digit	4	13
Middle East			Asia		
Imports:			Imports:		
one-digit	1	3	one-digit	4	9
two-digit	0	4	two-digit	1	12
Exports:			Exports:		
one-digit	1	3	one-digit	1	12
two-digit	0	4	two-digit	2	11
Africa			Other		
Imports:			Imports:		
one-digit	6	10	one-digit	2	2
two-digit	6	10	two-digit	2	2
Exports:			Exports:		
one-digit	6	10	one-digit	2	2
two-digit	6	10	two-digit	3	1

	Sign	
Total	*Positive*	*Negative*
Imports: one-digit	27	52
two-digit	16	62
Exports: one-digit	26	52
two-digit	20	58

those which dominated the import of certain items are receiving competition from those which formerly required little of those commodities.

At first glance, the results of these shift and share analyses, with their general confirmation of the import replacement/ export diversification model, conflict with those presented earlier in this chapter, which suggested considerable stability

TABLE 4.6

SHIFT AND SHARE ANALYSIS: CORRELATION BY COMMODITY[a]

One Digit

Commodity	Imports			Exports		
	Redistribution	Type	Correlation	Redistribution	Type	Correlation
1	18·7		0·49	16·7	S	0·43
2	20·4		0·36	13·4	S	0·54
3	13·4		0·22	13·4	S	0·32
4	15·5		0·01	35·5	S	0·50
5	14·1		0·39	23·8	S	0·72
6	11·9		0·04	12·3	F	-0·54
7	12·2		0·20	13·2	S	0·38
8	17·7		0·34	15·1	F	-0·57
9	15·4		0·09	19·4	F	-0·57

Two Digit[b]

Commodity	Imports			Exports		
	R	T	C	R	T	C
1	42·1	F	-0·44	47·3	S	0·72
2	27·2	S	0·79	38·4	S	0·74
3	27·7	S	0·75	28·4	S	0·42
4	30·0	S	0·26	23·3	S	0·67
5	23·4	S	0·24	25·0	S	0·66
6	12·3	S	0·41	18·6	S	0·62
7	16·1	S	0·51	17·2	S	0·75
8	19·3	S	0·81	17·3	S	0·54
9	31·3	F	-0·58	49·5	F	-0·51
10	89·5	F	-0·78	24·8	F	-0·76

Commodity	Imports			Exports		
	R	T	C	R	T	C
31	48·5	F	-0·59	75·1	S	0·34
32	28·8	F	-0·32	16·6	S	0·59
33	88·4	F	-0·80	57·4	F	-0·66
34	34·9	S	0·41	50·4	S	0·87
35	97·9	F	-0·91	47·0	S	0·82
36	29·5	F	-0·56	26·0	F	-0·73
37	48·0	F	-0·71	66·4	F	-0·88
38	51·4	F	-0·46	23·5	S	0·66
39	28·8	F	-0·28	41·4	F	-0·67
40	20·3	F	0·77	15·2	S	0·77

No.	R	T	C	R	T	C
11	26·9	S	0·30	7·1	S	0·17
12	22·8	S	0·74	19·0	S	0·77
13	17·6	S	0·46	24·9	S	0·39
14	23·2	S	0·10	24·9	S	−0·60
15	15·9	S	0·57	15·9	S	0·57
16	27·1	S	0·33	21·4	S	0·34
17	14·2	S	0·65	20·4	S	0·26
18	13·9	S	0·43	27·7	S	0·65
19	25·5	F	−0·67	63·2	F	−0·70
20	20·7	S	0·26	20·3	S	0·42
21	47·5	F	−0·76	32·8	F	−0·47
22	26·5	S	0·07	21·0	S	0·45
23	18·6	S	0·24	41·0	S	0·50
24	87·3	F	−0·71	84·0	F	−0·76
25	84·0	F	−0·80	54·8	F	−0·82
26	42·5	S	0·64	23·0	S	0·44
27	27·1	S	0·53	37·6	S	0·75
28	42·2	S	0·76	60·7	F	−0·68
29	28·7	F	−0·18	19·4	F	−0·49
30	26·5	S	0·08	21·0	S	0·45
41	17·4	S	0·10	15·4	S	0·36
42	37·4	F	−0·31	23·1	F	−0·37
43	17·5	S	−0·31	24·3	S	0·48
44	19·5	F	−0·32	19·5	S	0·56
45	14·9	F	0·01	11·7	F	−0·56
46	88·9	F	−0·85	96·7	F	−0·93
47	46·1	S	0·76	21·3	F	−0·52
48	65·3	F	−0·71	45·7	F	−0·60
49	97·5	F	−0·68	50·0	F	−0·60
50	62·5	F	−0·80	96·7	F	−0·80
51	25·9	F	−0·33	30·3	F	−0·56
52	84·2	F	−0·52	36·3	F	−0·32
53	22·2	F	−0·42	15·6	F	−0·58
54	34·2	F	−0·58	22·3	F	−0·71

a Correlations are between the structural and the regional advantage coefficients.
b The column headings R, T and C refer respectively to Redistribution Index, Type of Change (slow or fast growth relative to total change), and Correlation (see note a).

in the spatial structure of the world trade system. As previously noted, however, shift and share analysis focuses on change, on deviations from a predicted pattern based on a continuation of those distributions existing at the first date in the analysis. The investigations into changing trade concentration indicate that there has been a strong *status quo* in distributions of economic functions in the world economy over the 1960s decade, with but a relatively slight trend towards export and import diversification. The shift and share analyses have highlighted that slight trend, and have identified its strength and direction for both countries and commodities.

The general stability of the system is highlighted by the indices of redistribution for both countries and commodities, calculated using the equation

$$IR = (\Sigma |C_{ijt} - C_{ijv}|)/2 \qquad (28)$$

where C_{ijt} = percentage of trade of country i in commodity j
       at time t, and
    C_{ijv} = percentage of trade of country i in commodity j
       at time v.

Most of the countries have relatively small indices (Table A.14), particularly in the commodity composition of their imports. A few have large indices for exports, such as Libya — following the development of its oilfields — and Hong Kong, with its burgeoning industrial economy. Nevertheless, although the averages are higher, for exports, too, stability is the main element in these indices. By commodities, only one index is indicative of considerable redistribution — that for the export of oil (commodity 4)[12]. At the two-digit level, there was a greater range of index values, for both imports and exports, with the largest values most characteristic of the movements of some manufactured products (Table 4.6).

Trade Partners

Analysis of changes in trade partners by the shift and share method could be applied to a greater number of countries than in the study of commodity trade, because of the wealth of data. The import and export matrices were separately analysed, so that all of the reported correlations (Table A.15) are between original size of flows and regional advantage coefficients. Thus positive correlations indicate concentration of flows on the already heavily-traded routes, whereas negative correlations suggest more diffuse trading fields.

As with the analysis of commodity trade changes, the bulk of the evidence suggests support for the diversification rather than for the concentration hypothesis; most changes are towards a widening rather than a narrowing of markets. Tabulation of the correlation coefficients by sign shows that this conclusion is particularly valid for import linkages (Table 4.7). Again, the I.M.F. classification of countries into (a) developed, and (b) others, by continent, points up interesting differences. The concentration hypothesis is once more shown to be most valid in the developed nations, where it is indeed the majority trend in exports: on the other hand, it is clearly not as important in describing changes in the trade links of African countries as it was for describing

TABLE 4.7
CONCENTRATION OR DIVERSIFICATION IN TRADE LINKS:
INITIAL SIZE–REGIONAL ADVANTAGE CORRELATIONS

	Sign				*Sign*	
	Positive	*Negative*			*Positive*	*Negative*
Developed				Latin America		
Countries				Caribbean		
Imports	11	15		Imports	6	28
Exports	14	12		Exports	7	23
Middle East				Asia		
Imports	4	12		Imports	4	12
Exports	6	10		Exports	6	11
Africa				Others		
Imports	3	35		Imports	1	3
Exports	5	28		Exports	0	1

		Sign	
Total	*Positive*	*Negative*	
Imports	29	105	
Exports	38	85	

alterations in composition of their commodity trade. (Of the three examples of concentration in import flows, two are for Portuguese colonies.) Among the developed countries, nine of the ten correlations for E.E.C. nations are positive, suggesting the role of that institution as an internal trade-diverter. (The exception, for France's exports, is a very small negative correlation.) No such clear-cut pattern is revealed among the E.F.T.A. and C.A.C.M. countries, however, suggesting that in both cases and not only in the latter, as might have been expected, the trade agreements were emphasising links which were formerly not strong[13]. Finally, however, it must be stressed that these patterns of changing directions of trade are set within an overall situation of considerable stability, which has been illustrated in earlier analyses and is confirmed by the indices of redistribution (Table A.15). For both directions, but especially for imports, these indices are on average low and vary little.

From these two sets of findings from shift and share analyses, one fairly clear pattern stands out. Among the developed countries, and particularly those of Western Europe, the concentration hypothesis accounts for many of the changes; among countries in the rest of the world, there is much stronger support for the diversification hypothesis. This is in line with general notions of changing patterns of world trade. The developed nations in particular are becoming more introverted among themselves; increasingly their trade is in manufactured commodities, and increasingly it is with each other. Other countries tend to have a simple trading pattern, of exporting one or a few commodities, usually raw or partly-processed materials, to a small number of developed nation markets, from whom in turn they purchase manufactured goods. Many of them – notable exceptions at present are the oil exporters – are facing variable markets for their products, and markets which are not growing at particularly rapid rates. At the same time, their demands for manufactured goods are growing fast. To afford these, they must diversify, seeking more markets for their staple commodities and more commodities that they can successfully sell abroad. The result is the pattern of shifts just described; the consequences are taken up in the next chapter.

CHANGING PARAMETERS OF INTERACTION MODELS

The two interaction models introduced in the previous chapter related inter-country trade volumes to a range of independent variables, of which the salient one in this study of a spatial system is the distance separating those countries. How have the various parameters of those models changed during the 1960s? Were they relativ∠ly stable, with close correlations between the sets of values for the two dates, or has there been a considerable spatial reorganisation? The findings of the analyses reported earlier in this chapter suggest that stability should be a major characteristic. For most countries, and in particular the small, less-developed countries, there has been some trade diversification, with a widening of links. Such diversification could lead to a decline in the role of distance as a constraint to interaction, especially with exports as markets are widely sought, but the constraint of information may lead to a focusing of this search on local markets.

The Indifference and Total Interaction Models

The three major parameters of the indifference model, and four of those for the total interaction model, have been investigated for patterns of change over a population of seventy countries. They are:

1. The b_d coefficient, the slope of the relationship between trade volume and distance (in the total interaction model, holding all other variables in the equation constant).

2. The correlation coefficient (r for the indifference model; R for the total interaction model) which indexes the model's goodness-of-fit.

3. The b_s coefficient, which is the slope of the relationship between trade volume and distance, with distance standardised according to equation (16) — p. 75.

4. The t ratio for the b_d coefficient in the total interaction model, which is a measure of the strength of the relationship between trade volume and distance when all other variables in the equation are held constant.

The dependent variables were the values for these four in 1969. The independents were fed in using a three-stage approach. At the first stage, only the corresponding values for 1960 were input; at the second, measures of the relevant country's size and relative location were also included[14]; and at the third, the eight trade group memberships were added (Table 4.8).

Although all of the stage 3 multiple correlations for these analyses exceed 0·56, only in one is the explanation greater than 50 per cent (Exports, t ratio; Table 4.9). For the indifference model parameters, in all three cases between 26 and 31 per cent of the distribution of 1969 values can be accounted for by the 1960 values. There is thus some stability, but not a great deal, in the strength of the distance influence according to this model. For the import equations relating to the b_d coefficient, the measure of relative location is also significant, suggesting that those places favourably located relative to export markets had steeper distance-decay curves in 1969 than knowledge of their 1960 curve would

TABLE 4.8
CHANGES IN THE PARAMETERS OF THE INTERACTION
MODELS

Key to variables

Stage 1

1. b_d value, imports 1960
2. $r(R)$ value, imports 1960
3. b_s value, imports 1960
4. t ratio for b_d, imports 1960

5. b_d value, exports 1960
6. $r(R)$ value, exports 1960
7. b_s value, exports 1960
8. t ratio for b_d, exports 1960

Stage 2

9. Total imports, 1960
10. Total exports 1960
11. Population 1960

12. Import potential, 1960
13. Export potential, 1960

Stage 3

14. Member of 'British Trading Group'
15. Member of 'French Trading Group'
16. Member of 'Portuguese Trading Group'

17. Member L.A.F.T.A.
18. Member C.A.C.M.
19. Member E.E.C.
20. Member E.F.T.A.
21. Member O.E.C.D.

TABLE 4.9
REGRESSION ANALYSES: CHANGES IN PARAMETERS OF THE
INTERACTION MODELS

Significant variables at stage[a]	Indifference model			Total interaction model		
	1	2	3	1	2	3
b_d coefficient				b_d coefficient		
Imports	1	1,13	1,13,(−14),(−15),16,(−18)	none	13	13,16
R	0·42	0·47	0·63	0·03	0·39	0·59
Exports	5	5	5,(−15),(−21)	5	5	5,(12),15
R	0·52	0·53	0·59	0·24	0·29	0·62
r coefficient				R coefficient		
Imports	2	2	2,(−15),16,−18	2	2	2,(−15)
R	0·51	0·51	0·64	0·57	0·58	0·68
Exports	6	6	6,(−17)	6	6,12	6,(12),21
R	0·56	0·57	0·60	0·33	0·48	0·58
b_s coefficient				b_s coefficient		
Imports	3	3	3,16,−18	(3)	(3)	(3),(13),16
R	0·56	0·57	0·65	0·24	0·33	0·56
Exports	7	7	7,(−15),(−21)	none	(10)	10,15
R	0·51	0·53	0·57	0·14	0·25	0·58
				t ratio for b_d		
Imports				4	4	4,−16,(18),(−21)
R				0·41	0·42	0·65
Exports				8	8,(12)	8,(12),(−19)
R				0·74	0·76	0·79

[a] See text, p. 122.

predict, but in all other equations the only other significant variables related to membership of trade groups. Thus for all three coefficients, membership of the Portuguese group led to higher-than-predicted values for imports, whereas C.A.C.M. membership led to lower values; for the former this implies a stronger and steeper distance effect than was average, for the latter a weaker and shallower one. For the French group, the weaker, shallower pattern is also indicated, though less strongly; a similar relationship for that group, and also for O.E.C.D. members, is suggested for their export flows.

Compared to the findings for the indifference model, those for the total interaction model indicate very little stability in the role of distance as a constraint to trade. The highest stage 1 correlation for both b_d and b_s coefficients is 0·24; in two of the four cases for these coefficients the 1960 value is not a significant predictor for 1969. Overall, there is much more stability in the total fit of the equations, and also of the strength of the b_d coefficient; the latter finding suggests that although the relative positions of countries in terms of the steepness of their distance-decay curves has altered considerably, there has been much less change in which countries have a strong distance effect. Despite the poor correlations at stage 1 for b_d and b_s, however, by stage 3 the coefficients are generally larger than for the indifference model. In the spatial patterns of import flows, significant regression coefficients for variable 13, for both b_d and b_s, again suggest a steepening of the distance-decay curve for well-located countries, and there is also some suggestion of a similar relationship for exports. Of the other relationships noted for the indifference model, that relating to the Portuguese group is again the only one to stand out; no other variable is evident as a major influence on change.

Individual Commodity Flows

The total interaction model was applied to the import and export flows of each of nine commodities to and from twenty-nine separate countries; results of separate analyses for 1960 and 1969 are given in the previous chapter. The four parameters of the model abstracted for study from each regression were the regression coefficient for distance (b_d, and, in its standardised form, b_s), the t coefficient for b_d, and the multiple correlation coefficient, R. The 1960 and 1969 vectors of these coefficients, for each commodity, were correlated over the twenty-nine countries, to test for stability in these disaggregated flow patterns.

As with the comparative analyses for the total interaction model when fitted to total trade flows, these correlations

TABLE 4.10
COMMODITY TRADE FLOW: CHANGING PARAMETERS OF THE
TOTAL INTERACTION MODELS
(Correlation between 1960 and 1969 Values)

	Commodity								
	1	2	3	4	5	6	7	8	9
b_d coefficient									
Imports	0·70	0·41	0·41		0·73	0·55	0·29	−0·91	−0·40
Exports	−0·49	0·66	0·57	0·32		−0·09	0·65	0·29	
t coefficient for b_d coefficient									
Imports	0·53	−0·12	0·39		0·24	0·29	0·09	−0·03	0·43
Exports	0·14	0·67	0·33	0·19		0·03	0·10	0·08	
b_s coefficient									
Imports	0·47	0·70	0·51		0·93	0·67	0·33	−0·38	−0·67
Exports	−0·44	0·69	0·55	0·40		−0·08	−0·02	0·65	
R coefficient									
Imports	0·34	0·42	0·70		0·17	0·22	0·11	0·29	0·78
Exports	0·26	0·46	0·35	0·74		−0·16	0·19	−0·28	

suggest little stability in the role of distance as an influence on the movement of goods (Table 4.10). In some cases — such as the imports of food and of animal and vegetable oils and fats, the exports of beverages and tobaccos and of manufactures — there is some indication of stability in the intensity of the influence of distance (b_d and b_s); only in the imports of food and the exports of beverages and tobacco is this matched by stability in the strength of that influence (the t coefficient). And in others, notably the imports of machinery and miscellaneous manufactures, there is reversal in the relative ordering of the intensity of the distance variable.

The correlations involving the R coefficients also suggest little stability in the overall strength of the total interaction model. However, the mean values for these coefficients (Table 3.11) show that in both years the model was a very good fit to the data; the lack of stability in such a small range of values may indicate no more than random variations.

TIME SERIES ANALYSIS

Despite the great volume of data available on the I.M.F. file it proved possible, partly because of the absence of complete time series for 1948–72 and partly because of constraints of computer storage and programming, to analyse only longer-term trends for the twenty-six countries classified as 'developed' by the I.M.F. The data matrix factor analysed thus comprised each of those twenty-five years as the variables and each pair of countries as the observations.

A major element in the observed time trend is the increase in the value of trade brought about by changing currency values. Thus in the initial cross-product components analysis of the data, the first component accounted for 99 per cent of the variation in the matrix. To control for this influence, several methods of deflating the money value of trade were attempted. That adopted divided each pairwise trade value by the component loading for the relevant year; since the trend of loadings over the twenty-five years indexed the growing money value of trade, this had the effect of bringing all trade figures to a common base.

Cross-product components analysis of this deflated trade matrix emphasised the stability in trade flows which has already been identified. Only two components were interpretable. The first, accounting for 93 per cent of the variation, had a similar loading for each year, and thus emphasised the stability of the trade flow pattern. The second, accounting for 5 per cent, had high negative loadings for the initial years and high positive loadings for the end years; it indexed trade growth over the period. Inspection of the scores on this second component indicates that it refers mainly to exports from two countries; from the United States, which have expanded less rapidly than was general, and from West Germany, which have expanded more rapidly. This is, however, but a minor pattern within the overall matrix of stability.

CONCLUSIONS

The one obvious, and not unexpected, conclusion to be drawn from the analyses reported in this chapter is that, despite the massive growth in the volume of world trade during the 1960s, the predominant feature of the spatial system was its stability. The commodity composition and the direction of flows to and from most countries changed only slightly, as shown particularly well by the indices of redistribution listed in Tables A.14 and A.15. Thus the metropolitan-dominance of trading patterns has remained.

Apart from the stability, it was suggested that changes could take place in one of two directions. The first is towards diversification, with countries attempting to reduce their dependence on a few trading partners and, especially in their exports, on a few commodities. This is in line with the models from urban and regional growth theory which suggest movement towards greater internal self-sufficiency and, at the same time, a wider export base[15]. The second direction, based on notions derived from Janelle's work on time—space convergence[16], is for concentration, which involves an accentuation of existing patterns. According to this, countries would become even more specialised in the commodity composition of their exports as they concentrated on those goods which they are already successful in producing for a world market. Consequential on this would be greater demand for those goods not produced locally, and to which resources were not being directed, and a probable accentuation of the existing pattern of trading partner specialisation.

The overall patterns of change favour the first of those suggestions, since a majority of countries experienced trade diversification rather than increased specialisation. However, important differences were noted between the 'developed' nations and the others. In the former, and particularly in changing patterns of trade flows, the concentration hypothesis was much more frequently supported by the data. While the 'developing' nations seek widely for new markets and new commodities to trade in those markets, therefore, their 'developed' counterparts are becoming more introverted, concentrating on the goods which they are already successfully marketing among themselves. The nucleus of the world trade system is becoming more intense; the periphery is struggling to hang on.

In the pattern of trade flows, equations based on the gravity model analogy proved to be successful predictors of amounts exchanged, at both dates. The most important variable in these was clearly the size of the trade partner — its demand (either in total or for a particular commodity) relative to the other country's exports, its supply relative to imports. Distance between partners, the most significant (though not necessarily most important) variable when the focus is on *spatial* systems, frequently stood out as an independent influence on the amount of trade. Its significance varied in a somewhat random fashion, however, and there was little evidence of any stability in its role between 1960 and 1969. One result of interest did appear; for those countries which are located close to the main trading nations, the parameter for distance increased over time, suggesting a more localised pattern of trade in 1969. As several of these countries also underwent trade diversification during the period, this suggests that they are being 'drawn in' to the core.

Although these patterns of change, simply summarised as an intensifying and slowly expanding core surrounded by a peripheral set of countries struggling hard to maintain their attachment, are of considerable importance, it needs to be reiterated that the major element in these comparisons of the form of the world trade spatial system in 1960 and 1969 is stability. The shift and share analyses, like most measures of change, accentuate the deviations from the system's initial state, whereas it is the continuation of the latter structure which typifies trade patterns over the 1960s.

NOTES AND REFERENCES

1. O. D. Duncan, R. Cuzzort and B. Duncan, *Statistical Geography*, The Free Press, Glencoe, Illinois, 1961, 162 ff.
2. R. J. Johnston, Social area change in Melbourne 1961–1966: a sample exploration, *Australian Geographical Studies*, vol. 9, 1973, 79–98. K. E. Haynes, Spatial change in urban structure: alternative approaches to ecological dynamics, *Economic Geography*, vol. 47, 1971, 314–23.
3. M. A. Poole and P. O'Farrell, The assumptions of the linear

regression model, *Transactions, Institute of British Geographers,* vol. 52, 1971, 145–58.

4. R. B. Cattell, The meaning and strategic use of factor analysis, in R. B. Cattell (ed.), *Handbook of Multivariate Experimental Psychology,* Rand McNally, Chicago, 1966, 174–243.

5. For example, R. A. Murdie, *The Factorial Ecology of Metropolitan Toronto, 1951–1961,* University of Chicago, Department of Geography, Research Paper 116, 1969.

6. R. J. Johnston, *op. cit.*

7. D. J. Veldman, *Fortran Programming for the Behavioral Sciences,* Holt, Rinehart & Winston, New York, 1967; R. J. Johnston, The residential structure of major New Zealand urban areas: a comparative factorial ecology, in B. D. Clark and M. B. Gleave (eds), *Social Patterns in Cities,* Institute of British Geographers, Special Publication 5, 1973, 143–67.

8. There is a substantial literature on shift and share analysis, including a considerable debate on its value, particularly for prediction. For an introduction, see F. J. B. Stillwell, Regional growth and structural adaptation, *Urban Studies,* vol. 6, 162–78.

9. See L. J. King, E. Casetti, D. Jeffrey and J. Odland, Spatial-temporal patterns in employment growth, *Growth and Change,* vol. 4, 1972, 37–42.

10. It would have been possible to predict a country's 1960 indices from its values on the relevant independent variables and the equation derived for those data, but this would have involved assuming that those countries used to derive the equation were a random sample of all countries, which was clearly not the case.

11. This procedure would have 'classified' countries according to their change patterns over the commodities, or commodities over the countries. The latter classification would have been of little value. The former could have identified types of change, but these would have been specific to particular commodities and not general indicators of diversification or concentration. See R. J. Johnston, Regional development in New Zealand: the problems of a small, yet prosperous ex-colony, *Regional Studies,* vol. 5, 1971, 321–33.

12. Libya is the main contributor to this. Unfortunately, most of the major oil-producing nations (in the Middle East, plus Venezuela) were not in the 1960 matrix, so the amount of change in flows of this commodity engendered by the Libyan developments is clearly overstated.

13. In a study of Denmark's experience as a member of E.F.T.A., Burke has shown an increase in its trade with that grouping, relative to trade with other countries, but, within E.F.T.A., a lesser concentration of trade with specific partners. The latter finding is in line with those reported here. See J. D. Burke, The effects of economic integration on the geographic concentration of trade: a case study, *Tijdschrift voor Economische en Sociale Geografie,* vol. 64, 1973, 258–63.

14. The independent variables referred to 1960, on the argument that conditions at the start of the period would be the main determinants of system change.

15. These two notions seem somewhat contradictory, but the example of the developed nations, and trade blocs such as the E.E.C., shows that increasing self-sufficiency in finished goods may lead to greater imports of raw materials and intermediate products.

16. D. G. Janelle, Spatial reorganization: a model and concept, *Annals, Association of American Geographers*, vol. 59, 1969, 348—64.

5

Reflections

The model of an international space-economy outlined in Chapter 1 has been tested in the succeeding three chapters. These tests have been only partial, isolating particular hypotheses and comparing them with available data; unfortunately it was not possible to represent the model, and then test its validity, by a single set of equations. It remains, therefore, for some general threads to be drawn together, which is my purpose here. Two approaches are used. The first expresses the salient features of the empirical analyses, which allows some statement of the positivist aspects of the study; the aim is to provide some inputs to spatial theory. To many people, theory is practice[1], and the second section of the chapter is set within that definition, presenting an interpretation of the present results in the context of the problems of international inequalities.

SPATIAL VARIABLES AND SPATIAL SYSTEMS

The international economy can be studied from a variety of disciplinary or methodological viewpoints; that focused on here emphasises the role of space, or location, as an independent variable influencing the form and function of a system[2]. In order to sharpen this focus, some strict definitions of the spatial variable are needed; those used are based on the typology briefly introduced by Harvey[3].

Location is most frequently treated as a relative concept, as the position of one phenomenon *vis-à-vis* one or more others. The distance between each pair can be measured in a variety of ways, of which time, cost and linear distance are the most common. This notion of *relative location* is, in effect, a special case of a more general concept, of *relational location*. In the latter, position is not expressed separately for each pair of phenomena, but rather the total or average position of each phenomenon is assessed. Thus, in a four-place system, the relative location of point A can be measured separately for B, C and D; its relational location is its position relative to all other places in the system. This concept of relational location is analogous to the concept of population potential, borrowed from Newtonian physics and widely applied in geographical and regional science research[4]. The final member of the typology, *absolute location*, concerns the division of the continuous phenomenon of space into a set of discrete territories.

The independent variables employed in this study have all represented one or more of these concepts of location. Relative location, for example, was measured as the spherical distance between pairs of nodes, each of which represented a territory, and was employed in the various interaction models used to predict flow patterns. Relational location was indexed by the measures of import and export potential that were used to indicate the location of an individual territory relative to the main world import and export markets. Finally, absolute location was represented, not by a measure of area since this, in itself, bears little relation to the trading relations of a country, but rather by indices of the contents of area, such as population, G.N.P., and amount of trade. The succeeding paragraphs summarise the main findings for each of these.

Relative Location and Trade Patterns

In many ways this was the least important of the three sets of independent variables. The role of distance as a severe constraint on, and sometimes a determinant of, human activities is widely documented, though often results may be a self-fulfilling prophecy[5]. Furthermore, the particular inter-action models used here have been fitted in a wide variety of contexts, and have been suggested by at least one author as offering a firm base for a spatial theory of international trade[6]. And indeed, they were generally successful in this work, but not particularly through the predictive strength of the spatial variable.

This at least partial failure to produce results highlighting the role of the spatial variable in the prediction of trade flows may simply reflect the coarse specification of that variable. As pointed out in Chapter 3, many problems are involved in determining the coordinates of the end-points of a distance measurement, and the route between the two points finally decided on. Some of these problems were put to one side in this work, many of them because of the scale of the study. In an investigation of trade flows to and from one or a few countries, detailed experimentation and subsequent specification of the distance measure is possible. In one of the present size, however, involving more than 180 separate end-points, such experimentation and specification could have proceeded interminably; the problem of computing the total distance matrix, and of applying it to the flow matrix, would have consumed a vast amount of (computer as well as investigator) time. In consequence, after some study, the simple, universal approach was adopted.

Despite the above caveats, the distance variable did not prove totally irrelevant to the predictive power of the interaction models. The indifference model, which emphasised the relative location variable, indicated that often a considerable, though never a substantial, proportion of a country's trading pattern could be accounted for by its location relative to its various partners. The total interaction model indicated that, even when a range of other variables had been taken into consideration, distance still, in a vast majority of cases, accounted for a statistically significant proportion of the variation in flows.

Relational Location and Parameters of the Trade System

Greater general success relating aspects of the trade system to spatial variables occurred with the use of relational location measures as the predictors. Although, as indicated by the various references cited in Chapter 1, the importance of relational location has been previously recognised, it does not occupy as important a position in much spatial theory as does relative location.

The strongest influence of relational location on trade

patterns concerns the degree of commodity specialisation in a
country's trade, in particular, its export trade. The closer a
country is to major importing nations, the wider the range of
commodities it can sell. Reasons for this have been suggested
in Chapter 1, including the relationships between relational
location and access to market information. Cost factors are
undoubtedly important, also; Knox, for example, claims that[7]

> It is reasonable to assume that a small country cannot
> influence the prices of its exports or its imports, and thus
> has to bear transport costs on both. It follows that it
> makes quite a difference to its real living standard whether
> it is close to its markets and supplies or far from them.

Accepting that many of the non-metropolitan trading nations
are relatively small, then this argument clearly points out the
cost advantages, over and above those of access to information, of the 'well-located' countries.

Relational location was not strongly related to the pattern
of trading partner specialisation, the degree to which a
country's trade flows were focused on only a proportion of
the potential trade contacts available to them. This came
about because of interactions among relational and absolute
locations. Countries accessible to the European 'core nations'
traded more widely than did those which possessed similar
characteristics apart from poorer access; countries accessible
to the North American 'core', on the other hand, displayed
greater trading partner specialisation than their European
counterparts. The reason for this lies in the absolute spaces of
these two cores. The European pole is divided among several
nations, with whom peripheral countries may trade, but the
North American comprises but a single country, the United
States, on whom neighbours are strongly dependent.

Several studies of the parameters of interaction models,
including Linneman's work on international trade, have
suggested a relationship between relational location and the
influence of relative location on trade flows. Similar, though
by no means strong, relationships were identified here; they
indicate a negative correlation between the steepness of the
relative location influence and import/export potential,
suggesting that poorly-located places are more constrained to

trade with their neighbours. This fits in with notions concerning transport costs and trade, since it suggests that high costs for peripheral nations cause them to interact in a smaller area to counter the problems of the transport bill. Unfortunately, further evidence suggests that these findings are spurious and that the variations in the parameters of distance are themselves a function of relational location, irrespective of the trade flows. Once these 'map pattern' effects have been removed, there is no support for the expected relationship. Peripheral countries do not trade less widely than do those in or close to the 'metropolitan core'. In order to trade as widely, however, they must pay what was termed a 'locational penalty' in Chapter 3; some overcome this penalty by becoming supremely efficient in their production technology (New Zealand, for example), while others merely suffer economic repression.

Finally, relational location is associated with the importance of trade to an economy. This is a finding of Glejser's study[8], which is replicated with the data used here. Using trade volume per head as the dependent variable, and trade size plus potential as the independents, results of the regression equations are shown in Table 5.1.

TABLE 5.1
CORRELATIONS WITH TRADE INTENSITY

| Dependent | Independent | | | Independents | | | | |
	Potential r	r	t	Potential	t	size	t	R
1960								
Imports/head	−0·11	−0·9		4·9		−5·4	0·54	
Exports/head	0·37	3·4		4·0		−8·8	0·76	
1969								
Imports/head	0·33	3·0		3·0		−2·6	0·43	
Exports/head	0·49	4·9		4·9		−2·6	0·55	

The effect of size is always negative, indicating that per head of population the largest trading nations are less involved in the international economy — and thus are presumably more self-supporting — than are their smaller contemporaries. For potentials, the sign of the coefficient, when size is held constant, is positive; 'well-located' countries are better able to participate in the trade system than 'poorly-located'. This follows from the earlier finding relating position and commodity specialisation; the buying and selling advantages of access are reflected in volume as well as breadth of sales and purchases, presumably to the economic benefit of countries and their inhabitants. Such findings also suggest that 'well-located' countries are more dependent on others, and less able to develop self-sufficiency.

Absolute Location and Trade

The division of the world into territories of various sizes proved to be the most pervasive influence on the morphology of the international trade pattern. This was particularly the case in the analyses using interaction models and those involved with the range of trade partners. The system is arranged around a series of nations, here termed the core, among which there is a complex division of labour and a great volume of trade, but which act very much as a single focus of interaction with the majority of small peripheral countries. Of the latter, many direct their trade towards one or a few of the core members but the component analyses suggest that, in their trading with outside countries, the core nations tend to operate very much as a single unit. The total interaction model suggested that, holding size constant, several other variables were also significant, such as relative location and trade preferences, but this in no way plays down the dominating influence of nation size in determining the parameters of the trade system.

Nation-states are but one system of territories into which the world is divided. Several of the others were created, implicitly or explicitly, for the purpose of stimulating trade, particularly trade in certain directions. Unfortunately, few of the more recent supra-national territories had been in operation long enough for their influence on trade patterns to be very apparent in the data used here; of these, it is of interest that only one — the Central American Common Market — has had any marked effects. (For the E.E.C. and, to a lesser extent, E.F.T.A., this may reflect the generalised nature of the study, involving, for example, little use of the very detailed commodity trade classifications.) The former imperial trade systems, which form 'looser' supranational territories, are clearly still important trade channellers.

Location and Change

The general patterns reported in the preceding sections refer to both the 1960 and the 1969 analysis, thereby demonstrating marked stability in the system's morphology. During the period studied, some alterations to the structure did occur, most of them indicative of diversification, in commodities traded and in partners involved. The major deviation from this involved the countries of the 'core', which tended to become slightly more specialised than was average, and to become more inwardly-orientated within that core. These countries also extended their influence over those located close to them, resulting, for example, in steeper distance-decay coefficients (i.e. more local trade) for their neighbours.

SPACE, TRADE AND DEVELOPMENT

The conclusions summarised in the preceding paragraphs present a partial description of the world trade system during the 1960s. Many other analyses could have been conducted and reported; those included here were considered sufficient as a demonstration of the basic spatial parameters of the system. The remainder of this chapter is concerned with possible implications of those parameters.

The Nature of Development

Much of what is written in this section is based on a number of assumptions. Most important of these are that there are inequalities in levels and qualities of living among the countries of the world, and that policies are needed to right these inequalities. Furthermore, it is assumed that, in general terms, the differences should be corrected by raising all countries to those levels now enjoyed by the most favoured. Thus, throughout this book, the latter countries have frequently been referred to as 'developed' or 'advanced', whereas those still striving for material 'progress' are termed 'developing' or 'underdeveloped'.

A further assumption concerns the relationships between the results of the present set of analyses and other character-istics of the international system. In particular, it is taken as axiomatic that the social and economic inequalities referred to here are associated with various parameters of a country's trade patterns. Those which are dependent on selling one or a few commodities, usually to one or a few countries, are those with the lowest levels of individual welfare – high infant mortality rates, low life expectancies, poor diets, few 'material' posessions, etc. There are some obvious exceptions to this generalisation – Luxembourg and New Zealand, for example – but only in one direction: some countries have limited trade horizons but high living standards; none has low living standards but wide trade relationships[9]. Thus further analyses have not been conducted; instead, the evidence of studies such as Berry's is considered sufficient to indicate the relationships assumed here[10].

Development in the present context, therefore, concerns the improvement of living standards in a number of countries which occupy particular positions in the world trade system. Many factors contribute to the generation of such develop-ment, but those concerned with the spatial parameters of the system are the focus here. (This does not imply that the other factors are considered irrelevant or are simply ignored, but only that within the constraints that they set and the opportunities that they offer, the spatial variables are stressed in the present discussion.) It is thus assumed that alteration of the trade system, or of the trading patterns of countries, will assist in the development process, thus inferring a temporal and causal relationship from the cross-sectional associations between trade parameters and 'development levels' observed in the previous chapters.

Finally, it is assumed that development is not an inexor-able process, and that present inequalities are not a passing stage towards the great 'upwards levelling'. This is not an assumption shared by all. Some of the literature on regional development, for example, argues that initial polarisation of growth and inequalities is a transient state, to be followed by a more equitable spatial distribution of jobs and welfare[11]. Others argue that there is nothing inherently 'bad' about the structure of the present system and that development is possible within its parameters. According to Cairncross[12] for example:

> There is nothing necessarily regrettable about dependence on foreign trade. It is true that engaging in trade a country puts itself at the mercy of external events: this is the price that any international division of labour exacts. But a country that seeks development must invite foreign influences if it is to succeed . . . . Most of the countries that we now think of as advanced have been at one time or another dependent on just as narrow a range of exports [as those now considered 'underdeveloped'] . . . . If you want to make a start you must use what you have, not lament that the other fellow who is ahead of you is less highly specialised . . . . Far too much emphasis is put in current literature on the forces operating to limit or diminish the demand for primary produce and far too little on the constant opening up of new requirements.

Absolute Location, Export Specialisation and Development

Several spatial parameters have been related to various aspects of the trade system in this book; the contention in this chapter is that their significance as determinants can be ordered, and that absolute space — the size of the country — is top of this list. Hence major attention is paid in the present reflections to the role of that variable.

Size and export specialisation — in both commodities and the countries they are traded with — are closely related, though with some obvious exceptions. In what way does this specialisation hinder the development process? Given that a country is small in population, it probably has few natural resources, as well as few human resources, whose potential can be tapped. It is therefore necessary to import resources, both the raw and semi-processed materials, the capital goods — machinery, for example — with which to work them, and the human resources needed to motivate such work[13].

To pay for these imports, exports are needed to earn the necessary foreign exchange.

The export of a few commodities, to a few markets, is, as shown here, the usual method by which small countries earn foreign exchange. In doing this, however, they expose themselves to the manipulations of their customers, as several authors have demonstrated. They are, for example, usually expected to pay the transport costs on both their exports and their imports, being in too weak a bargaining position to be able to do otherwise. And since, as shown in this book, many of these small countries are 'unfavourably' located within the world trade system's spatial structure, and so have to bear 'locational penalties' in order to trade with the 'metropolitan core', these payments are accentuated in size and reduce the proportion of the earned foreign exchange that can be spent on the needed goods.

Most of the small, specialised exporters are selling primary, mostly agricultural and pastoral, products in the world market. In doing this, they have established niches within the system, providing materials wanted by the larger trading nations but which, for lack of resources, they are unable to provide for themselves. In a stable marketing situation, in which demand for those products was expanding, occupation of such a niche might be comfortable, reflecting the 'ease with which the small countries can fit into the interstices of the international trade network'[14].

But unfortunately, all is usually not well in such a position. The prices of many primary products fluctuate widely on the world markets, so that countries which specialise in their export, with some notable exceptions depending on the product, suffer most from these variations in receipts for their produce[15]. And since such countries are also often those most dependent on trade — i.e. with the highest ratios of export earnings to G.N.P. — there is a positive relationship between degree of commodity specialisation of export trade and annual variations in G.N.P.[16]. Such economic fluctuations are not in the best interests of planning for internal economic development.

The concentration of trade on a few partners, which is a frequent concomitant of commodity specialisation, also can impede a country's development plans. As Hirschman demonstrated for the 1930s, the large trading nations favour obtaining their imports from small exporters since this gives immense economic and political power to the former. A country which gears its production to the needs of a particular customer, developing a comparative advantage in that market, will find it extremely difficult, and probably impossible in the short term, to change its orientation. Thus the larger country is able to dominate the smaller, and to manipulate its terms of trade; it also has the power to interrupt that trade, with possibly little impact on itself, and thereby force impoverishment on its weak supplier[17]. Furthermore, in many cases it operates these trade relationships to its benefit in that it invests in, and often owns, the resources in the supplier country, with the result that it, or its financial institutions, reap a large proportion of the profits of that trade[18].

During the 1960s, a trend of previous decades was continued with the more rapid growth of trade in manufactured goods as against that of primary products. This reflects the operation of several factors, among them the relatively low elasticity of demand for agricultural and pastoral products in the well-fed nations of the metropolitan core, the initiation of policies designed to protect local agriculture in those countries (of which those of the E.E.C. are a prime example), the greater economies gained from the re-use of materials, such as metal scrap, and the growing use of synthetics, as in fibres[19]. As a result, the income of many primary producing countries is falling, and the terms of trade are moving against them. Returns from exports are insufficient to meet the consumer demands of a local population made increasingly aware of the living standards overseas, and prevent the import of the resources necessary to produce such goods locally. Increasing local production, to make good the deficit, may merely further depress the price.

The situation described in the previous paragraph does not apply to all products, nor to all countries: it is probably most relevant to temperate latitude agricultural and pastoral producers. For some products, demand is such that the producers can, as with oil in 1973, take the initiative and drive their own bargains, even where their resources are being exploited by firms based in the metropolitan core. Unilateral action is probably rarely feasible, however, and some international sellers' cartel (like O.P.E.C.) is necessary. Success of such a policy depends on demand elasticity for the product, which is probably related to its substitutability. For oil, at least in the short run, the seller can probably dominate the market, but the producers of coffee and cheese are much more vulnerable. And, because the resources are almost all held in the 'advanced' countries, these probably have the upper hand in the long term, since they are able to develop substitutes. In any case, as several observers are strong in pointing out, the small countries do not necessarily dominate in the export of many primary products and the advanced countries are in many cases increasing their relative proportion of these exports[20]: the difference between the two types of country is their dependence on this trade, not their significance in it. Thus, for example, as prospecting continues, it may be that the present near-hegemony of the small countries of the Middle East in the oil trade is a temporary phenomenon, and they will eventually return to their dependent position.

All of this discussion is based on the country as the unit. In some cases, particularly among the 'developing' countries, the validity of this approach is in some doubt. Some resources are exploited in these countries by finance from other states; in some cases they are owned by overseas companies. Thus, for primary exporters the return from exports may not all be available, either for imports or for investment in local development. Some countries, realising the constraints of foreign ownership of, and investment in, their resources, have acted to remove them, either by making arrangements with the companies or by nationalisation. Authors such as Frank argue that overseas ownership has deprived countries of much capital which should have been available for internal investment[21]; whether this capital would have been generated without the initial foreign investment is doubtful, however.

Scale Economies and Integration

One of the most frequent explanations for the failure of small countries to 'develop', and therefore increase the standard of living of their inhabitants, is their inability to achieve economies of scale. Internal economies are achieved by large-scale production, which allows for efficient use of, and maximum productivity from, resources. For many productive functions these economies are only attainable when large markets are being served, and both their small populations and low purchasing powers mean that small countries do not possess sufficient markets. Jewkes has argued that the role of such economies, and the thresholds of market size needed for their achievement, has been over-stressed. His case is based on American data, from which he asks[22]

> Might it not be that ... the industrial strength of the United States resides just as much in the extraordinary multiplicity of small factories and firms as it does in the small number of large factories and firms?

This introduces the second type of scale economy, the external or agglomeration effect which is gained from the existence of an extensive industrial and commercial infra-structure. Each industrial unit has contacts with a wide range of other units; many of them are set up by former employees of existing firms[23]. It may be, therefore, that a country meets the threshold for the internal size of a plant producing for a local market, but establishment of such a plant will require either an existing infrastructure or the concurrent introduction of the factories and services required to provide the needed links. And since development needs imported inputs, it is doubtful whether some countries earn sufficient from their exports for establishment of the needed complexes[24].

Other arguments that small size is not a constraint to development quote examples of small countries which enjoy high living standards. Most of these overlook two important aspects of those 'deviant' countries, however: their initial advantage in the development process, and their special relationship with the countries of the 'metropolitan core'. An example of the latter aspect is New Zealand which, although treated in many respects in the typical colonial manner by British capital, was populated by members of the metro-politan society. These people retained some of the capital and, through their access to many of Britain's resources and technological abilities, developed their country's agriculture to its high level of efficiency and provided for themselves a high standard of living. In this respect, New Zealand and other 'temperate-zone colonies' differed from the 'enclave colonies' typical of tropical plantations, in which the European population was a shifting one whose members developed few ties with their country of residence[25]. Nevertheless, New Zealand is at present suffering the same problems as many other small, primary produce exporters.

Switzerland, Belgium and Luxembourg are often quoted as countries with high standards of living which have overcome the problems of smallness. Concerning Switzerland, for example, Jöhr and Kneschavrek have suggested thirteen reasons for that country's high ratio of gross domestic product to labour unit[26]:

1. freedom from war;
2. political stability;
3. high levels of industrialisation;
4. high levels of exports per caput;
5. subsidiaries in foreign countries;
6. large stocks of real capital (the proverbial 'Swiss thrift');
7. high rate of investment;
8. high quality of labour;
9. high level of research and entrepreneurial energy;
10. flexibility and adaptability;
11. highly diversified production;
12. highly diversified exports; and
13. dispersion of foreign markets.

Apart from reasons (1) and (2), and possibly (6), however, these are not causes of success but rather effects of it, and the question still remains as to whether Switzerland's development can be emulated by others. At the time when the Swiss moved towards their present prosperity they were able to invade other markets, partly through ability and expertise in technology (and finance), partly because the markets were there to be created, and partly because of their good location relative to those expanding markets. (In addition, it could be argued that they were able to exploit local labour through the capitalist system.) For current developing countries the problem of market creation is much more severe, for they must face the twin competition of the existing developed countries, with their more efficient industries and their established trading networks, and the developing countries who wish to develop their own industries to serve their markets. In the international system, as in the urban system, initial advantage has played an important role in determining the present morphology and is a major constraint on significant structural changes[27].

To many observers, critics and economic advisers the economic integration of countries has been an obvious solution, or at least part-solution, to the problems of development for small nations. By combining their markets, and by cooperating in the development process, they can more realistically hope to achieve improvement in their position. From an abstract viewpoint, the logic of integration appears sound. Larger markets assist in the attainment of internal scale thresholds; larger areas mean a wider range of resources which can be developed, for the wider good; development of internal markets, and an internal division of labour, lessens the group's dependence on export receipts to produce the national income; a larger total budget gives greater flexibility in development programming: these are but some of the advantages offered by integration.

Movement from the abstract to reality, however, introduces two sets of constraints. The first are political. Integration involves loss of sovereignty, with the replacement of national goals by supra-national goals. To many countries — and a large number of the small 'developing' countries have only recently gained political independence — such potential loss of sovereignty is too high a price to pay for possible economic gains. In many cases, the potential economic gains are, at least to some, hard to discern. Smaller countries entering a union with slightly larger neighbours may fear a 'new colonialism', because the group will be dominated by the larger members; the latter, in turn, may fear that the union will be used by their smaller counterparts

to 'milk' their larger, and therefore potentially more prosperous, colleague, thereby reducing its rate of development[28].

The second set of constraints is spatial. Although it is not
necessary for a union to comprise contiguous countries —
even non-contiguous countries separated only by water
barriers — a dispersed pattern is likely to create many
difficulties of communication and integration. Yet neighbouring countries, especially small neighbouring primary
exporters, are likely to have common resource bases and to
be producing the same goods for export; economic integration and the formation of a larger market is therefore not,
of itself, likely to make for lesser dependence on outside
purchasers, though it may reduce the ability of the latter to
manipulate prices. And if the countries are not similar, is
each likely to benefit equally from the integration programme? To ensure efficiency in what may still be a tenuous
situation, and to gain the internal scale economies, it may
well be that certain locations will be the 'obvious' sites for
new industries to be established. Almost certainly, too,
development of infrastructure complexes to provide external
economies will only be possible in one or a few places. Thus,
in countering their peripheral location in the international
metropolitan situation, a group of countries may develop a
similar pattern at a smaller scale, with one or a few metropolitan nodes within their boundaries and large, still
specialised peripheries — perhaps involving whole countries.
The trade-off is thus between international income and
welfare disparities, and inter-regional (intra-union) disparities: the latter may be more desirable and more easily
resolved, if countries within the union are prepared to accept
the need to introduce policies to ensure spatial equality, and
thereby probably to lose sovereignty.

The economic integration of small countries is not a
straightforward path to development, therefore. In at least
one case, the Central American Common Market, some
considerable success has been achieved in little more than a
decade[29]. Whether it can continue to divert trade from the
developed countries, whether it can build up a complete
industrial infrastructure, and whether it can, concurrently,

ensure that all areas of the group benefit, are crucial
questions. Any group of small countries which integrates
economically must accept that it is still dependent on trade
with the rest of the world for much of its prosperity, which
involves, among other things, the development of other
export lines in competition with the existing vested
interests[30].

The Added Variable—Relational Location

That smallness is not the only locational problem in the
righting of the international inequities which have resulted
from the trade system, erected largely by the activities of the
'metropolitan' core, was realised by several contributors to a
seminar series on the problems of smaller territories[31]. Thus

> Smallness in whatever form it may exist is only one of the
> variables. The issue is complicated still further by the
> significant factors of remoteness, whether simple geo-
> graphical remoteness or remoteness from the intellectual
> mainstream of the world[32].

and Luxembourg is

> highly integrated economically with surrounding countries,
> and yet maintains a considerable degree of economic
> independence. Of course, it has special advantages in its
> geographical location, the possession of large iron deposits,
> and the proximity of prosperous neighbours. Yet it shows
> that economic integration can be combined with political
> separateness[33].

Such statements lead to a conclusion that

> Wherever possible, the best solution for small territories is
> to look for some form of economic integration with their
> neighbours. Small continental territories close to pros-
> perous neighbours are most favourably placed for this[34].

The above quotations would be logical inferences to draw
from the results of the analyses reported in this book, which
indicated the value of good relational locations for both a
widening of export markets and a reduction of the 'locational
penalties' discerned in the parameters of the interaction

models. A partial 'solution' to the trade and development problem would seem to be the international application of growth pole theory, which is presently a popular mechanism for inducing regional development (though whether it is a successful mechanism is far from clear)[35]. This suggests that investment in, for example, an industrial infrastructure at a favourable location will generate development in adjacent locations – the 'trickling down' or 'spread' effect[36]. In the international context, such an effect clearly does occur. The European 'periphery' is a good example; one of more recent growth pole activity is the rapid expansion of Japan in recent decades and its effect on the trade patterns of Asian and Australasian countries.

Inducement of development through growth poles would have many major drawbacks in the international context. As well as 'trickling down' effects, such development also has 'polarisation' or 'backwash' effects, in which the pole develops at the expense of the hinterland. Application of the growth pole notion within an individual country can result in 'polarisation' over large areas concurrent with 'trickling down' over smaller areas, the latter adjacent to the pole. The inequalities which it creates can be corrected by a welfare state system of differential payments – though they rarely are, and the nomination and nurturing of growth poles often creates as much intra-regional strife (albeit perhaps at a different spatial scale) as the initial inter-regional inequalities which the poles were supposed to right. In the international context, strife is likely to be much greater, because of the sovereignty and national aspirations of individual nations. The choice of country(ies) to be the poles for a selected part of the world; the channelling of much of the investment capital of several countries into such poles; the problems of payments to correct inter-regional inequities (as in the E.E.C.) – which payments could themselves harm the economic viability of the pole: all these lead to the despairing question[37]:

> are there any 'solutions' for the smaller territories, any ways in which their inhabitants can satisfy their demands for political self-determination and a higher standard of living?

Swaziland could become a 'southern African Luxembourg' because of its iron resources, but could it also get the independence it, like so many other nations, yearns for.

FINALE

Geographers have recently been castigated, from within the discipline, for their failure to provide, through their research, findings which will allow solution of the pressing problems of the world's population. For example[38],

> There is an ecological problem, an urban problem, an international trade problem, and yet we seem incapable of saying anything of any depth of profundity about any of them. When we do say something it appears trite and rather ludicrous.

With regard to the international trade problem, it may well be that the analyses and discussions of the present book will be so categorised. These have isolated the relevance of locational variables in accounting for the dimensions of the trade problem. They have also indicated that these locational variables could be manipulated to alter the morphology of the international trade system and thereby possibly correct some of the obvious inequalities which it presently maintains. It has also been demonstrated, however, that such manipulation will probably only partly solve the problem, and will generate other inequalities and strife so that, rather than providing a solution, they will merely be transferring or restructuring the basic problem. Perhaps, therefore, the conclusions must be pessimistic; that it is in the nature of such a spatial system, as it has evolved and currently exists, to produce inequalities. Perhaps this is a product of the division of labour, especially the spatial division of labour, itself.

The international trade system is the product of international capitalism. Each country's roles are a function of comparative advantages but those advantages exist not in the vacuum of economic models but in the matrix of the history of international capitalism, in which the major comparative advantage is initial advantage. Economic growth was initiated in a few places according to an economic system which was developing contemporaneously[39]. Slowly at first, and then rapidly, this system spread its growth processes across the earth[40]. Some of the areas were allowed to 'grow' through the system and join the upper echelons of its hierarchy of control; most were prescribed a role and the system was so structured that they have been unable to escape from the imposed strait jacket.

It may be that the pessimistic tone of these conclusions results from overly-optimistic aspirations, particularly those represented in the earlier-stated assumption (p. 137) that 'the differences should be corrected by raising all countries to those levels enjoyed by the most favoured'. Such an aim may be Utopian, and it may be more realistic to accept some levelling down by the 'developed' countries, as a process of redistribution of wealth to their 'developing' counterparts. Indeed, the current experience of Britain and some other countries in the first group may indicate the beginning of such a 'levelling down', and, furthermore, there are undoubtedly many environmental and other externalities of the 'developed' countries that their would-be emulators would wish to avoid. Nevertheless, it is clear that the major aim of the 'developing' nations, as firmly expressed by many at the 1974 Bucharest World Population Conference, is to attain the standards presently enjoyed in the metropolitan core. It would certainly be Utopian, of course, to assume that an equitable equilibrium among all countries could be attained and maintained; what is disturbing, however, is that disequilibrium seems to be permanently weighted in favour of the relatively few countries that have enjoyed initial advantage in the evolution of the system.

The morality of such a system is excellently summarised by Dell[41]

First we tell the underdeveloped countries that nature herself has ordained that their economies are best suited to primary production, thereby complementing our own self-evident superiority in manufacturing. Then we insist that they expand their capacity to meet our needs which,

> we say, are growing more rapidly than any conceivable growth in available supplies. But no sooner have they complied with our wishes than they begin to find that our demand is not growing anywhere near as quickly as we had promised, and as they had expected. The result is that commodity surpluses begin to appear and prices fall. Whereupon we preempt a substantial segment of the market for our own producers, keeping out the additional supplies from abroad which we ourselves had earlier been encouraging and helping to develop ... the Treaty of Rome ... seeks to put the clock back and revive policies associated with the colonial period ... so long as the channels of trade of the underdeveloped countries run exclusively to and from the developed countries, the former are bound to be at the mercy of the economic policies of the latter.

The problem is the economic system. The spatial system is a part of it, but not independent of it; manipulation of the spatial system alone cannot solve the problems of the economic system.

Investigation of the spatial parameters of the economic system which organises world trade indicates constraints which are possibly likely to exist whatever the economic system. It should be possible, therefore, to develop programming models which incorporate spatial constraints within different economic systems. Three Dutch researchers have laid the foundations for such work with a model whose basic aims are to meet growth criteria for various economic sectors in various 'regions'[42]. Expansion of such a model with all the necessary spatial and political constraints, as well as the economic, would be a mammoth task. In the interim, partial models can be used to simulate possible futures, futures which are more equitable but which are only attainable under alternative economic systems.

152   THE WORLD TRADE SYSTEM

NOTES AND REFERENCES

1. D. W. Harvey, *Social Justice and the City*, Edward Arnold, London, 1973, 12.
2. This spatial focus must be embedded within a study of all elements of the system, since the spatial variables are not independent. See R. D. Sack, The spatial separatist theme in geography, *Economic Geography*, vol. 50, 1974, 1–19.
3. D. W. Harvey, *op. cit.*, p. 13.
4. By J. Q. Stewart and W. Warntz, Macrogeography and social science. *Geographical Review*, vol. 48, 1958, 167–84.
5. The conflicting influence of social and spatial variables is emphasised by D. W. Harvey, *op. cit.*, 38–41; for research which avoids this, see the methodology of N. R. Ramsøy, Assortative mating and the structure of cities, *American Sociological Review*, vol. 31, 1966, 773–86.
6. M. H. Yeates, A note concerning the development of a geographic model of international trade, *Geographical Analysis*, vol. 1, 1969, 399–404.
7. A. D. Knox, Some economic problems of small countries, in B. Benedict (ed.), *Problems of Smaller Territories*, The Athlone Press, London, 1967, 38.
8. H. Glejser, An explanation of differences in trade-product ratios among countries, *Cahiers Economiques de Bruxelles*, vol. 37, 1968, 47–58.
9. The question of wealth distributions within a nation is avoided here: cognisance of it would involve a more complex typology than that used.
10. B. J. L. Berry, Basic patterns of economic development, in N. S. Ginsburg (ed.), *Atlas of Economic Development*, University of Chicago Press, Chicago, 1961, 110–19; L. F. Schnore, The statistical measurement of urbanization and economic development, *Land Economics*, vol. 37, 1961, 229–46.
11. J. G. Williamson, Regional inequality and the process of national development, *Economic Development and Cultural Change*, vol. 13, 1965, 3–84. See also B. J. L. Berry, City size and economic development, in L. Jakobson and V. Prakash (eds), *Urbanization and National Development*, Sage Publications, Beverly Hills, 1970, 110–56; and W. Alonso, Urban and regional imbalances in economic development, *Economic Development and Cultural Change*, vol. 17, 1969, 584–95.
12. A. K. Cairncross, *Factors in Economic Development*, Allen & Unwin, London, 1962, 214–16.
13. S. B. Linder, *Trade and Trade Policy for Development*, Pall Mall Press, London, 1967.
14. S. Kuznets, Economic growth of small nations, in E. A. G. Robinson (ed.), *Economic Consequences of the Size of Nations*, Macmillan, London, 1960, 30.

15. M. Michaely, *Concentration in World Trade*, North-Holland, Amsterdam, 1962, 72.
16. *Ibid*, p. 100.
17. A. O. Hirschman, *National Power and the Structure of Foreign Trade*, University of California Press, Berkely, 1945. One possibility open to developing countries is that, with the split of the metropolitan core into several blocs — notably the Euro-American, the Soviet, the Chinese, and the Japanese, each wishing economic and political power — small countries can play one bloc off against another.
18. A. G. Frank, *Capitalism and Underdevelopment in Latin America*, Monthly Review Press, New York, 1969.
19. R. Nurske, *Patterns of Trade and Development*, University of Stockholm, Stockholm, 1959.
20. A. K. Cairncross, *op. cit.*, p. 199.
21. A. G. Frank, *op. cit.*, p. 108.
22. J. Jewkes, Are the economies of scale unlimited?. in Robinson, *op. cit.*, p. 102.
23. See J. Jacobs, *The Economy of Cities*, Random House, New York, 1969; B. Chinitz, Contrasts in agglomeration: New York and Pittsburgh, *American Economic Review*, vol. 61, 1965, 279—89.
24. S. B. Linder, *op. cit.*
25. J. D. Gould, *Economic Growth in History*, Methuen, London, 1972, 248.
26. W. A. Jöhr and F. Kneschavrek, Study of the efficiency of a small nation — Switzerland, in Robinson, *op. cit.*, 54—77. Similar arguments are produced in P. J. Lloyd, *International Trade Problems of Small Nations*, Duke University Press, Durham, 1968.
27. A. R. Pred, Industrialization, initial advantage, and American metropolitan growth, *Geographical Review*, vol. 55, 1965, 158—85.
28. D. P. J. Wood, The smaller territories: some political considerations, in B. Benedict, *op. cit.*, 23—34; examples are cited of failed federations within the British Commonwealth, such as Rhodesia and Nyasaland, Malaysia, and the West Indies.
29. E. C. Conkling and J. E. McConnell, A cooperative approach to trade and development, *Tijdschrift voor Economische en Sociale Geografie*, vol. 64, 1973, 363—77.
30. The Soviet bloc is no exception to the problem of metropolitan-periphery disparities within a trade union, though most of the peripheral countries are, on a world scale, relatively large.
31. B. Benedict, *op. cit.*
32. D. P. J. Wood, *op. cit.*, p. 29.
33. B. Benedict, Introduction, in B. Benedict, *op. cit.*, p. 3.
34. *Ibid*, p. 9.
35. N. M. Hansen (ed.), *Growth Centers in Regional Economic Development*, The Free Press, Glencoe, 1972.

36. A. O. Hirschman, *The Strategy of Economic Development*, Yale University Press, New Haven, 1958; G. Myrdal, *Economic Theory and Under-Developed Regions*, Duckworth, London, 1957.
37. B. Benedict, *op. cit.*, p. 9.
38. D. W. Harvey, *op. cit.*, p. 129.
39. S. Kuznets, *Modern Economic Growth*, Yale University Press, New Haven, 1966; T. Parsons, *The Systems of Modern Societies*, Prentice-Hall, Englewood Cliffs, 1971.
40. E. Casetti, L. J. King and F. Williams, Concerning the spatial spread of economic development, *International Geography*, vol. 2, 1972, 897–9.
41. S. Dell, *Trade Blocs and Common Markets*, Constable, London, 1963, 143–7.
42. L. B. M. Nennes, J. Tinbergen and J. G. Waardenburg, *The Element of Space in Development Planning*, North-Holland, Amsterdam, 1969.

Appendix I

Detailed Tables

TABLE A.1
INDICES OF COMMODITY SPECIALISATION, 1960

Country	Imports One-digit	Imports Two-digit	Imports Three-digit	Exports One-digit	Exports Two-digit	Exports Three-digit
U.S.	86·38	77·96	69·78	85·10	73·31	69·52
Canada	81·47	72·71	61·97	71·72	62·47	58·46
Japan	71·45	65·69	59·93	67·13	61·51	52·00
U.K.	83·81	77·30	70·70	71·41	62·14	60·62
Austria	86·89	76·75	67·72	78·99	64·02	52·51
Belgium	86·81	79·85	69·22	66·11	58·16	49·18
Denmark	86·44	76·43	61·11	64·72	61·18	55·19
France	89·13	75·92	65·04	82·89	72·56	61·98
W. Germany	85·92	80·03	70·45	69·72	64·00	57·34
Italy	86·46	77·28	65·63	82·70	66·73	59·61
Netherlands	88·51	77·78	69·27	85·99	77·86	66·40
Norway	81·57	67·72	57·19	74·39	59·03	52·65
Sweden	86·08	75·12	66·65	65·72	61·82	52·14
Switzerland	88·75	81·44	68·97	72·78	62·89	55·22
Finland	81·54	73·44	62·30	54·40	42·45	35·95
Greece	73·72	65·60	53·42	67·86	46·94	44·37
Iceland	82·21	70·16	57·60	25·01	24·18	17·57
Ireland	89·31	79·21	67·63	62·02	60·37	47·27
Portugal	86·12	73·59	60·88	80·67	65·96	53·14
Spain	90·25	68·89	58·00	76·83	56·92	53·77
Turkey	75·05	59·95	53·92	56·55	49·97	43·71
Yugoslavia	78·93	69·25	65·38	81·52	74·57	62·68
Australia	80·99	67·62	60·92	58·90	54·62	43·75
New Zealand	78·27	71·89	59·09	39·70	39·18	33·98
S. Africa	76·64	71·94	64·97	70·39	72·55	59·36
Argentina	68·30	57·90	54·36	43·32	50·78	45·79
Brazil	58·26	60·55	55·54	32·48	34·65	30·23

Table continued overleaf

TABLE A.1 (cont.)
INDICES OF COMMODITY SPECIALISATION, 1960

Country	Imports One-digit	Imports Two-digit	Imports Three-digit	Exports One-digit	Exports Two-digit	Exports Three-digit
Colombia	74·02	67·31	54·47	34·04	19·20	16·06
Costa Rica	78·06	70·51	58·34	11·85	23·27	19·44
Ecuador	78·56	70·85	53·96	9·08	22·56	21·61
El Salvador	83·33	74·64	43·23	33·97	18·36	9·86
Guatemala	92·70	79·96	65·89	20·71	24·60	17·79
Honduras	79·88	70·02	60·70	31·97	34·84	30·10
Mexico	68·04	61·95	54·43	63·73	64·62	53·68
Nicaragua	81·09	70·89	49·21	32·72	35·42	25·47
Panama	83·66	70·73	39·48	3·14	17·40	14·41
Guadeloupe	88·78	76·12	64·29	24·00	22·81	17·74
Guyana	80·49	60·51	52·72	43·74	26·27	20·43
B. Honduras	81·02	70·83	40·36	31·49	29·17	22·55
Jamaica	85·09	78·38	41·96	46·72	28·31	21·41
N. Antilles	33·32	20·98	18·09	4·56	1·45	3·80
Surinam	82·43	62·49	—	25·27	4·28	—
Trinidad	80·03	58·17	45·20	30·09	13·53	13·03
Cyprus	87·25	81·01	74·71	42·00	24·74	19·95
Israel	81·22	71·65	63·84	63·91	54·05	40·84
Aden	68·00	36·03	37·91	34·00	34·31	27·13
Egypt	86·98	71·09	63·82	29·10	22·60	17·91
Afghanistan	68·01	58·71	47·61	40·58	29·77	33·71
Burma	72·35	62·02	57·07	28·54	30·02	25·08
Ceylon	77·14	75·04	54·07	37·67	26·44	20·06
Hong Kong	83·06	78·24	71·90	52·25	55·22	52·57
India	79·23	60·88	57·69	63·69	47·75	49·85
Indonesia	70·50	59·35	56·42	51·73	39·07	32·80
S. Korea	82·41	61·84	45·79	57·73	39·09	32·04
Malaya	88·11	76·83	61·78	40·64	30·44	23·24
Pakistan	83·94	68·28	60·91	44·65	34·54	37·64
Philippines	78·11	64·76	—	43·34	43·73	—
Sabah	91·46	68·04	54·11	28·61	31·13	21·86
Sarawak	62·36	23·23	19·92	38·31	28·63	27·40
Singapore	80·80	59·67	45·33	74·98	49·19	37·06
Thailand	76·96	66·13	55·72	35·33	42·87	35·62
Cameroons	86·95	77·57	65·68	62·15	37·54	35·17
Congo	80·13	74·11	64·59	44·96	32·75	29·67
Dahomey	82·84	72·97	61·43	39·61	26·14	18·63
Gambia	84·89	44·03	42·10	7·31	—	—
Ghana	78·32	68·62	60·83	38·49	18·61	16·88
Ivory Coast	80·00	75·01	64·08	38·26	25·70	28·56
B.E. Africa	75·41	62·73	57·71	46·77	44·23	41·04
Liberia	79·07	68·88	39·95	3·31	22·88	16·69
Libya	76·09	65·16	43·64	44·06	46·64	25·44
Madagascar	84·97	78·96	65·37	65·54	51·72	41·54
Mauritius	78·83	46·06	40·17	0·0	1·36	1·06

Table continued

TABLE A.1 (*cont.*)
INDICES OF COMMODITY SPECIALISATION, 1960

Country	Imports			Exports		
	One-digit	Two-digit	Three-digit	One-digit	Two-digit	Three-digit
Morocco	83·08	77·26	67·21	55·62	60·64	54·24
Niger	82·42	71·05	57·65	37·61	28·66	22·29
Nigeria	76·12	65·74	46·66	48·77	49·50	38·33
Reunion	83·51	66·00	50·00	20·55	13·44	10·45
Rhodesia	79·56	71·92	59·10	49·32	25·38	16·99
Senegal	84·97	73·60	64·38	59·72	50·19	38·33
Sierra Leone	84·05	66·28	50·39	37·42	29·44	23·70
Somalia	74·24	59·42	33·65	27·01	15·77	12·26
Sudan	82·11	74·61	63·74	16·30	27·12	30·99
Togo	79·11	74·60	56·74	35·80	30·73	30·43
Fiji	82·85	56·58	37·56	29·72	18·69	14·53
New Guinea	81·42	60·84	—	58·13	37·00	28·76
Papua	81·42	78·19	—	2·63	18·77	14·60
W. Samoa	81·87	52·39	—	30·77	16·18	—
Cook I.	78·70	56·72	—	52·17	31·73	—
Niue	84·25	53·66	—	26·39	0·01	—
Cuba	77·70	73·42	64·89	30·65	16·01	6·27
Mean	80·27	67·81	51·77	44·92	38·11	31·63
SD	8·00	11·08	17·15	22·32	19·52	17·84
CV	0·10	0·16	0·33	0·49	0·51	0·57

TABLE A.2
IMPORTS AND EXPORTS BY COMMODITIES 1960 (ONE-DIGIT):
SCORES FROM CROSS-PRODUCT COMPONENT ANALYSES

Analysis and component	Commodity category								
	1	2	3	4	5	6	7	8	9
Imports									
1	1·12	0·18	0·48	0·73	0·07	0·60	1·78	1·77	0·52
2	0·45	0·00	0·04	−0·56	−0·02	0·14	−0·58	0·48	0·03
3	0·19	−0·06	0·35	0·70	0·06	0·68	−0·24	−0·55	0·00
4	0·65	0·08	0·58	2·39	−0·04	−0·37	−0·87	−0·56	0·00
Exports									
1	2·44	0·11	1·68	0·13	0·11	0·08	0·37	0·12	0·09
2	−1·77	0·00	2·39	0·11	0·05	0·03	0·36	0·12	−0·01
3	−0·02	−0·15	−0·13	1·58	−0·06	0·11	−0·68	0·64	0·17
4	−0·11	0·18	−0·58	1·00	−0·03	0·34	2·54	0·91	0·34

TABLE A.3
IMPORTS AND EXPORTS BY COMMODITIES 1960 (ONE-DIGIT):
LOADINGS FROM CROSS-PRODUCT COMPONENT ANALYSES
(expressed as percentages of variance)

Country	Imports				Exports			
	1	2	3	4	1	2	3	4
U.S.	76	−23			45			40
Canada	66	15	−9		68	−28		
Japan	22		5	18	77	−18		
U.K.	54		7	9			38	18
Austria	85				19	15	27	12
Belgium	71	−15					−15	74
Denmark	86				62	−14	11	
France	59	−8		11	42			49
W. Germany	60	−9					44	18
Italy	59	−3	7	5	11		35	24
Netherlands	83	−11			31		33	18
Norway	84				23		−20	42
Sweden	85	−11			17	21	18	12
Switzerland	88						29	9
Finland	90				32	44		17
Greece	56	29	−5		15		−9	
Iceland	85		−10		68	−28		
Ireland	95				77	−18		
Portugal	84				16		−40	32
Spain	49	−4	13	5	77	−9		
Turkey	75				61			
Yugoslavia	71	16			62			23
Australia	80	−10			87			
New Zealand	71	−24			98			
South Africa	84		−7		68	19		
Argentina	74		−10		89	−8		
Brazil	24	47			81	−18		
Colombia	64	17			68	−26		
Costa Rica	71		14	−10	68	−32		
Ecuador	82			−11	68	−32		
El Salvador	74		15		82	−18		
Guatemala	16	22	53		74	−25		
Honduras	69	−10	11	−6	86	−12		
Mexico	41	41			90			
Nicaragua	47		36		80	16		
Panama	71	−9			67	−32		
Barbados	72	19			69	−30		
Guadeloupe	51	26	12		64	−32		
Guyana	83	8			96			
B. Honduras	54	40			96			
Jamaica	96				90			
N. Antilles	8	−23	6	49			44	10
Surinam	87				43	54		
Trinidad	52	−25		17			45	10
Cyprus	81				77	18		
Israel	88				24		−25	34

Table continued

TABLE A.3 (*cont.*)
IMPORTS AND EXPORTS BY COMMODITIES 1960 (ONE-DIGIT):
LOADINGS FROM CROSS-PRODUCT COMPONENT ANALYSES
(expressed as percentages of variance)

Country	Imports				Exports			
	1	*2*	*3*	*4*	*1*	*2*	*3*	*4*
Aden	16	−36		35			37	14
Egypt	41	42			80	15		
Afghanistan	53	−36			96			
Burma	40	−48			86	−13		
Ceylon	55	21			93			
Hong Kong	61	−19					27	55
India	72	19			36		32	28
Indonesia	63	−17		−6	41	42	9	
S. Korea	16		74		83	16		
Malaya	54	32			38	60		
Pakistan	75				45	47		
Philippines	74	16			76	21		
Sabah	31	24	−17	−10	34	61		
Sarawak	19	22	−6	44	14	17		
Singapore	32			20	56	35		
Thailand	62	−30			93			
Cameroons	50		11		60		−18	19
Congo	75		−17		38	59		
Dahomey	59	−31			39	46		
Gambia	63	−18			33	63		
Ghana	92				93			
Ivory Coast	82	−10			98			
B.E. Africa	69	−23			94			
Liberia	67	10	−10		33	62		
Libya	69	17	−7		52	38		
Madagascar	64	−21			84			
Mauritius	61	23	6		65	−34		
Morocco	92				95			
Niger	53	−35			56	37		
Nigeria	65	−26			68	73		
Reunion	44	44			64	−32		
Rhodesia	84						41	45
Senegal	39	31			91			
Sierra Leone	49	−40			12	70	−32	41
Somalia	39	40			93			
Sudan	21	32	11		40	55		
Togo	63	−12	−12		94			
Zanzibar	41	18			72	−25		
Fiji	81	−8			63	−26		
New Guinea	70	18			28			
Papua	49	35			33	63		
W. Samoa	80				84	11		
Cook I.	66	−16			52			
Niue	83				54	−26		
Cuba	45	−27			67	−30		
% Variance	56	19	8	5	52	21	9	7

TABLE A.4

IMPORTS AND EXPORTS BY COMMODITIES 1960 (TWO-DIGIT):
SCORES FROM CROSS-PRODUCT COMPONENT ANALYSES[a]

Imports Commodity	Component 1	2	3	4	5	6	7
1	6	0	3	3	0	9	27
2	37	24	24	-26	-25	96	-25
3	37	5	26	19	-11	13	-27
4	29	27	24	17	3	-46	-22
5	183	26	228	35	-64	-631	87
6	50	11	40	11	28	-10	53
7	62	35	-253	-492	461	43	-44
8	37	-2	16	3	22	36	89
9	11	-5	-2	10	8	-9	18
10	3	1	4	3	-1	1	-6
11	32	1	22	-6	-24	-9	-53
12	37	5	55	-67	54	-20	-21
13	6	-2	9	9	13	8	31
14	16	-1	3	20	31	-13	63
15	26	-21	2	24	35	2	175
16	32	15	-10	0	19	-32	101
17	8	-1	0	14	20	4	46
18	53	-1	12	88	114	26	316
19	12	1	1	14	16	12	46
20	20	-4	10	19	46	14	177
21	5	1	4	2	-1	9	22
22	20	2	2	33	34	26	94
23	360	-616	-143	-80	-10	14	-42
24	1	0	0	2	2	0	-4
25	0	0	0	0	0	0	0
26	2	1	1	4	2	-2	7
27	12	-1	4	17	14	13	34

Commodity	Component 1	2	3	4	5	6	7
28	0	0	0	0	0	-1	0
29	22	5	1	28	25	16	42
30	20	2	2	33	34	26	94
31	17	7	9	14	3	11	-2
32	53	27	34	13	-21	22	-46
33	13	5	11	-2	-13	9	-36
34	31	7	21	43	37	-14	62
35	1	0	0	-1	-1	1	-4
36	37	17	5	34	19	42	33
37	3	1	1	2	0	6	5
38	33	16	13	14	-7	54	-52
39	11	12	9	-21	-15	-37	24
40	50	18	21	43	11	31	-8
41	278	115	340	-185	-446	247	114
42	52	17	29	16	-16	0	-67
43	173	41	23	223	184	142	332
44	85	38	26	46	-10	83	-111
45	327	133	134	362	221	68	-316
46	50	42	33	12	-22	16	-196
47	339	344	-504	-211	-9	-69	20
48	8	5	4	2	-5	8	-17
49	5	2	3	-2	-5	0	-16
50	0	0	0	0	-1	0	1
51	48	11	24	-4	-27	11	-81
52	16	3	10	-6	-18	21	-42
53	30	8	6	21	11	35	5
54	41	13	16	10	-16	62	4

Exports

Commodity	Component 1	2	3	4	5	6	7	8
1	15	-3	22	15	-6	17	-20	-2
2	38	-19	-9	9	12	75	-17	15
3	9	-1	9	3	12	41	-14	14
4	27	11	51	-8	8	26	11	0
5	41	16	42	24	50	104	4	143
6	365	178	350	-501	19	-99	-97	23
7	217	592	-327	193	-53	-14	-46	24
8	519	-379	-330	35	-75	-80	70	-26
9	17	-1	32	34	-15	19	-21	8
10	6	0	0	0	2	1	0	1
11	12	12	9	-5	9	5	10	-1
12	22	5	27	-1	13	37	3	27
13	25	3	39	-6	2	37	-31	-3
14	147	-35	366	421	-276	-203	-180	-97
15	67	-25	105	156	166	-81	153	570
16	90	-1	31	62	-6	-31	-2	88
17	4	1	7	5	6	11	11	23
18	151	-50	72	97	51	608	-264	-25
19	11	3	12	-6	5	11	4	1
20	130	88	192	100	72	158	596	-259
21	19	-2	23	9	0	20	-8	1
22	2	1	4	2	4	7	8	-2
23	73	-16	19	140	637	-190	-163	-201
24	0	0	0	0	0	1	0	0
25	0	0	0	0	0	1	0	1
26	1	0	2	0	1	4	0	2
27	27	13	27	50	-23	-19	-22	8

Commodity	Component 1	2	3	4	5	6	7	8
28	1	0	0	0	0	1	2	1
29	2	1	3	0	4	4	0	5
30	2	1	4	2	4	7	8	2
31	2	0	2	1	2	4	0	3
32	2	0	3	1	5	6	0	6
33	6	11	-10	5	-1	0	-2	2
34	3	1	4	0	7	8	1	18
35	0	0	0	1	0	0	0	0
36	4	-1	4	-1	5	8	-1	5
37	2	-1	1	0	1	4	0	0
38	2	1	3	6	3	2	0	4
39	7	0	9	5	0	0	0	5
40	6	-1	9	5	10	15	11	24
41	43	-4	31	11	62	102	2	30
42	7	0	6	1	9	16	0	7
43	43	-5	36	20	60	86	47	215
44	5	0	8	2	12	13	2	20
45	22	-4	29	24	22	25	-2	57
46	0	0	0	0	1	1	0	1
47	13	1	17	9	30	28	4	55
48	0	0	0	0	0	0	0	1
49	0	0	0	0	0	1	0	0
50	0	0	0	0	0	0	0	0
51	12	5	23	-14	3	-2	-7	9
52	1	0	2	0	2	3	0	2
53	2	0	2	1	4	7	0	9
54	4	1	7	-2	7	9	-2	11

a To two decimal places: decimal points omitted.

TABLE A.5
IMPORTS AND EXPORTS BY COMMODITIES 1960 (TWO-DIGIT): LOADINGS FROM CROSS-PRODUCT COMPONENT ANALYSES
(expressed as percentages of variance)

Country	Imports							Exports							
	1	2	3	4	5	6	7	1	2	3	4	5	6	7	8
U.S.	52						10						8		
Canada	78													13	
Japan	27	−8			7		19						5		
U.K.	50	−7					14								
Austria	68	9		8											11
Belgium	66			5			13								6
Denmark	80														
France	51	−5		7	10		11					7	6		6
W. Germany	46			7			23								5
Italy	53	−5		10	7		15	9		7		9			
Netherlands	83						5	11				25			
Norway	76	6	−9												7
Sweden	81													7	
Switzerland	79														
Finland	71						9								
Greece	58	12	−24					5		5			7		
Iceland	83		−9												
Ireland	84														
Portugal	65			6	13		5								

	1	2	3	4	5	6	7	8	9	10	11	12	13	14	15
Spain	53	−22			6			31	6	24	−28	16			
Turkey	69	7		10	9			27	6	13	−7	8		8	
Yugoslavia	53			17	11			7				70			9
Australia	86					6		10				41			
New Zealand	66					8						30		7	
S. Africa	79	7						20		16		20		11	
Argentina	60														
Brazil	43	9		17	10			30	−9	−8					
Colombia	62			19	7			53	−24	−16					
Costa Rica	59			6	5			74	−10						
Ecuador	66	14		15				57		5	−7				
El Salvador	83							54	−25	−18	−33				
Guatemala	47							65	−20	−12					
Honduras	82			6				56		8	−29				
Mexico	50	16		6	5		9	41	−5			40			
Nicaragua	78							30		17	7	38		−11	
Panama	80							30	65	−18	−41				
Barbados						8		9	66		6				
Guadeloupe	49		12					27	57		9			10	
Guyana	62		5	12			−7	13	25	−5					
B. Honduras	75						−7	20	25				75		
Jamaica	86							16						43	−8
N. Antilles	26	−68											−6	−5	−8
Surinam	38	6	13	14			−14			7			−6	66	12
Trinidad	60	−36											73	−5	−7
Cyprus	83							19	6	24	−7			33	
Israel	74							24	5	20	−34				
Aden	35	−59											74	−6	−7

Table continued overleaf

TABLE A.5 (cont.)
IMPORTS AND EXPORTS BY COMMODITIES 1960 (TWO-DIGIT): LOADINGS FROM CROSS-PRODUCT COMPONENT ANALYSES
(expressed as percentages of variance)

Country	Imports							Exports							
	1	2	3	4	5	6	7	1	2	3	4	5	6	7	8
Egypt	68			7		-13							68	-14	
Afghanistan	45		13	-11	-17			24		17	-24			-5	
Burma	40	6	14		-19	13									6
Ceylon	63		7			-14		54	-23	-11					
Hong Kong	46		17	18	-6		12	25	-5						
India	58				9			7							
Indonesia	53		21		-12						12	35	-5		26
S. Korea	20		10	5			7			8			11	48	-9
Malaya	68										6	6		8	64
Pakistan	61			8		-14		5		5		5	69	-11	
Philippines	63	23						25	26	5	27				
Sabah	55							5		6	10				
Sarawak	29	-67						5			9	66	-8		5
Singapore	17	-7					6	6			7	18			49
Thailand	80					10				6					36
Cameroons	74						-10	55	-23	-11					
Congo	67	6													
Dahomey	81		23	-10				6		26	34	-13	-6	-7	
Gambia	43	6			-12					27	35	-14	-8	-6	

	48	16	9	7	5	3	3	18	13	10	10	8	7	6	5
Ghana	78	7						53	−23	−15					
Ivory Coast	76	7		−5				58	−21	−12					
B.E. Africa	86	10					5	46	−14				28	48	12
Liberia	76	12			−6			12	−11	9	8	−9			
Libya	75	5						67	64	39	17				
Madagascar	74		12		−32			9		−15					
Mauritius	46		5					19		−19	6				
Morocco	75		11	−10				5		17	−12	−14	−7	−7	
Niger	53	7		−12	5			42	−8	30	32				
Nigeria	70				6			10	63	8	30				
Reunion	21	22	−47	−8						−19	6				
Rhodesia	83	7	7												8
Senegal	63		19	−7				20		7	6				
Sierra Leone	74		8		−8					15	18			29	−13
Somalia	47		19			−8		6			6			−16	
Sudan	80							62		5	5		58		
Togo	74			−6											
Zanzibar	48	15	15			−23									
Fiji	66	−15						10	63	−15	7		−5		
New Guinea	66					−6		17		6	21	−8	−7		21
Papua	65	6					−5			22	32				
W. Samoa	26	9		−13		−11		34	37		−21				
Cook I.	39	10	13	−6	−7			24	6	31	−16				
Niue	28	15	−5	−5				25		20	−44				
Cuba			13	−45	40			6				24			
% Variance	48	16	9	7	5	3	3	18	13	10	10	8	7	6	5

TABLE A.6
INDICES OF COMMODITY SPECIALISATION 1969

Country	Imports			Exports		
	One-digit	Two-digit	Three-digit	One-digit	Two-digit	Three-digit
U.S.	78·49	79·91	69·00	77·90	73·18	68·41
Canada	70·33	68·12	58·95	75·50	69·52	47·61
Japan	79·64	75·05	63·80	63·66	62·33	62·17
U.K.	88·34	83·71	74·10	71·70	69·15	66·89
Austria	84·92	81·43	73·22	73·61	73·49	69·65
Belgium	86·65	83·60	71·44	82·47	74·36	66·62
Denmark	84·13	80·80	69·55	79·03	75·50	63·72
France	88·15	83·05	71·19	82·41	78·97	73·78
W. Germany	88·05	83·72	75·08	68·55	66·58	63·39
Italy	87·88	82·47	71·43	77·49	71·29	64·70
Netherlands	88·16	83·90	73·10	87·75	85·08	73·81
Norway	82·43	76·46	67·25	75·34	68·32	56·82
Sweden	84·67	79·66	72·21	67·85	67·60	58·86
Switzerland	85·56	81·83	73·49	74·24	68·86	58·39
Finland	82·76	76·04	69·24	65·86	62·12	47·87
Greece	84·73	77·41	66·51	80·57	64·62	57·98
Iceland	86·72	79·63	69·55	33·47	29·98	24·22
Ireland	85·74	80·69	72·96	73·27	73·27	62·98
Malta	85·18	82·70	73·80	74·77	57·71	48·34
Portugal	86·71	77·94	68·94	82·00	71·98	62·44
Spain	81·24	80·26	69·68	91·24	78·70	68·95
Turkey	72·80	68·43	63·14	63·64	49·81	43·63
Yugoslavia	79·00	75·68	71·48	82·51	80·55	70·77
Australia	78·50	69·92	69·10	70·93	68·07	53·34
New Zealand	80·41	72·15	67·30	49·10	48·92	43·55
S. Africa	73·31	69·92	63·99	74·04	74·18	59·49
Argentina	79·13	72·09	69·56	53·23	58·06	52·00
Brazil	80·32	69·85	63·70	52·77	56·47	45·09
Chile	79·36	72·71	65·10	33·42	22·69	18·54
Colombia	70·06	66·04	66·20	45·97	38·58	28·31
Costa Rica	79·08	75·48	66·73	36·21	48·12	35·05
Ecuador	53·07	—	—	14·00	26·50	24·66
El Salvador	82·95	79·73	69·67	64·69	51·33	42·60
Guatemala	74·75	75·87	65·53	61·28	58·28	42·93
Honduras	79·28	73·44	66·47	48·16	41·53	30·52
Mexico	76·31	66·71	62·48	72·52	74·71	59·35
Nicaragua	79·04	75·57	62·85	58·04	58·36	40·20
Peru	78·88	74·55	—	58·83	48·84	—
Venezuela	71·78	67·06	59·86	16·48	8·89	17·55
Barbados	86·32	80·34	61·96	65·24	41·96	31·75
Guadeloupe	86·58	81·67	71·49	19·44	26·92	20·93
Guyana	81·45	70·87	60·77	40·61	27·44	19·15
B. Honduras	82·65	79·98	69·34	24·18	27·39	22·58
Jamaica	80·78	77·15	58·82	53·73	36·70	29·35
Martinique	85·69	83·23	70·34	30·55	23·40	24·75

Table continued

TABLE A.6 (cont.)
INDICES OF COMMODITY SPECIALISATION 1969

Country	Imports One-digit	Imports Two-digit	Imports Three-digit	Exports One-digit	Exports Two-digit	Exports Three-digit
N. Antilles	44·12	32·24	22·81	14·41	6·82	3·19
Surinam	83·59	77·59	—	35·41	19·79	9·19
Trinidad	67·97	51·71	34·64	38·55	18·09	19·53
Cyprus	81·66	79·13	64·92	57·14	37·46	26·53
Iran	67·97	67·04	63·94	26·31	14·67	23·55
Israel	76·03	72·53	70·56	64·17	54·10	44·17
Jordan	82·54	81·10	70·94	65·38	46·38	37·69
Kuwait	75·09	75·04	67·10	10·18	6·71	5·01
Lebanon	86·35	82·14	69·25	81·47	76·74	63·96
Yemen, P.D.R.	77·75	65·48	43·62	36·51	22·42	9·04
Syria	81·39	75·89	68·25	62·72	52·00	41·27
Egypt	90·36	79·29	66·64	64·69	44·25	38·11
Afghanistan	81·10	59·18	50·10	57·40	41·00	41·13
Brunei	76·65	73·68	65·74	10·47	5·47	4·08
Burma	66·90	65·71	63·07	39·01	40·78	37·61
Khmer R.	78·74	73·97	64·11	32·25	38·25	32·47
Sri Lanka	72·62	74·09	59·22	39·95	29·75	23·56
China (Taiwan)	78·71	71·25	63·42	73·75	66·21	57·67
Hong Kong	83·38	78·26	68·55	58·09	59·29	48·82
India	83·92	66·46	62·95	68·02	68·96	62·38
Indonesia	74·04	69·08	63·85	63·46	43·27	39·05
S. Korea	80·32	68·88	64·53	71·94	62·11	49·43
Sabah	82·60	75·00	67·86	30·10	26·73	21·04
Sarawak	72·43	58·50	42·94	52·89	35·49	33·75
W. Malaysia	87·13	79·55	69·48	55·86	42·52	30·45
Pakistan	75·26	70·81	69·36	55·81	41·59	45·60
Philippines	78·01	68·97	64·50	61·05	54·76	40·39
Singapore	89·44	75·74	64·64	80·80	62·91	45·13
Thailand	77·62	71·32	60·38	53·88	48·89	42·31
S. Vietnam	79·61	71·87	59·18	27·19	17·80	13·94
Cameroons	79·65	73·27	65·93	51·57	36·12	35·11
C. African R.	83·08	74·95	64·86	55·32	34·46	26·47
Chad	87·39	73·69	61·22	19·49	15·65	7·52
Congo	77·00	71·97	67·33	55·52	35·73	29·72
Zaire	76·52	75·66	—	31·98	23·47	25·46
Dahomey	80·28	73·78	63·92	68·28	43·48	31·85
Ethiopia	80·99	73·80	66·14	29·41	34·22	26·64
Gabon	74·51	68·20	65·08	43·08	32·72	29·60
Gambia	77·93	63·06	—	43·35	24·30	18·90
Ghana	75·07	77·19	65·93	43·37	28·80	24·24
Ivory Coast	77·74	74·73	65·99	43·64	35·01	35·24
Kenya	76·41	72·51	63·99	55·74	51·11	37·75
Liberia	78·86	73·75	61·49	6·12	19·98	15·83
Libya	74·62	73·29	63·67	0·39	0·02	0·02
Malagasy R.	81·15	74·73	68·30	49·27	53·87	45·38

Table continued overleaf

TABLE A.6 (cont.)
INDICES OF COMMODITY SPECIALISATION 1969

Country	Imports			Exports		
	One-digit	Two-digit	Three-digit	One-digit	Two-digit	Three-digit
Malawi	81·20	76·48	64·06	56·21	62·07	32·40
Mali	82·87	73·14	61·88	42·31	39·70	29·43
Mauritania	70·61	64·47	55·23	15·32	11·41	8·23
Mauritius	83·01	54·47	46·35	0·0	4·30	3·34
Morocco	84·31	76·43	68·48	58·95	54·78	50·74
Niger	76·43	66·97	56·50	38·87	32·60	25·38
Nigeria	75·86	71·89	63·73	61·18	41·61	34·02
Reunion	86·08	82·26	71·52	26·25	14·66	11·16
Rhodesia	82·71	77·11	64·50	83·83	67·21	59·00
Rwanda	86·45	70·33	42·13	31·52	22·38	20·56
Senegal	81·36	73·41	67·22	77·94	57·72	43·47
Sierra Leone	81·66	75·26	64·87	35·38	22·38	19·25
Somalia	87·29	75·99	64·80	27·41	32·35	25·65
Sudan	79·21	71·75	63·70	17·42	31·24	24·19
Tanzania	77·66	71·11	65·05	60·69	55·24	45·78
Togo	83·67	74·98	62·98	46·18	32·69	30·88
Tunisia	85·64	78·79	70·20	85·81	62·17	52·30
Uganda	69·82	70·38	62·44	39·75	29·79	26·02
Upper Volta	82·15	76·53	65·01	43·35	40·03	28·01
Zambia	77·55	76·35	65·59	2·96	1·51	3·90
Cook I./Niue	80·26	73·02	—	45·86	37·16	—
Fiji	85·16	78·49	62·52	51·32	34·90	19·68
New Guinea	79·60	77·89	47·56	47·09	32·43	31·94
Papua	79·50	77·98	51·73	22·29	29·81	16·02
Cuba	74·67	67·77	56·56	12·51	19·61	12·45
Czechoslovakia	86·39	80·70	69·99	68·89	66·85	61·78
Mean	79·81	73·28	62·81	51·81	44·19	37·51
S.D.	6·63	9·70	11·59	22·13	21·03	18·48
C.V.	0·08	0·13	0·18	0·42	0·48	0·49

TABLE A.7
IMPORTS AND EXPORTS BY COMMODITIES 1969 (ONE-DIGIT):
SCORES FROM CROSS-PRODUCT COMPONENT ANALYSES

Analysis and component	Commodity category								
	1	2	3	4	5	6	7	8	9
Imports									
1	0·91	0·13	0·37	0·56	0·06	0·69	1·63	2·07	0·52
2	0·00	0·05	−0·60	0·91	−0·02	−0·12	−0·21	−0·06	0·15
3	−0·15	0·13	0·27	−0·02	−0·07	−0·65	0·09	0·01	0·53
4	1·02	0·00	0·80	1·59	0·04	0·27	0·07	−1·26	0·36
Exports									
1	2·40	0·13	1·61	0·25	0·11	0·13	0·66	0·22	0·18
2	−1·81	−0·03	2·09	0·57	0·05	0·05	0·95	0·26	0·09
3	0·14	0·04	−1·12	2·57	−0·02	0·24	0·87	0·47	0·27
4	−0·06	0·08	−0·83	−1·44	−0·03	0·33	2·23	0·90	0·56
5	−0·10	0·08	0·19	−0·07	0·02	1·27	−1·34	2·18	0·89

TABLE A.8
IMPORTS AND EXPORTS BY COMMODITIES 1969 (ONE-DIGIT):
LOADINGS FROM CROSS-PRODUCT COMPONENT ANALYSES
(expressed as percentages of variance)

Country	Imports				Exports				
	1	2	3	4	1	2	3	4	5
U.S.					17	4	6	18	45
Canada	75	7		−9	31	21		15	15
Japan	12	−49	8	−18	8	7	11	55	14
U.K.	51	−27	6	7	7	7	11	42	26
Austria	84				18	18	10	52	
Belgium	39	−7	7	22	34	7	13	33	
Denmark	91		6		62	−5		10	18
France	80		12		28		10	37	19
W. Germany	46	−31	13	9	6	6	11	35	36
Italy	47	−34		10	13		15	36	27
Netherlands	77		12	6	52		16	18	12
Norway	83		9		27	10	9	49	
Sweden	79		10		19	25		29	14
Switzerland	68		11	6	7		8	35	44
Finland	97				28	37		33	
Greece	66	−24			62			13	
Iceland	94				71	−28			
Ireland	98				83	−10			
Malta	86				29	8		30	

Table continued overleaf

TABLE A.8 (*cont.*)
IMPORTS AND EXPORTS BY COMMODITIES 1969 (ONE-DIGIT):
LOADINGS FROM CROSS-PRODUCT COMPONENT ANALYSES
(expressed as percentages of variance)

Country	Imports				Exports				
	1	2	3	4	1	2	3	4	5
Portugal	22	−50		24	35	11	6	43	
Spain	45	−12		12	21	8	20	32	14
Turkey	65		−23		91				
Yugoslavia	75	−21			41		8	42	
Australia	88				92	7			
New Zealand	94				95				
S. Africa	83			−7	63	16		15	
Argentina	78	−18			81	−19			
Brazil	70	8	−19		94	−5			
Chile	85				13	7	5	47	−16
Colombia	75		−6	−6	76	−21			
Costa Rica	80		−7		69	−30			
Ecuador	52	5	−16	5					
El Salvador	41		−33	10	84	−11			
Guatemala	70		−14		95				
Honduras	89				85	−15			
Mexico	75				98				
Nicaragua	69		−16		95				
Peru	93				79	14			
Venezuela	87			−8		−22	70	−23	
Barbados	77	6		5	67	−22	8		
Guadeloupe	55	12	6	8	65	−34			
Guyana	88	8			90		5		
B. Honduras	75				72	28			
Jamaica	95				71	15	−6	−6	
Martinque	52	7		12	66	−32			
N. Antilles	7	65		12			74	−21	
Surinam	70	11	−13		41	51	−6		
Trinidad	14	70		6			75	−19	
Cyprus	94				95		71	−21	
Iran	83	−6		−8			71	−21	
Israel	79	−10			31		9	51	−5
Jordan	75				94				
Kuwait	73		10				73	−25	
Lebanon	74	−17		6	62		5	27	5
Yemen, P.D.R.	20	63		11	4	6	69	−21	
Syria	87		−6		85	10			
Egypt	44	−8	−42		81	17			
Afghanistan	63			5	90	5		5	
Brunei	85			−9			74	−21	
Burma	86			−9	96				
Khmer R.	81		−11		91	−6			
Sri Lanka	61		−12		90	−7			

Table continued

TABLE A.8 (*cont.*)
IMPORTS AND EXPORTS BY COMMODITIES 1969 (ONE-DIGIT): LOADINGS FROM CROSS-PRODUCT COMPONENT ANALYSES
(expressed as percentages of variance)

Country	Imports 1	2	3	4	Exports 1	2	3	4	5
China (Taiwan)	50	−41			43		8	36	
Hong Kong	62	−17	5	8	5			22	8
India	57	−15	−18		53	5		32	−7
Indonesia	79		−13		23	14	55		
S. Korea	50	−39			19	8		29	
Sabah	61	10		−7	33	48	−12	−6	
Sarawak	14	72		5	43	34	4	−18	
W. Malaysia	73	−18			42	54			
Pakistan	83		−9		36	33		32	−8
Philippines	91				67	21	−7		
Singapore	58	−7	21	6	55	34			
Thailand	93				98				
S. Vietnam	52		−40		36	51	10		
Cameroons	91				90	−9			
C. African R.	86	11			48	25		17	
Chad	55	39			42	38	−12	−8	
Congo	89			−6	54	41			
Zaire	77		−5		11	11	7	51	−18
Dahomey	74				65				
Ethiopia	87				85	−14			
Gabon	84			−10	29	51		−17	
Gambia	69				49	23	−10	−7	
Ghana	76		−16		91	−7			
Ivory Coast	92				95				
Kenya	86				85	−11			
Liberia	84		9		31	47	−13	−8	
Libya	81		11				73	−22	
Malagasy R.	93				79	−20			
Malawi	87				63				
Mali	98				87	−11			
Mauritania	76			−7	34	45	−13	−7	
Mauritius	47		−20	10	64	−36			
Morocco	77	−15			96				
Niger	82			−7	57	25	−11		
Nigeria	93				42	6	33	−18	
Reunion	60			11	64	−35			
Rhodesia	97				26	6		6	
Rwanda	72	−5	6		91		−5		
Senegal	71				63				
Sierra Leone	83		8		20	20		40	−16
Somalia	86				76	−23			
Sudan	87				38	41	−12	−8	
Tanzania	87	8			99				

Table continued overleaf

TABLE A.8 (*cont.*)
IMPORTS AND EXPORTS BY COMMODITIES 1969 (ONE-DIGIT):
LOADINGS FROM CROSS-PRODUCT COMPONENT ANALYSES
(expressed as percentages of variance)

Country	Imports				Exports				
	1	2	3	4	1	2	3	4	5
Togo	66				97				
Tunisia	73	−10			50	11	22	−5	
Uganda	87			−6	90	−9			
Upper Volta	84	−6			91		−5		
Zambia	79	14			5	11	9	−55	19
Cook I./Niue	68	17	8		70	−18			
Fiji	50	29	8		70	−25			
New Guinea	78	9			92	−5			
Papua	69	6	16		38	46	−11	−5	
Cuba	62		−25		64	−35			
Czechoslovakia	69	−9	11		8	6	9	26	37
% Variance	67	13	7	5	51	18	12	11	4

TABLE A.9
IMPORTS AND EXPORTS BY COMMODITIES 1969 (TWO-DIGIT): SCORES FROM CROSS-PRODUCT COMPONENT ANALYSES[a]

Imports Commodity	Component 1	2	3	4	5	6	7
1	10	3	9	7	-2	49	30
2	32	13	29	-14	58	211	-92
3	42	13	28	30	35	48	-100
4	22	4	11	11	6	62	-42
5	143	63	124	124	662	-15	-41
6	50	17	31	15	30	168	54
7	37	10	9	83	11	-24	5
8	35	13	6	41	-48	44	141
9	14	11	7	-10	1	72	28
10	9	2	8	2	-1	22	-51
11	26	-3	12	27	0	83	-121
12	31	-3	-8	59	15	31	-36
13	4	4	2	-8	-1	17	44
14	9	6	6	-15	8	31	90
15	12	6	8	-14	-6	4	78
16	26	13	20	-25	21	102	182
17	8	1	9	-22	8	14	68
18	41	4	47	-55	41	25	286
19	22	-1	16	-14	0	24	73
20	17	14	9	-40	16	105	277
21	12	4	1	15	9	13	38
22	12	2	10	-24	-2	14	103
23	250	637	-248	-81	-55	-45	-24
24	3	0	2	-5	0	12	8
25	2	-1	4	-6	-5	-2	-6
26	6	-1	2	-3	4	-18	14
27	12	5	8	20	32	-19	33

Commodity	Component 1	2	3	4	5	6	7
28	1	0	1	1	2	0	0
29	25	0	22	-2	-17	-20	15
30	12	2	10	-24	-2	14	103
31	23	-4	19	-1	-5	7	7
32	63	-7	39	63	-26	-22	-13
33	24	3	13	26	-9	61	-83
34	36	6	34	-4	120	-90	20
35	4	-3	2	2	-2	-2	-18
36	44	-6	31	-12	-15	-39	32
37	4	0	2	0	-7	18	26
38	40	-6	18	43	-38	-17	-56
39	11	0	1	4	-7	50	-8
40	64	-4	44	12	0	45	-6
41	229	10	125	605	-196	-136	107
42	70	-1	44	45	25	223	24
43	66	6	69	-66	19	48	353
44	104	-18	64	37	-41	73	-216
45	420	-100	369	-331	-93	-244	-67
46	166	-21	107	-45	-86	398	-46
47	373	-343	-524	75	59	-17	20
48	12	-2	8	8	-5	25	-40
49	11	-2	6	6	0	73	-51
50	1	0	0	1	1	7	-6
51	50	6	10	39	-43	217	-109
52	17	5	5	30	-18	42	-39
53	49	-5	30	-28	40	86	36
54	80	-6	33	18	-70	200	-41

Table continued overleaf

TABLE A.9 (cont.)

IMPORTS AND EXPORTS BY COMMODITIES 1969 (TWO-DIGIT): SCORES FROM CROSS-PRODUCT COMPONENT ANALYSES[a]

Exports

Commodity	1	2	3	4	5	6	7	8
1	14	23	11	23	110	-7	68	-8
2	21	31	1	20	65	5	75	-13
3	4	4	2	7	16	2	14	-3
4	20	21	42	19	24	20	29	5
5	33	42	26	82	133	16	93	402
6	123	198	154	33	480	-205	-384	-70
7	117	152	584	-340	-129	154	73	11
8	305	504	-332	-156	-206	-2	-43	-33
9	15	18	1	16	24	16	32	13
10	2	2	2	-1	2	0	-1	-1
11	8	10	20	5	32	-14	-26	-6
12	19	31	12	10	44	-4	-6	-4
13	16	19	-3	7	38	-6	13	-13
14	47	61	-25	17	91	19	156	93
15	44	34	-1	107	-1	79	-1	333
16	76	55	-1	35	1	2	-4	421
17	3	2	3	10	4	7	-2	6
18	85	124	-22	78	292	70	519	-202
19	26	36	6	25	51	-28	-52	-16
20	102	114	234	462	-297	-377	97	-62
21	14	18	2	13	19	-6	25	4
22	1	1	2	3	3	1	2	0
23	613	-411	-22	-20	4	0	-13	-30
24	2	2	2	3	15	-3	-1	-6
25	0	0	1	1	1	1	0	0
26	1	1	1	2	2	2	2	0
27	25	23	1	9	29	21	46	27

Commodity	1	2	3	4	5	6	7	8
28	1	2	1	0	3	0	-2	-1
29	6	0	1	4	7	2	2	-2
30	1	1	2	3	3	1	2	0
31	2	2	0	3	3	1	1	1
32	4	4	2	3	6	2	3	0
33	5	7	14	-8	-2	5	5	1
34	8	2	2	6	10	0	-6	0
35	0	0	0	0	0	0	0	0
36	3	4	1	4	7	2	3	0
37	3	4	1	4	9	0	6	-2
38	11	-2	0	5	6	1	6	2
39	11	8	2	7	6	-2	0	33
40	6	6	4	15	9	12	-2	13
41	34	34	12	35	98	6	75	-22
42	32	45	2	51	55	-2	47	21
43	60	85	53	383	-51	563	-192	-113
44	7	7	4	10	15	3	0	4
45	20	15	15	42	49	18	1	38
46	15	7	18	18	30	12	1	12
47	18	13	17	46	42	25	-1	29
48	0	0	0	1	1	0	0	0
49	0	2	0	2	3	1	0	0
50	0	0	0	0	1	-1	0	0
51	16	16	21	22	47	-8	1	-1
52	4	5	2	5	11	0	1	0
53	3	2	2	6	9	2	1	3
54	12	15	17	14	47	-4	-12	0

[a] To two decimal places: decimal points omitted.

TABLE A.10

IMPORTS AND EXPORTS BY COMMODITIES 1969 (TWO-DIGIT): LOADINGS FROM CROSS-PRODUCT
COMPONENT ANALYSES
(expressed as percentages of variance)

Country	Imports							Exports							
	1	2	3	4	5	6	7	1	2	3	4	5	6	7	8
U.S.	76		−8			7					5				
Canada	79	−10	−5					5			16				
Japan	28	23					25								
U.K.	63	11				6	7								
Austria	86														
Belgium	80						9	7			14	5	11		
Denmark	92										5	7			
France	84			−5											
W. Germany	68	6				6	10								
Italy	68	16					7	7				10			
Netherlands	88					5		21				10			
Norway	86		−5								21				
Sweden	88					8					7				
Switzerland	87														
Finland	88														
Greece	72		13	−6		6		5	8		7	31		−7	
Iceland	74	6	5												
Ireland	93			5		8						9			
Malta	80											10			
Portugal	84														
Spain	71	7	5	−11				14				35		−12	
Turkey	82	12	−5	−8				6	12	−5	0	52			
Yugoslavia	82										18	5	11		

Table continued overleaf

TABLE A.10 (cont.)

IMPORTS AND EXPORTS BY COMMODITIES 1969 (TWO-DIGIT): LOADINGS FROM CROSS-PRODUCT COMPONENT ANALYSES

Country	Imports							Exports							
	1	2	3	4	5	6	7	1	2	3	4	5	6	7	8
Australia	92				−5			5	7	5	18	8		32	8
New Zealand	91				−5							9		17	
S. Africa	91										17	13			
Argentina	70		8	−13				14	6	7		12			
Brazil	78			−10				25	59					5	9
Chile	85			−8						−7	36		47	−6	
Colombia	74	−10		−11				32	42	−15					
Costa Rica	77							21	52						
Ecuador	25	−22	−51					13	32			18	−5	−11	
El Salvador	69							23	50	−13				−23	
Guatemala	75							23	57	−5					
Honduras	82							12	18						
Mexico	72	−8		−14				21	26	9		28	−9	−24	
Nicaragua	81		6					11	24			21		39	
Peru	90	−8						12	10	12		7	17	5	
Venezuela	70			−8				71	−29		28				−7
Barbados	76					16		15	47	54	−16				
Guadeloupe	72					12		20	7	10	−17				
Guyana	76		5					5	9	51	8	−15	−9		
B. Honduras	77		5				5	5	7	66	−15				
Jamaica	93							7	9	27	23				
Martinique	73					12			9	11		−11	−23	−25	
N. Antilles	16	72	−10					69	30			37	−6		
Surinam	81									12	54	−15	−9		
Trinidad	26	66	−7					72	−27	9			−17		
Cyprus	94								10	9	6	27		21	

Country	1	2	3	4	5	6	7	8	9	10	11	12
Iran	71	−6			7	71		−29	17	31		
Israel	61	−7			6	71	7			−5	−18	
Jordan	81		9			71		−28		40		
Kuwait	78				8	71	9	−28			−8	
Lebanon	82		−9									
Yemen, P.D.R.	45	38				71		−28				30
Syria	89								29		39	
Egypt	71			22						42		
Afghanistan	34		37	22		69	7	−30				
Brunei	80		−6	−7								
Burma	83								11			58
Khmer R.	88			7								45
Sri Lanka	82	8	26			19	47	−16		21		
China (Taiwan)	77		−5		8	5	6	7				
Hong Kong	43		9	21		10	19					
India	35	10		10								
Indonesia	78					75	−12					
S. Korea	76											
Sabah	80	−8				48			17			40
Sarawak	27	64										23
W. Malaysia	85								14		26	15
Pakistan	75		5									
Philippines	91	17	−12			6	7	18	13			14
Singapore	60					34				11		15
Thailand	91								12			33
S. Vietnam	75			12					5			19
Cameroons	92					21	52	−18		−5		
C. African R.	93					5	11			17		
Chad	71	13							17	16	53	−7
Congo	87	−7										32
Zaire	84					5			29	54	−6	
Dahomey	60		34								15	

Table continued overleaf

TABLE A.10 (cont.)

IMPORTS AND EXPORTS BY COMMODITIES 1969 (TWO-DIGIT): LOADINGS FROM CROSS-PRODUCT COMPONENT ANALYSES

(expressed as percentages of variance)

Country	Imports							Exports							
	1	2	3	4	5	6	7	1	2	3	4	5	6	7	8
Ethiopia	92							20	52	-16					8
Gabon	80	-9						47	-5		9		-6		8
Gambia	36			57										5	5
Ghana	81		5					21	49	-15		-8			
Ivory Coast	93		-12					21	44	-14					
Kenya	80		5					43	31	-16					
Liberia	84									9	41	-15			
Libya	96							69	-30				-23		
Malagasy R.	90							29	49	-9					
Mali	77							10	24	-5					
Malawi	78	8	-10	6										7	
Mauritania	84									11	40	7	-26		
Mauritius	32				50				6	60	-22	28			
Morocco	70		7	11	-6			5	10	6		5	-9	-16	
Niger	95													7	
Nigeria	70					9		83							
Reunion	70									62					
Rhodesia	89	-5									-20				
Rwanda	66			21				17	39		5		-11		
Senegal	60				23							-22			
Sierra Leone	81			14											
Somalia	75				13							18			
Sudan	78			16								18		55	
Tanzania	95							29	25			13		14	-5

Togo	73			18				16	40	−14					
Tunisia	76	−10						55	−7	−17					
Uganda	84		10		7			21	52						
Upper Volta	87			6							27	21	57	25	
Zambia	83		17								−19	31		−7	−15
Cook I./Niue	60						6	5	10						
Fiji	75	6				7		10	46	18	−19				
New Guinea	83							18	60	−17					
Papua	82					7									16
Cuba	67	5			13			6	68		−13				
Czechoslovakia	70	9		−13											5
% Variance	65	12	8	5	3	2	1	19	15	10	7	7	6	6	5

TABLE A.11
INDICES OF TRADING PARTNER SPECIALISATION BY COUNTRY

Country	Imports 1960	Imports 1969	Exports 1960	Exports 1969
U.S.	61·24	55·90	64·99	62·31
U.K.	67·35	66·81	70·58	69·43
Austria	37·27	36·50	55·00	55·70
Belgium	51·47	47·78	54·78	45·62
Denmark	47·45	49·63	50·28	53·97
France	61·46	54·33	63·44	61·54
W. Germany	60·19	56·38	65·35	60·31
Italy	57·53	56·42	64·05	59·40
Netherlands	53·72	52·72	56·43	49·03
Norway	47·68	50·78	55·00	53·01
Sweden	50·30	52·36	57·56	58·26
Switzerland	43·12	44·85	62·47	61·73
Canada	25·46	24·43	32·66	27·60
Japan	49·75	56·50	62·88	59·22
Finland	45·86	48·81	53·57	53·09
Greece	51·96	52·95	55·47	56·23
Iceland	46·90	48·77	53·17	49·31
Ireland	38·22	33·50	16·53	24·74
Malta	42·47	40·12	34·35	45·34
Portugal	54·24	54·82	59·38	53·45
Spain	54·50	57·04	57·65	60·82
Turkey	42·78	45·50	54·78	57·15
Yugoslavia	49·13	50·76	60·21	58·54
Australia	46·67	49·31	52·69	54·08
New Zealand	39·89	43·15	34·35	38·82
S. Africa	46·12	47·69	46·04	40·39

Country	Imports 1960	Imports 1969	Exports 1960	Exports 1969
Argentina	48·95	52·36	52·22	56·51
Bolivia	42·32	42·41	26·35	33·67
Brazil	47·70	50·40	46·29	54·94
Chile	42·90	46·34	39·30	46·57
Colombia	35·88	40·25	27·98	46·90
Costa Rica	41·17	46·38	32·23	43·49
Dominican R.	37·82	36·18	36·75	13·09
Ecuador	39·74	42·59	33·80	44·77
El Salvador	43·70	45·70	34·95	43·79
Guatemala	37·54	44·14	30·21	47·68
Haiti	29·14	37·57	30·67	29·89
Honduras	34·25	41·33	35·25	41·22
Mexico	24·40	30·94	28·97	32·19
Nicaragua	37·98	44·11	40·13	44·62
Panama	44·46	47·99	10·08	25·28
Paraguay	44·84	43·48	33·53	37·16
Peru	41·62	51·20	45·08	44·33
Uruguay	49·49	52·87	53·95	57·19
Venezuela	35·08	39·28	37·05	44·60
Bahamas	24·55	28·41	12·93	24·19
Barbados	33·82	39·99	34·56	32·09
Bermuda	26·91	25·82	45·05	9·21
Falkland I.	30·25	9·48	15·56	4·99
Greenland	18·10	12·66	27·01	15·20
Guadeloupe	10·26	15·71	6·20	16·24
Fr. Guiana	22·61	20·16	31·66	16·45

Guyana	36·38	40·33	58·32	41·19
B. Honduras	31·83	36·59	31·61	35·46
Jamaica	34·94	37·60	30·46	33·75
Leeward I.	30·17	35·11	16·49	29·09
Martinique	7·60	17·12	1·98	11·44
N. Antilles	17·37	26·63	55·59	41·90
Panama Canal	32·87	35·08	26·11	41·53
St. Pierre	23·46	20·58	31·86	20·06
Surinam	36·43	36·20	20·01	37·53
Trinidad	39·65	43·32	36·37	33·96
Virgin I.	—	24·54	—	12·90
Windward I.	25·30	27·39	8·16	5·61
Bahrein	41·39	37·37	48·04	54·38
Cyprus	48·18	49·04	47·32	46·11
Iran	44·61	45·87	56·23	54·21
Iraq	50·26	59·74	48·23	51·19
Israel	44·26	43·54	56·37	57·45
Jordan	51·31	49·40	41·97	44·30
Kuwait	46·64	51·75	42·13	49·31
Lebanon	56·06	56·29	54·49	55·57
Oman	33·28	37·55	36·78	39·94
Qatar	24·05	39·15	29·18	39·62
S. Arabia	52·94	53·44	55·61	54·75
Yemen, P.D.R.	52·90	54·51	50·00	56·63
Syria	53·49	55·89	57·39	56·17
Trucial S.	15·65	33·48	15·76	30·81
Egypt	50·46	56·20	60·20	59·47
Yemen, A.R.	12·02	49·90	31·53	35·57
Afghanistan	39·52	44·16	34·35	39·48
Bhutan	—	—	—	—
Brunei	29·89	32·84	4·12	5·98

Burma	46·12	48·73	51·01	58·55
Khmer R.	44·61	44·08	42·39	49·87
Sri Lanka	50·57	55·38	47·82	52·27
Taiwan	27·36	34·44	43·71	42·71
Hong Kong	52·42	50·46	58·42	50·91
India	48·36	50·48	56·28	58·43
Indonesia	49·96	45·26	48·89	39·31
Korea	27·71	32·85	28·88	32·32
Laos	32·69	35·86	28·37	33·52
Macao	12·97	9·97	29·42	47·40
Malaysia	—	49·03	—	51·45
Maldive I.	—	29·86	—	—
Nepal	—	17·44	—	26·03
Pakistan	46·84	46·02	61·91	65·80
Philippines	36·46	40·54	29·72	30·91
Ryukyus	11·76	14·82	7·94	9·05
Singapore	44·99	52·44	45·44	57·26
Thailand	43·95	44·75	51·82	50·91
Timor	—	37·01	—	39·38
Vietnam	38·25	38·16	45·34	35·69
Afars-Issas	49·84	44·37	35·96	20·18
Algeria	16·41	35·23	17·40	34·57
Angola	39·66	42·69	45·05	43·06
Botswana	—	20·69	—	26·82
Burundi	—	48·83	—	22·07
Cameroons	35·48	36·14	30·26	42·60
Cape Verde I.	37·83	35·01	15·24	27·06
C. African R.	23·93	31·90	24·38	38·37
Chad	20·07	35·86	22·38	28·15
Comoro	—	17·86	—	21·37
Congo	16·13	37·72	41·06	52·74

Table continued overleaf

TABLE A.11 (cont.)
INDICES OF TRADING PARTNER SPECIALISATION BY COUNTRY

	Imports 1960	Imports 1969	Exports 1960	Exports 1969		Imports 1960	Imports 1969	Exports 1960	Exports 1969
Zaire	45·92	49·46	37·62	32·79	Sudan	50·45	53·76	56·38	55·93
Dahomey	12·77	42·58	27·58	41·67	Swaziland	–	34·83	–	19·32
Eq. Guinea	30·17	38·58	16·28	24·37	Tanzania	–	51·40	–	56·05
Ethiopia	48·84	49·38	48·59	43·47	Togo	37·57	44·80	29·05	40·02
Gabon	17·13	33·53	30·12	41·08	Tunisia	29·67	39·35	40·97	51·55
Gambia	36·47	39·14	29·61	36·60	Uganda	28·35	42·97	51·92	53·58
Ghana	42·22	46·84	42·26	46·79	U. Volta	16·77	29·60	20·34	38·46
Port Guinea	14·76	33·07	16·27	21·94	Zambia	–	51·03	–	43·45
Guinea R.	40·04	43·04	44·53	41·19	B. Solomon I.	–	–	–	–
Ivory C.	22·04	39·99	32·91	41·72	Faroe I.	7·66	10·67	23·76	13·15
Kenya	40·51	50·58	51·63	55·83	Fiji	40·05	38·22	33·47	38·05
Lesotho	–	28·50	–	–	Gibraltar	45·50	41·23	28·04	32·12
Liberia	40·18	47·05	29·43	41·09	Gilbert E.I.	–	1·65	–	–
Libya	43·22	45·69	42·37	41·52	Guam	10·73	26·82	–	–
Malagasy R.	28·62	35·52	33·85	38·30	Nauru	17·43	13·82	20·05	20·65
Malawi	–	43·01	–	31·91	New Caledonia	17·71	27·90	15·07	20·04
Mali	28·46	30·27	37·64	48·23	New Guinea	26·71	21·42	24·67	33·46
Mauritania	20·16	36·16	31·69	39·43	New Hebrides	–	2·22	11·46	22·25
Mauritius	40·04	53·40	14·57	18·28	Norfolk I.	–	–	–	–
Morocco	42·68	45·19	46·46	50·65	Papua	15·57	10·97	11·72	17·57
Mozambique	50·66	50·52	43·14	41·14	St. Helena	–	1·60	–	–
Niger	25·23	31·04	17·91	28·11	A. Samoa	–	10·43	–	–
Nigeria	40·11	47·40	31·60	46·14	W. Samoa	29·82	34·06	28·41	38·50
Reunion	22·66	25·14	12·20	13·70	Tonga	–	28·89	–	–
Rhodesia	–	44·22	–	31·91					

	Col1	Col2	Col3	Col4
Rwanda	—	46·77	—	29·33
S. Tome	23·28	17·98	12·66	3·12
Seychelles	—	25·39	—	13·15
Senegal	18·72	44·82	18·79	33·16
Sierra Leone	31·94	46·79	16·83	22·11
Somalia	37·71	49·54	19·53	24·21
S.W. Africa	—	—	—	4·95
Mean	36·74	37·19	40·81	40·21
SD	15·83	15·83	11·62	14·74
CV	43·09	42·57	27·23	36·66

TABLE A.12

REGRESSION ANALYSES OF TRADE FLOWS: PARAMETERS OF THE INDIFFERENCE MODEL[a]

Country	Imports 1960			Imports 1969			Exports 1960			Exports 1969		
	b_d	r	b_s	b_d	r	b_s	b_d	r	b_s	b_d	r	b_s
U.S.	−78	−37	−39	−93	−41	−49	−48	−25	−27	−58	−35	−31
U.K.	−10	−06	−4	−16	−08	−7	2	01	1	−6	−05	−2
Austria	−88	−57	−53	−120	−47	−74	−81	−66	−58	−90	−62	−65
Belgium	−30	−25	−25	−52	−30	−39	−34	−31	−28	−41	−44	−33
Denmark	−64	−36	−41	−84	−39	−52	−60	−46	−41	−47	−41	−38
France	−39	−20	−23	−53	−24	−35	−23	−14	−14	−32	−21	−21
W. Germany	−40	−23	−27	−51	−30	−36	−38	−33	−26	−39	−47	−27
Italy	−68	−46	−39	−78	−42	−46	−48	−47	−24	−56	−57	−31
Netherlands	−16	−15	−15	−35	−31	−28	−30	−38	−24	−33	−39	−26
Norway	−65	−37	−42	−89	−40	−54	−50	−40	−35	−62	−34	−44
Sweden	−62	−40	−37	−106	−45	−64	−67	−53	−46	−79	−52	−55
Switzerland	−87	−60	−53	−110	−48	−67	−27	−27	−20	−41	−39	−26
Canada	−96	−36	−48	−90	−26	−51	−108	−49	−54	−112	−53	−59
Japan	−157	−48	−65	−116	−32	−50	−108	−38	−48	−107	−47	−49
Finland	−107	−59	−58	−90	−38	−56	−84	−55	−48	−101	−56	−63
Greece	−84	−57	−39	−98	−43	−53	−109	−48	−54	−161	−71	−76
Iceland	−132	−46	−66	−139	−43	−57	—	—	—	−228	−60	−108
Ireland	−36	−27	−28	−66	−28	−44	−32	−22	−30	−55	−29	−41
Malta	−90	−59	−54	−63	−23	−44	−73	−45	−49	−92	−41	−61
Portugal	−79	−33	−34	−68	−23	−35	−51	−24	−22	−66	−24	−38
Spain	−60	−39	−31	−44	−25	−33	−63	−48	−32	−73	−41	−44
Turkey	−79	−48	−31	−117	−54	−54	−129	−70	−52	−169	−68	−91
Yugoslavia	−65	−41	−41	−61	−34	−38	−72	−42	−46	−118	−58	−73
Australia	−144	−43	−40	−209	−44	−53	−240	−66	−83	−263	−75	−103
New Zealand	−184	−60	−56	−225	−42	−72	−138	−42	−38	−186	−79	−49

S. Africa	−61	−19	−26	−52	−01	−37	−85	−24	−8	49	8	10
Argentina	−68	−35	−29	−112	−32	−57	−97	−43	−50	−139	−47	−77
Bolivia	−111	−59	−42	−51	−24	−29	−42	−27	−8	−77	−24	−38
Brazil	−97	−30	−27	−62	−14	−41	−74	−24	−31	−99	−30	−51
Chile	−100	−44	−40	−114	−34	−45	−109	47	−41	−130	−52	−52
Colombia	−46	−34	−21	−38	−17	−24	−74	−42	−38	−121	−53	−61
Costa Rica	−81	−71	−50	−146	−71	−91	−92	−71	−51	−92	−39	−70
Dominican R.	−10	−08	−04	−102	−52	−55	−16	−12	−16	−109	−47	−64
Ecuador	−88	−58	−28	−60	−33	−38	−107	−64	−43	−26	−11	−24
El Salvador	−106	−80	−64	−139	−79	−93	−106	−70	−66	−140	−56	−98
Guatemala	−100	−80	−63	−144	−71	−96	−84	−65	−57	−97	−45	−75
Haiti	−63	−47	−11	−65	−24	−35	−12	−60	−5	−129	−57	−76
Honduras	−91	−72	−56	−144	−74	−93	−105	−69	−63	−149	−63	−91
Mexico	−68	−30	−21	−89	−31	−34	−105	−53	−48	−164	−57	−77
Nicaragua	−82	−76	−42	−134	−74	−82	−69	−61	−38	−94	−46	−69
Panama	−76	−55	−61	−71	−39	−60	−113	−77	−49	−129	−57	−94
Paraguay	−88	−53	−36	−91	−42	−52	−154	−88	−43	−181	−91	−53
Peru	−60	−34	−19	−39	−14	−27	−113	−57	−54	−63	−20	−42
Uruguay	−82	−52	−39	−103	−47	−54	−6	−04	−2	−80	−25	−43
Venezuela	−20	−11	−8	−60	−26	−32	−128	−59	−70	−165	−62	−95
Bahamas	−128	−70	−33	−125	−47	−54	−57	−40	−14	−147	−56	−64
Barbados	−30	−22	−3	−103	−60	−38	−33	−19	−2	−172	−63	−93
Bermuda	−92	−56	−24	−159	−49	−57	6	3	3	−8	−3	−2
Greenland	476	56	61	87	21	15	−421	−62	−63	−104	−38	−31
Guadeloupe	18	12	7	−87	−53	−51				−72	−29	−55
Fr. Guiana	−150	−33	−66	−117	−46	−35	−140	−88	−50	−354	−80	−62
Guyana	−83	−54	−42	−71	−35	−40	−141	−66	−57	−157	−54	−89
B. Honduras	−70	−58	−29	−50	−29	−34	−104	−73	−31	−113	−53	−53
Jamaica	−55	−38	−18	−89	−47	−50	−136	−58	−45	−208	−65	−85
Leeward I.	−143	−79	−62	−147	−66	−76				−96	−59	−18
Martinique				−118	−59	−59				−100	−49	−62

Table continued overleaf

TABLE A.12 (cont.)

REGRESSION ANALYSES OF TRADE FLOWS: PARAMETERS OF THE INDIFFERENCE MODEL[a]

Country	Imports						Exports					
	1960			1969			1960			1969		
	b_d	r	b_s	b_d	r	b_s	b_d	r	b_s	b_d	r	b_s
N. Antilles	−74	−44	−35	−88	−46	−54	−59	−34	−30	−94	−38	−64
Panama, C.Z.	−137	−73	−54	−115	−61	−76	−109	−81	−61	−106	−74	−56
Surinam	−87	−49	−45	−75	−37	−43	−105	−65	−46	−58	−24	−33
Virgin I.	−60	−44	−24	−134	−70	−54						
Windward I.	−194	−47	−25	−181	−28	−16	−594	−45	−35	9	5	11
Bahrein	−81	−32	−30	−90	−32	−56	−5	−05	−1			
Cyprus	−72	−46	−46	−75	−35	−29	−39	−37	−17	−121	−56	−49
Iran	−89	−40	−33	−143	−45	−47	−42	−15	−21	−63	−24	−32
Iraq	−58	−41	−43	−81	−41	−59	−15	−09	−14	−95	−41	−64
Israel	−85	−43	−33	−118	−40	−54	−100	−55	−54	−95	−42	−55
Jordan	−90	−67	−59	−99	−50	−53	−128	−79	−55	−188	−55	−104
Kuwait	−92	−43	−23	−79	−36	−32	59	21	11	56	19	9
Lebanon	−90	−66	−62	−126	−62	−88	−144	−71	−81	−201	−76	−131
Oman	−192	−71	−35	−123	−46	−33	−106	−52	−16	129	44	30
Qatar	−140	−43	−39	−162	−52	−37	70	24	17	43	21	24
S. Arabia	−157	−60	−57	−138	−47	−74	8	4	13	16	08	10
Yemen P.D.R.	−235	−55	−44	−221	−45	−48	−117	−26	−28	−96	−18	−50
Syria	−85	−65	−62	−122	−67	−86	−104	−69	−59	−140	−61	−84
Trucial States				−51	−31	−53				25	10	9
Egypt	−86	−44	−26	−96	−48	−45	−115	−49	−43	−127	−44	−59
Yemen, A.R.	−165	−38	−27	−66	−26	−43	−87	−37	−21	−74	−25	−29
Afghanistan	−201	−65	−49	−211	−77	−63	−88	−66	−16	−249	−63	−78
Brunei	−153	−79	−50	−146	−70	−58	−228	−89	−91	−188	−62	−92
Burma	−104	−54	−25	−119	−44	−23	−180	−62	−32	−161	−40	−49
Khmer R.	−125	−74	−58	−60	−36	−23	−83	−51	−36	−80	−35	−50

	1	2	3	4	5	6	7	8	9	10	11	12
Sri Lanka	−163	−61	−45	−239	−65	−106	−89	−33	−19	−91	−32	−47
Taiwan	−115	−59	−46	−121	−48	−53	−159	−65	−62	−107	−45	−57
Hong Kong	−121	−66	−78	−150	−54	−98	−111	−51	−78	−96	−45	−73
India	−148	−50	−63	−150	−38	−82	−119	−44	−63	−182	−56	−100
Indonesia	−134	−51	−60	−129	−36	−43	−182	−68	−85	−140	−146	−57
Korea	−138	−60	−50	−201	−54	−66	−156	−85	−43	−119	−51	−36
Laos	−183	−85	−72	−122	−54	−68	−120	−92	−28	−148	−78	−59
Macao	−105	−75	−61	−104	−81	−60	−39	−30	−23	−50	−17	−40
Malaysia				−194	−63	−108				−115	−69	−59
Nepal				−204	−70	−76				−155	−57	−72
Pakistan	−140	−62	−57	−205	−62	−69	−107	−49	−54	−104	−37	−47
Philippines	−107	−58	−38	−57	−53	−22	−64	−30	−26	−104	−53	−40
Ryukyus	−168	−75	−47	−87	−63	−32				−81	−45	−14
Singapore	−172	−81	−70	−173	−65	−97	−134	−65	−71	−153	−71	−89
Thailand	−84	−46	−42	−103	−39	−57	−110	−49	−50	−161	−65	−76
Timor	−99	−58	−50	−133	−41	−23				−76	−40	−20
Vietnam	−206	−56	−64	−148	−68	−83	−88	−53	−48	−18	−10	−10
Afars Issas	−62	−27	−35	−115	−42	−37	−212	−84	−56	−162	−74	−59
Algeria	−127	−22	−35	−36	−46	−61	−11	−05	−15	−73	−29	−27
Angola				−97	−11	−14	−290	−69	−82	−148	−37	−52
Botswana				−168	−61	−26				−198	−80	−49
Burundi	−157	−72	−81	−114	−80	−81				−137	−78	−70
Cameroons	−127	−29	−35		−47	−65	−134	−70	−70	−156	−56	−103
Cape Verde I.	−206	−42	−70	110	33	15				101	66	14
C. African R.	−107	−32	−16	−219	−65	−82	−211	−63	−40	−160	−46	−77
Chad				−200	−69	−94	−333	−78	−63	−313	−67	−107
Comoro				−469	−70	−43				−436	−78	−45
Congo	−354	−60	−80	−178	−44	−61	−198	−57	−29	−116	−41	−30
Zaire	−171	−42	−25	−87	−22	−6	−173	−43	−27	−79	−19	−30
Dahomey	−203	−78	−53	−43	−21	−23	−115	−57	−41	−107	−60	−60
Eq. Guinea	−106	−84	−44	−131	−80	−67				−76	−70	−23
Ethiopia	−150	−67	−66	−125	−41	−56	−147	−60	−65	−198	−55	−100

Table continued overleaf

TABLE A.12 (cont.)

REGRESSION ANALYSES OF TRADE FLOWS: PARAMETERS OF THE INDIFFERENCE MODEL[a]

Country	Imports						Exports					
	1960			1969			1960			1969		
	b_d	r	b_s	b_d	r	b_s	b_d	r	b_s	b_d	r	b_s
Gabon	−308	−64	−75	−160	−64	−83	−122	−57	−51	−92	−38	−47
Gambia	−84	−61	−41	−69	−34	−43	−114	−61	−28	−170	−56	−83
Ghana	−93	−50	−52	−63	−31	−36	−76	−54	−39	−6	−02	−16
Port. Guinea	−371	−38	−27	82	17	50	−76	−09	−16	−71	−46	−33
Guinea	−73	−41	−28	−78	−42	−36	−70	−24	−20	−25	−12	−7
Ivory C.	−157	−55	−43	−92	−33	−46	−83	−35	−11	−195	−65	−63
Kenya	−89	−46	−16	−178	−56	−93	−132	−52	−61	−231	−76	−113
Liberia	75	24	25	66	11	16	−32	−05	−24	20	5	25
Libya	−95	−51	−63	−122	−51	−74	−92	−57	−47	−78	−25	−33
Malagasy R.	−83	−36	−28	−145	−38	−56	−140	−47	−57	−214	−50	−76
Malawi				−123	−52	−80				−171	−70	−74
Mali	−175	−58	−43	−104	−23	−27	−306	−70	−49	−109	−22	−31
Mauritania	86	16	03	−71	−23	−18	−114	−27	−41	−69	−23	−05
Mauritius	−192	−68	−39	−169	−39	−58	−81	−48	−35	−164	−45	−77
Morocco	−72	−32	−36	−132	−48	−64	−100	−44	−44	−149	−51	−88
Mozambique	−100	−29	−39	11	04	6	−238	−52	−39	−204	−52	−115

Niger	−196	−60	−49	−164	−62	−82	−216	−80	−56	−287	−82	−99
Nigeria	−65	−41	−38	−070	−34	−52	−73	−46	−22	−91	−34	−59
Reunion	−113	−45	−36	−156	−53	−60	−116	−38	−30	−176	−51	−48
Rhodesia				−110	−53	−46				−264	−80	−101
Rwanda				−161	−61	−86				−203	−90	−92
S. Tome				−179	−66	−32						
Senegal	−293	−66	−47	−87	−30	−55	−112	−49	−53	−154	−56	−74
Sierra Leone	−161	−51	−39	−28	−13	−13	−108	−62	−43	−141	−59	−69
Somalia	−81	−36	−31	−86	−25	−27	−232	−74	−47	−167	−50	−60
Swaziland	−179	−61	−58	−120	−71	−55				−43	−34	−13
Sudan	−175	−63	−69	−68	−23	−40	−173	−67	−67	−122	−37	−49
Tanzania				−97	−30	−68				−135	−49	−67
Togo	−117	−61	−36	−67	−37	−34	−82	−46	−37	−104	−41	−51
Tunisia	−79	−53	−43	−64	−32	−31	−64	−33	−38	−89	−42	−39
Uganda	−178	−67	−38	−155	−58	−89	−102	−38	−41	−110	−38	−71
U. Volta	−316	−72	−47	−183	−61	−86	−132	−68	−54	−185	−61	−81
Zambia				−190	−59	−108				−164	−45	−80
Fiji	−64	−30	−14	−119	−37	−37	−209	−82	−74	−366	−82	−181
Gibraltar	−4	−03	−01	−65	−35	−38	−92	−54	−19	138	51	35
N. Caledonia				−134	−56					−119	−31	−14
N. Hebrides	−322	−93	−58	−211	−84	−77	−21	−11	−5	−147	−67	−49
W. Samoa				−231	−60	−67	−101	−53	−30	−186	−94	−92

aDecimal points omitted, to two decimal places.

TABLE A.13
REGRESSION ANALYSES OF TRADE FLOWS: PARAMETERS OF THE TOTAL INTERACTION MODEL[a]

		Imports					Exports		
							1960		
	R	b_d	b_s	b_1	Other	R	b_d	b_s	b
U.S.	91	−80	−36	104	7,8,−9,−10	93	−57	−28	96
U.K.	91	−37	(−14)	107	4,−5,−8	94	−35	−13	102
Austria	92	−100	−50	101		92	−87	−81	63
Belgium	90	(−28)	−22	85		94	−36	−27	71
Denmark	88	−47	−25	68	9,10	90	82	−70	82
France	89	−58	−26	105	−4,5,−8,−10	90	−54	−27	94
W. Germany	93	−36	(−14)	98	−4,8,10	94	−42	−19	88
Italy	92	−82	−54	82	3	94	−68	−46	87
Netherlands	93	(−21)	(−43)	106	7	95	−36	−23	89
Norway	88	−49	−29	89	10	90	−47	−32	79
Sweden	92	−42	−23	119	−3,7,9,10	94	−62	−41	95
Switzerland	93	−76	−35	78	3,−4,10	95	−21	−12	92
Canada	89	−122	−51	123	−3,4	92	−118	−48	107
Japan	84	−145	−53	78	3,8	88	−121	−48	68
Finland	92	−101	−26	115	−4,10	90	−75	−25	94
Greece	91	−82	−30	106	−4	85	−105	−62	114
Iceland						79	(17)	(13)	(−42)
Ireland	86	−86	−40	86	4	86	−122	−60	91
Malta	90	−63	−65	108	4				
Portugal	88	−87	−33	100	6,9	86	−77	−53	63
Spain	89	−74	−30	108	8	92	−80	−44	73
Turkey	87	(−6)	(8)	59	9	84	−122	−77	88
Yugoslavia	83	(−39)	−28	(29)	3,10	79	−71	−65	(30)
Australia	87	−91	−43	132	4,−7	88	−223	−79	104
New Zealand	88	−104	−37	136	4,−7	84	(−81)	−47	127
S. Africa	85	−167	−122	122		83	−82	−3	103
Argentina	91	−72	−11	144	7	88	−96	−31	85
Brazil	84	(−79)	(−18)	173	−3,−4	87	−118	−42	119
Chile	95	−155	−44	124	3,−4,10	87	−254	−59	121
Colombia	95	−101	−74	99	3,−4,−6,−7,−8	93	−150	−100	220
Costa Rica	96	−85	−77	143	−4,−5,8				

					1969					
			Imports					*Exports*		
Other	R	b_d	b_s	b_1	*Other*	R	b_d	b_s	b_1	*Other*
,−4,−5,−10,·	87	−101	−47	112		96	−65	−27	116	−5,7,8,−9,−10.
,−5,−9	90	−51	−19	099	4,−8	95	−40	−17	89	4,−5,10
,	87	−134	−67	084	10	95	−102	−94	93	3,−5,6,7,8
,−5,9,10	89	−46	−29	099	3,−4	96	−47	−29	86	−4,9
,7	88	−91	−40	099	6	94	−76	−66	88	−3,−5
-4,5,−8	89	−61	−31	101	−4,5,−8	93	−52	−28	84	3,−4,5,−8
,−5,7,10	91	−36	(−16)	111	−4,8	97	−30	−16	92	3,−4,7,10
-5,7	90	−84	−57	106	−4	95	−66	−31	97	7,−10
,10	91	−42	−28	115	6,7,−10	96	−35	−21	89	
0	89	−77	−36	123	−3,−5	91	−76	−43	108	4,7
,9,10	91	−92	−47	125	−5,7,10	96	−76	−46	107	−5,7,10
,7,10	88	−122	−59	058	3,10	96	−42	−23	100	3,−5,7
,5,7,8	84	−131	−50	135	4	93	−135	−51	101	3,4,7,−9
,4,−5,7,8,−9,−10	85	−112	−42	111	3,8,−9,−10	92	−98	−42	89	3,4,−5,−10
,9	89	−61	−23	107	8,10	94	−103	−37	102	−5,7,10
	87	−86	−42	087	10	90	−170	−119	98	
,−5,−7,10	86	(−63)	−28	128	−3,10	85	−120	−77	137	−3
,8,−10	88	−91	−29	085	4,10	91	−110	−59	103	4,5,7,−8
	88	−64	−60	079	−8	81	−115	−67	70	4,9
	87	−80	−37	088	3,6	91	−65	−50	95	6,10
,7,10	92	−53	−22	116	7,−8	91	−100	−54	104	−4,7
	89	−124	−48	122	−7	90	−122	−92	111	−4,−7
	89	−69	−37	052	3,−5,−6,10	86	−114	−88	65	3,−5
,4,6,−7,9	89	−202	−107	143	4,−7,−8	88	−246	−85	96	4,9
,9	91	−112	−44	141	4,−7	94	−107	−33	90	3,4
,6,9	98	−168	−138	153	−7	97	(137)	(19)	92	3,4,−8,9,10
,9,10	84	−96	(−26)	141	7,−8	86	−113	−45	92	−4,−5,7,9
4	91	−89	−39	173	−3,−4,−8	87	−84	−40	121	−4,7,−8
,−7	93	−213	−49	191	−8	88	−103	−36	(49)	3,9
,4,−7,−9,10	91	−91	−39	177	7,−8	83	−161	−61	139	−4
	93	−132	−55	134	8	84	(−18)	(−17)	122	−4,−6,−7,8

Table continued overleaf

TABLE A.13 (cont.)

REGRESSION ANALYSES OF TRADE FLOWS: PARAMETERS OF THE TOTAL INTERACTION MODEL[a]

	1960								
	Imports					Exports			
	R	b_d	b_s	b_1	Other	R	b_d	b_s	b
Dominican R.	98	−89	−85	77	3,−5,−7	82	(−12)	(−9)	6
Ecuador	96	−74	−18	144	−4,−5	77	(−40)	(−35)	
El Salvador									
Guatemala	96	−85	−36	113	3,−4,−5,8	83	−60	−35	9
Haiti						85	−98	−23	13
Honduras	97	(−46)	−37	157	−4,−5,−7, 8,−9	85	−71	−46	17
Mexico	90	−148	−50	94	−7,−8	91	−125	−46	11
Nicaragua						93	(−26)	(−48)	13
Panama	87	−65	−64	154	−4				
Paraguay									
Peru	95	−108	−28	177	−3,−4	84	−144	−56	11
Uruguay	84	−68	−20	115		91	−54	−14	8
Venezuela	88	−57	−20	107	−4	81	−119	−61	15
Bahamas									
Barbados									
Guyana	94	−113	−96	70	4	94	−160	−134	10
Jamaica	95	−39	−16	91	4,8				
N. Antilles	85	−122	−119	120		70	(−26)	(−7)	8
Surinam									
Trinidad	91	−111	−102	96	4				
Bahrein	88	(107)	(67)	(17)	4,−5	82	(1)	(1)	(2
Cyprus	82	−45	(−25)	24	3,−7,9,10	84	−33	−13	4
Iran	85	(−1)	(−11)	66	−7,9	86	−82	−46	10
Iraq	84	(−16)	−21	51	−5,−7	75	(−11)	(−13)	(4
Israel	85	−63	−27	98	−4,8	86	−90	−40	10
Jordan	91	−71	−68	81	3,−5,8				
Kuwait	81	(−22)	(−10)	(17)	3,−6,−7,9	91	−131	−36	(8
Lebanon	86	−79	−54	84		76	−98	−52	10
S. Arabia	78	(−67)	−56	(41)	−7	77	(39)	(−2)	6
Yemen						48	(5)	(1)	(−2
Syria	86	−62	−46	48	3,−4,−7,9	77	−81	−41	8
Egypt	83	−68	(−17)	71	3	76	−99	−28	4
Burma	90	−287	−264	96	4	85	−209	−181	(2
Khmer R.	91	−206	−198	113	5				
Sri Lanka	86	−73	(−10)	84	3,4	92	(91)	(22)	(4
Taiwan	90	−172	−144	169	8,−9	86	−100	−50	6

					1969					
		Imports					Exports			
Other	R	b_d	b_s	b_1	Other	R	b_d	b_s	b_1	Other
-10	92	-128	-61	113	3,-7,8	76	-95	(-33)	91	-8,-10
	95	-103	-41	141	-4,-8,-10	77	(-37)	-31	126	-4
	96	-109	-45	133	-4,-5,-6,-7,8	88	-102	-50	199	-3,-4,-5,-7,8
	95	-121	-52	143	-4,8	83	-60	-37	74	-5,-7,8
-4,-7	91	-84	-32	137	-7	86	-127	-64	117	-7,9
-4	95	-127	-55	160	-4,7,8	82	-119	-62	101	-7
3,-4,-5,-10	84	-147	-62	126	4,-8	89	-187	-79	117	7,-10
3,6,8,-10	95	-170	-46	148	-4,5,8	86	-101	-42	133	-5,6,-7,8,-10
	86	-121	-92	143	-4	75	-122	-118	(101)	-5,-7
	92	-108	-53	092	3,-6					
-6,9	91	-132	-52	176	7,-8	86	-98	-55	166	-4,-10
-6,9	92	-88	-28	135	-3,7,-8	80	(-68)	(-23)	82	-8,9
-3,6,7	90	-87	-42	157	7	80	-180	-96	148	6,7,8
	89	-128	-52	145	-3	80	-195	-71	115	-5,-8
	88	-139	-133	118	4	79	-156	-69	73	4
-7,-9	86	-75	-39	(28)	4,-7	76	-195	-100	138	4
	94	-143	-80	156	4,8	86	-185	-54	225	8,-9
3	83	-126	-50	139	-3	64	-82	-53	105	-10
	92	-99	-90	138	-7	74	(17)	(17)	96	
	92	-167	-105	164	4,7	76	-171	-107	83	
4,6,9,10	83	-113	-56	111	4,-7,8	84	(8)	(4)	114	-3,-5,6,-9
9,10	81	-71	(-19)	73	4,9,10	83	-126	-35	125	-3,9
●	88	-155	-58	127	3	83	-46	-28	83	4,-8
9	82	-86	-61	84	3,-7,8	73	-109	-69	71	6,9
-7	90	-102	-42	112	-6,7,10	91	-101	-48	119	-7
	84	-135	-78	80	3,8	89	-150	-56	(17)	-9,-10
3,4	84	-69	-25	66	3,-7	81	(112)	(15)	52	-6,9
4,-9,-10	90	-120	-80	77	3	82	-170	-104	80	-7
	76	-111	-66	49	3,-7	79	(21)	(-14)	98	4
	52	-116	(-22)	(30)		40	(-27)	(-24)	(68)	3,4
5,8,-9,-10	88	-120	-80	74	3	74	-103	-56	(-04)	3,-7
3,4,-7	90	-105	-43	64	-6	81	-106	-47	(27)	3,-8
3,4,-5	86	(-69)	-56	131		73	-151	-39	(-16)	3,9,10
	95	-334	-326	55	3,4,5,8,-10	88	-92	-54	145	4,5,-10
3,4,-5,-7	89	-182	-89	64	3,4,-8	78	(157)	(5)	(-10)	3,4,-7
	90	-149	-53	149	-4,8,-9,-10	85	-105	-52	135	5,-7,-10

Table continued overleaf

TABLE A.13 (*cont.*)
REGRESSION ANALYSES OF TRADE FLOWS: PARAMETERS OF
THE TOTAL INTERACTION MODEL[a]

	1960								
	Imports					*Exports*			
	R	b_d	b_s	b_1	*Other*	R	b_d	b_s	b_1
Hong Kong	83	−135	−91	90	3,−6	73	−93	−67	6
India	80	−113	−50	95	4,−9	80	−100	−48	5
Indonesia	81	(−74)	(−28)	46	−6	82	−183	−137	15
Korea	94	(−51)	(−15)	114	−4,−7,−9, −10				
Malaysia									
Pakistan	90	−127	−66	87	3,4,−7	81	−95	−46	7
Philippines	89	(−77)	(−71)	132	4,6,−10	88	(−87)	(−80)	20
Singapore	90	−154	−56	84	3,−7	86	−237	−77	18
Thailand	83	−66	(−25)	127		62	−107	−43	9
Vietnam	89	−140	−42	131	−4,5	88	−141	−49	14
Algeria	87	(−28)	(−24)	98	−4,5	85	−85	−62	4
Angola	89	−315	−34	186	−3,−4,6, −9	84	−110	−75	8
Cameroons	89	(15)	(14)	68	5,−7	96	−243	−239	20
Chad									
Congo									
Zaire	84	(−64)	(−41)	93	9	90	−210	−164	8
Ethiopia	82	−152	−135	(41)	−5	55	−162	−51	11
Gabon									
Gambia									
Ghana	83	(−91)	(−89)	132	4	91	−100	−92	12
Ivory Coast									
Kenya	85	−94	−72	(35)	3,10	89	(−76)	(−67)	13
Liberia	88	(51)	(11)	132	−4,−7				
Libya	83	−119	−58	88					
Malagasy R.	93	−141	116	87	5	84	(−109)	(−35)	8
Mali									
Morocco	87	(−28)	(−22)	46	3,−4,5,9	89	−116	−93	7
Mozambique	89	−148	−30	115	4,6,−7	79	−163	−27	5
Nigeria	76	(5)	(6)	87					
Senegal									
Sierra Leone									
Somalia									
Sudan						85	−189	−57	9
Togo									
Tunisia	91	(−26)	(−28)	74	3,5	83	−115	−51	3
Uganda						93	−101	−81	13
Zambia									

[a] Decimal points omitted to two decimal places.

					1969					
		Imports					Exports			
Other	R	b_d	b_s	b_1	Other	R	b_d	b_s	b_1	Other
4	85	−177	−118	102	3,4,5,7,10	88	−92	−68	100	−3,4
3,4	79	−146	−79	100		86	−139	−72	62	3,4,−5
−3	88	−187	−95	171						
	88	−202	−52	143		87	−98	−27	149	−9,−10
	87	−215	−104	151	4	86	−122	−69	127	4,7,−10
3,4,6,−10	91	−162	−49	135	3,4,−7	79	−85	−36	69	4,6
−3,−4,−5, −7,−9	87	(−33)	(−12)	155		84	−95	−31	124	−4,−9, −10
−3,7,8	85	−185	−87	130		84	−137	−72	108	4,−10
	84	−126	−74	133	5,−7	83	−132	−58	92	−7,−10
5,7,−10	87	−198	−98	160	−10	88	−178	−37	158	5,6,−10
5,9	89	−85	−58	120	−4,5	82	−148	−85	55	5
6	91	(77)	(69)	79	6,−7,10	77	−103	−34	126	6
−3,−4,5, −10	84	−71	−44	91	5	81	−190	−114	138	5,−10
	93	−141	−138	(72)		67	(−22)	(−9)	(−30)	4,5,9
	87	(−81)	(−70)	107	5	82	−111	−23	50	−6,−7,9
3,−7,9, −9	86	(0)	(19)	117	5,6,−7	83	(−48)	(−31)	55	3,9
−9	81	−127	−78	87	−6	72	−283	−111	156	−7,−10
	93	−85	−61	111	5,−7	77	−150	−60	168	−3,5, −10
	81	(9)	(89)	67	4	90	−160	−150	(09)	4,9,10
	87	(−16)	(−14)	77	6	78	(−38)	(−38)	151	4
	85	(12)	(11)	111	5	88	−121	−18	75	3,5,9
4,−10	88	−117	−102	120	4,−7	61	(−20)	(−36)	(15)	3,−7,9
	87	(32)	(11)	110	10	76	(96)	(5)	(30)	3,9
	87	−97	−55	84	−6,−7	84	(−19)	(−10)	84	9,10
5,−9,−10	83	(−92)	−80	57	3,5	88	(199)	(199)	(−143)	3,4,5,9
	85	(−25)	(40)	141	5	80	(188)	(103)	(−171)	3,5,−6, 9,10
5,−6,−7	90	−104	−54	101	3,5	86	−151	−87	94	5,−6
3,6	91	(−24)	(−23)	115	6	82	−190	−179	101	6,−7,10
	87	−68	−46	111	−7	90	−170	−88	175	10
	75	(−42)	(−34)	76	5	83	−52	−23	43	5,9
	84	(−61)	(−58)	68	3,4,−6	80	−342	−139	306	−3,4
	72	(57)	(46)	(07)	3,−7	51	−405	−380	156	
	79	−77	−64	65	3,8	82	−147	−48	129	−7
	88	(92)	(88)	59	5,9	80	(−67)	(−30)	97	5,9
5	91	−83	−40	65	3	82	−117	−50	34	3,−4,5
4,−5,6,−10	91	(−70)	(−71)	80	3,−7, −10	79	−123	−76	113	5,−7,−9, −10
	90	−180	−167	(43)	5	85	−215	−185	51	

TABLE A.14

SHIFT AND SHARE ANALYSES: COMMODITY TRADE

| | Imports | | | | Exports | | | |
| | One-digit | | Two-digit | | One-digit | | Two-digit | |
Country	Correlation	Redistribution	Correlation	Redistribution	Correlation	Redistribution	Correlation	Redistribution
U.S.	−0·12	22·9	−0·15	37·1	−0·86	11·5	−0·65	24·6
Canada	0·27	15·6	0·18	28·8	−0·22	31·0	−0·11	41·5
Japan	0·82	13·8	0·52	25·5	0·67	18·0	−0·11	43·8
U.K.	−0·90	18·7	−0·63	27·9	−0·92	3·9	−0·77	27·8
Austria	−0·71	12·1	−0·64	26·6	0·73	14·9	−0·54	36·1
Belgium	−0·56	16·6	−0·22	21·1	−0·83	25·2	−0·30	48·6
Denmark	0·09	11·5	−0·13	30·4	−0·95	20·3	−0·41	30·8
France	0·01	24·9	−0·13	40·4	−0·51	13·0	−0·45	32·4
W. Germany	0·33	14·5	−0·10	30·0	−0·42	6·8	−0·28	23·1
Italy	0·52	11·4	0·08	26·0	0·81	14·6	−0·15	27·1
Netherlands	−0·31	9·1	−0·30	27·4	0·24	9·0	−0·38	28·7
Norway	−0·90	9·1	−0·61	29·3	0·33	16·7	0·36	37·3
Sweden	−0·85	9·8	−0·45	27·7	−0·12	12·8	−0·33	26·6
Switzerland	−0·20	10·7	−0·49	16·5	−0·62	4·9	−0·16	15·1
Finland	−0·88	6·2	−0·26	26·0	−0·27	20·6	−0·85	36·7
Greece	−0·88	4·9	−0·56	26·6	−0·23	27·3	−0·19	45·3
Iceland	−0·87	11·5	−0·88	37·1	0·07	9·7	−0·47	11·0
Ireland	0·11	12·3	−0·07	24·0	0·15	16·1	−0·47	29·7
Portugal	0·08	7·8	−0·25	27·3	0·59	12·8	−0·24	33·5
Spain	0·63	20·2	0·34	48·4	0·38	32·4	0·47	42·8
Turkey	−0·93	14·2	−0·80	34·4	−0·16	5·9	0·47	23·7
Australia	0·72	13·3	0·49	22·6	0·96	12·9	0·73	26·1
New Zealand	0·77	31·4	−0·15	34·4	0·92	9·5	0·76	19·8
S. Africa	−0·98	12·3	−0·22	15·1	−0·24	18·2	−0·19	26·1

Argentina	−0·94	19·2	−0·91	42·4	−0·73	12·2	−0·28	21·7
Brazil	−0·99	43·1	−0·76	32·9	−0·90	20·9	−0·79	42·5
Colombia	−0·99	10·8	−0·51	37·4	−0·89	12·8	−0·70	20·6
Costa Rica	−0·67	6·1	−0·16	23·4	0·13	18·9	−0·40	25·8
Ecuador	−0·70	42·5	−0·30	83·6	−0·99	2·1	−0·93	9·6
El Salvador	−0·66	11·8	−0·23	21·2	−0·92	28·2	−0·85	34·3
Guatemala	−0·56	13·5	−0·14	16·6	−0·74	35·1	−0·63	46·7
Honduras	0·04	7·5	0·07	20·2	0·98	10·2	0·74	16·6
Mexico	−0·98	3·8	−0·32	17·6	0·02	12·0	0·09	26·2
Nicaragua	0·35	7·9	−0·16	26·4	0·25	24·0	0·19	44·2
Barbados	−0·43	9·1			−0·92	38·6	−0·87	51·3
Guadeloupe	0·58	8·6	−0·09	32·5	−1·00	4·4	−0·61	37·6
Guyana	−0·83	5·2	−0·75	19·2	−0·20	20·7	0·08	27·2
B. Honduras	−0·36	7·1	−0·29	25·7	0·15	39·6	−0·18	37·3
Jamaica	−0·32	7·6	−0·06	14·1	−0·14	14·2	−0·16	16·6
N. Antilles	−1·00	8·2	−0·99	11·7	−0·99	5·0	−1·00	6·8
Surinam	−0·77	10·4	−0·50	40·5	0·83	17·1	0·75	23·0
Trinidad	0·12	18·7	0·30	26·7	−0·97	9·7	−0·99	7·6
Cyprus	−0·18	14·9	−0·11	23·7	−0·35	31·9	−0·22	38·8
Israel	0·34	11·5	−0·39	34·0	0·78	16·6	−0·68	54·9
Yemen P.D.R.	−0·91	27·6	−0·94	39·1	−0·53	17·6	−0·92	22·1
Egypt	−0·86	7·9	−0·85	30·7	−0·86	43·3	−0·75	37·7
Afghanistan	−0·87	20·3	−0·59	30·8	−0·47	19·6	−0·85	27·5
Burma	−0·99	26·0	−0·97	41·7	−0·99	19·5	−0·98	43·0
Sri Lanka	−0·73	10·5	−0·07	24·8	−0·99	1·5	−0·98	4·9
Hong Kong	0·74	9·2	−0·12	27·6	−0·20	63·9	−0·13	74·7
India	−0·61	13·3	−0·26	29·7	−0·95	10·0	−0·83	32·6
Korea	0·23	25·9	0·07	50·0	−0·06	63·8	0·02	75·5
Malaya	−0·76	12·6	−0·59	22·4	−0·97	14·4	−0·02	18·8
Pakistan	−0·91	20·8	−0·73	43·3	−0·49	30·9	−0·13	32·7
Philippines	−0·82	3·6	−0·23	28·8	−0·44	15·4	−0·57	36·1
Sabah	0·17	16·8	−0·21	32·3	0·97	6·9	0·74	35·8

Table continued overleaf

TABLE A.14 (cont.)
SHIFT AND SHARE ANALYSES: COMMODITY TRADE

Country	Imports One-digit Correlation	Redistribution	Imports Two-digit Correlation	Redistribution	Exports One-digit Correlation	Redistribution	Exports Two-digit Correlation	Redistribution
Sarawak	−0·97	14·1	−0·99	37·0	−0·86	25·2	−0·84	38·4
Singapore	−0·84	25·6	−0·72	33·8	−0·85	12·7	−0·83	26·5
Thailand	0·00	17·8	−0·15	33·5	−0·57	18·3	−0·18	29·2
Cameroon	0·18	17·1	−0·11	23·5	0·83	6·8	0·96	12·6
Dahomey	−0·19	10·4	−0·39	29·7	−0·82	38·6	−0·89	52·8
Gambia	0·55	11·1	0·80	31·4	−0·97	37·7	−0·70	40·8
Ghana	−0·35	12·7	−0·36	35·4	0·97	6·1	0·80	20·9
Ivory Coast					0·96	19·0	0·85	22·4
Liberia	−0·83	4·0	−0·23	27·1	1·00	1·4	0·41	36·0
Libya	0·74	5·8	0·06	31·5	−0·32	99·9	−0·32	99·9
Malagasy R	−0·79	12·5	−0·23	17·5	−0·84	8·0	0·23	11·0
Mauritius	−0·59	15·3	−0·43	26·3		0·0		3·2
Morocco	−0·85	17·6	−0·27	26·5	−0·87	10·0	−0·66	20·3
Niger	0·35	15·0	0·12	20·9	−0·01	5·6	−0·65	14·5
Nigeria	−0·92	17·5	−0·35	35·4	−0·52	45·4	−0·27	49·7
Reunion	0·78	8·8	0·70	80·6	−0·96	3·4	−0·08	2·9
Senegal	−0·72	11·3	−0·21	24·6	−0·96	27·7	−0·92	35·7
Sierra Leone	0·58	11·5	0·07	30·3	0·92	18·9	−0·32	84·0
Sudan	−0·91	6·6	−0·29	12·1	−1·00	1·2	−0·30	9·7
Togo	−0·55	9·1	0·01	13·6	0·62	18·3	0·45	39·3
Fiji	−0·44	12·8	−0·36	48·1	−0·15	18·2	0·24	26·3
New Guinea	0·92	10·3	0·47	31·6	0·01	37·5	0·06	51·1
Papua	0·94	11·8	0·34	14·8	0·99	13·1	0·70	16·2
Cuba	−0·93	27·9	−0·93	26·9	−0·99	9·9	−0·90	12·0

TABLE A.15
SHIFT AND SHARE ANALYSES: TRADE PARTNERS

Country	Correlation		Redistribution	
	Imports	Exports	Imports	Exports
U.S.	0·76	−0·08	20·8	11·1
U.K.	−0·84	−0·09	18·1	17·0
Austria	−0·73	−0·19	10·2	16·9
Belgium	−0·53	0·49	14·9	20·9
Denmark	−0·49	−0·45	15·9	18·3
France	0·64	−0·06	25·4	23·1
W. Germany	0·24	0·44	20·8	14·5
Italy	0·21	0·16	20·9	17·2
Netherlands	0·19	0·06	15·8	17·1
Norway	−0·47	0·14	16·1	14·4
Sweden	−0·54	−0·09	15·4	12·3
Switzerland	−0·53	−0·04	8·1	12·0
Canada	−0·83	0·58	9·7	13·1
Japan	0·24	0·82	19·2	18·8
Finland	−0·44	0·13	16·8	17·1
Greece	0·09	0·17	18·2	20·0
Iceland	−0·70	0·32	15·7	25·1
Ireland	0·97	0·27	9·0	12·2
Malta	−0·09	−0·14	19·8	29·5
Portugal	−0·25	0·37	18·0	17·7
Spain	0·49	0·10	20·1	22·7
Turkey	−0·95	−0·61	12·4	19·5
Yugoslavia	0·03	0·48	21·3	20·1
Australia	−0·67	−0·47	21·7	27·9
New Zealand	−0·96	−0·13	22·3	19·0

Country	Correlation		Redistribution	
	Imports	Exports	Imports	Exports
Argentina	−0·95	−0·69	21·8	22·0
Bolivia	−0·48	0·18	16·9	18·8
Brazil	−0·94	−0·93	16·9	21·8
Chile	−0·90	−0·73	13·9	29·2
Colombia	−0·98	−0·99	16·3	29·7
Costa Rica	−0·69	−0·29	26·7	32·2
Dominican R.	0·75	−0·44	14·3	35·3
Ecuador	−0·75	−0·76	19·1	33·6
El Salvador	−0·73	−0·81	23·8	34·1
Guatemala	−0·87	−0·80	26·8	43·3
Haiti	−0·98	0·76	19·3	22·1
Honduras	−0·26	0·54	27·2	27·6
Mexico	−0·99	−0·26	9·5	9·4
Nicaragua	−0·40	−0·35	26·5	23·9
Panama	−0·78	0·94	25·5	25·5
Paraguay	−0·22		19·1	13·7
Peru	−0·95	0·17	24·9	23·0
Uruguay	−0·91	−0·81	28·8	32·0
Venezuela	−0·99	−0·76	12·2	20·9
Bahamas	0·67	0·98	26·0	19·6
Barbados	−0·16	−0·72	31·5	33·3
Bermuda	0·67	0·10	33·4	78·9
Falkland I.			64·4	19·3
Greenland			23·1	27·4
Guadeloupe	−0·99		8·7	22·0

Table continued overleaf

TABLE A.15 (cont.)
SHIFT AND SHARE ANALYSES: TRADE PARTNERS

Country	Correlation Imports	Correlation Exports	Redistribution Imports	Redistribution Exports	Country	Correlation Imports	Correlation Exports	Redistribution Imports	Redistribution Exports
S. Africa	−0·29	−0·04	19·5	26·1	Fr. Guiana	0·95	−0·82	20·1	55·8
Guyana	−0·86	−0·65	18·4	26·0	Sri Lanka	−0·84	0·01	21·0	20·5
B. Honduras	−0·45	−0·50	40·7	33·2	Taiwan	−0·08	0·09	29·2	38·9
Jamaica	0·15	−0·37	31·3	23·2	Hong Kong	0·65	−0·60	18·6	29·0
Leeward I.	0·27		26·7	54·1	India	−0·97	−0·16	25·3	29·3
Martinique	−0·95	−0·99	13·2	12·7	Indonesia	−0·92	0·45	27·7	27·9
N. Antilles	−0·97	−0·09	51·3	31·2	Korea	0·34	−0·10	29·9	48·9
Panama C.Z.	−0·81	−0·98	65·7	50·9	Laos	−0·78		47·3	44·7
St. Pierre/M.			9·6	67·3	Pakistan	−0·96	−0·02	18·6	28·4
Surinam	−0·79	−0·28	13·4	36·0	Philippines	−0·89	−0·81	26·9	20·1
Trinidad	−0·60	−0·16	27·0	46·3	Ryukyus			6·4	2·0
Windward I.	0·25		26·1	8·4	Singapore	−0·26	0·03	44·0	62·2
Bahrein	−0·09	−0·23	58·0	70·0	Thailand	−0·08	−0·07	20·4	30·9
Cyprus	−0·37	0·01	15·4	18·3	Vietnam	0·12	−0·04	26·9	29·6
Iran	−0·54	−0·09	12·7	45·9	Afars-Issas	−0·60		49·1	83·6
Iraq	−0·92	−0·60	37·3	36·3	Algeria	−0·99	−0·85	32·9	30·5
Israel	0·79	0·43	14·8	22·5	Angola	0·65	0·17	16·3	31·2
Jordan	−0·34	0·01	19·0	31·2	Cameroons	−0·86	−0·84	20·9	28·8
Kuwait	−0·36	−0·86	19·0	28·6	Cape Verde I.	−0·35		26·6	71·0
Lebanon	−0·67	0·43	16·1	27·2	C. African R.	−0·86	−0·68	28·6	44·0
Oman	−0·02	−0·30	73·1	84·5	Chad	−0·91	−0·94	40·7	18·1
Qatar	−0·44	−0·72	33·6	52·7	Congo	−0·99	−0·29	34·2	39·9
S. Arabia	0·58	−0·46	23·8	38·4	Zaire	−0·86	−0·96	24·6	23·0
Yemen, P.D.R.	−0·91	−0·01	31·3	57·3	Dahomey	−0·97	−0·95	42·0	43·8
Syria	−0·87	−0·61	32·5	42·9	Eq. Guinea	−0·65		55·7	73·7
Trucial S.	0·97	0·56	26·9	59·9	Ethiopia	−0·69	−0·02	19·0	24·9

Egypt	−0·95	0·20	30·6	26·0
Yemen, A. R.	−0·61	−0·34	63·1	49·5
Afghanistan	0·57	0·22	28·8	26·1
Brunei	0·07	−0·99	57·8	5·3
Burma	−0·91	0·10	21·5	35·8
Khmer R.	−0·97	−0·07	26·5	37·4
Kenya	−0·52	−0·06	32·7	44·4
Liberia	−0·83	−0·56	43·6	35·3
Libya	0·78	0·76	21·1	40·4
Malagasy R.	−0·99	−0·39	22·5	33·6
Mali	−0·98	−0·81	40·2	24·2
Mauritania	−0·97	0·14	46·4	75·3
Mauritius	−0·92	−0·26	39·2	14·3
Morocco	−0·98	−0·64	16·3	17·1
Mozambique	−0·27	−0·15	28·7	28·7
Niger	−0·48	−0·92	29·4	22·9
Nigeria	−0·82	−0·84	27·4	25·9
Reunion	−0·51		15·9	16·5
São Tomé			47·2	37·5
Senegal	−0·99	−0·99	40·7	24·4
Sierra Leone	−0·88	−0·84	32·7	10·1

Gabon	−0·83	−0·67	30·2	34·6
Gambia	−0·67	0·23	23·2	47·0
Ghana	−0·92	−0·95	26·6	18·2
Port Guinea	0·43		33·3	22·8
Guinea R.	−0·98	−0·88	41·1	64·5
Ivory Coast	−0·96	−0·59	33·8	29·5
Somalia	−0·78	−0·43	39·2	70·5
Sudan	−0·68	−0·43	20·3	30·5
Togo	−0·81	−0·64	35·6	50·8
Tunisia	−0·98	−0·48	26·5	38·1
Uganda	−0·14	0·01	66·2	40·3
U. Volta	−0·86	−0·23	35·2	75·0
Faeroe I.			5·4	34·3
Fiji	−0·04	−0·53	31·0	28·0
Gibraltar	−0·75		35·3	61·1
Nauru			15·3	27·9
New Caledonia	0·89		21·4	14·0
New Hebrides			14·3	32·2
Papua			19·0	45·6
W. Samoa	−0·36		18·6	51·2

Appendix II
Commodity Categories

One-Digit

1. Food and Live Animals
2. Beverages and Tobacco
3. Inedible Crude Materials (not fuels)
4. Mineral Fuels
5. Animal and Vegetable Oils and Fats
6. Chemicals
7. Manufactured Goods
8. Machinery and Transport Equipment
9. Miscellaneous Manufactures

Two-Digit[a]

1.
   1. Live Animals
   2. Meat/Meat Preparations
   3. Dairy Products and Eggs
   4. Fish/Fish Preparations
   5. Cereals
   6. Fruit and Vegetables
   7. Sugar and Honey
   8. Coffee, Tea, Cocoa, Spices
   9. Animal Feeding Stuffs
   10. Miscellaneous Foods
2.
   11. Beverages
   12. Tobacco
3.
   13. Undressed Hides, Skins, Furs
   14. Oil Seeds, Nuts, Kernels
   15. Crude Rubber
   16. Woods, Lumber, Cork
   17. Pulp and Waste Paper
   18. Textile Fibres
   19. Crude Fertilisers and Minerals
   20. Metal Ores and Scrap

   21. Crude Materials N.E.S.
4.
   22. Coal and Coke
   23. Petroleum and Products
   24. Gas
   25. Electric Energy
5.
   26. Animal Oils and Fats
   27. Fixed Vegetable Oils and Fats
   28. Processed Oils and Fats
6.
   29. Chemical Elements and Compounds
   30. Mineral Tar and Coal, Petrol, Gas Chemicals
   31. Dyeing, Tanning, Colouring Materials
   32. Medicinal, Pharmaceutical Products
   33. Essential Oils, Perfume Materials
   34. Manufactured Fertilisers
   35. Explosives
   36. Chemicals N.E.S.

[a]The figure in the left-hand column refers to the one-digit classification.

7. 37. Leather, Fur Manufactures
    38. Rubber Manufactures
    39. Wood and Cork Manufactures (excl. Furniture)
    40. Paper and Paperboard
    41. Textile Yarns, Fabrics
    42. Non-Metallic Mineral Manufactures N.E.S.
    43. Non-Ferrous Metals
    44. Metal Manufactures N.E.S.
8. 45. Machinery (not Electric)

    46. Electrical Machinery, Appliances
    47. Transport Equipment
9. 48. Sanitary, Plumbing, Heating, Lighting Fixtures
    49. Furniture
    50. Travel Goods, Handbags
    51. Clothing
    52. Footwear
    53. Professional, Scientific Equipment
    54. Miscellaneous Manufactures N.E.S.

Three-Digit[a]

1. 1. Live Animals
2. 2. Fresh, Chilled, Frozen Meat
    3. Dried, Salted, Smoked
    4. Other Meats
3. 5. Milk and Cream
    6. Butter
    7. Cheese
    8. Eggs
4. 9. Fresh and Simply Preserved Fish
    10. Other Fish
5. 11. Unmilled Wheat
    12. Rice
    13. Unmilled Barley
    14. Unmilled Maize
    15. Other Unmilled Cereals
    16. Wheat Meal and Flour
    17. Other Meals and Flours
    18. Cereal Preparations
6. 19. Fresh Fruits and Nuts
    20. Dried Fruit
    21. Preserved Fruit
    22. Fresh, Frozen Vegetables
    23. Preserved Vegetables
7. 24. Sugar and Honey
    25. Confectionery
8. 26. Coffee
    27. Cocoa

    28. Chocolate
    29. Tea and Mate
    30. Spices
9. 31. Animal Feeding Stuffs
10. 32. Margarine and Shortening
    33. Food Preparations N.E.S.
11. 34. Non-alcoholic Beverages
    35. Alcoholic Beverages
    36. Unmanufactured Tobacco
    37. Tobacco Manufactures
13. 38. Undressed Hides and Skins
    39. Undressed Furs
14. 40. Oil Seeds, Nuts, Kernels
15. 41. Crude Rubber
16. 42. Fuel Wood and Charcoal
    43. Wood in the Rough
    44. Wood Shaped
    45. Raw and Waste Cork
17. 46. Pulp and Waste Paper
18. 47. Silk
    48. Wool, Animal Hair
    49. Cotton
    50. Jute
    51. Vegetable Fibres (not Cotton, Jute)

[a]The figure in the left-hand column refers to the two-digit classification.

52. Synthetic and Regenerated Fibres
53. Textile Wastes
19. 54. Crude Fertilisers
55. Other Crude Minerals
20. 56. Iron Ore
57. Iron and Steel Scrap
58. Nonferrous Ores
59. Nonferrous Scrap
60. Silver, Platinum Ore
61. Uranium, Thorium Ore
21. 62. Crude Animal Materials N.E.S.
63. Crude Vegetable Materials N.E.S.
22. 64. Coal and Coke
23. 65. Crude Petroleum
66. Petroleum Products
24. 67. Gas
25. 68. Electric Energy
26. 69. Animal Oils and Fats
27. 70. Fixed Vegetable Oils and Fats
28. 71. Processed Oils and Fats
29. 72. Chemical Elements and Compounds
30. 73. Mineral Tar and Coal, Petrol, Gas Chemicals
31. 74. Synthetic Organic Dyestuffs
75. Dyeing, Tanning Extracts
76. Pigments, Paints, Varnishes
32. 77. Medicinal, Pharmaceutical Products
33. 78. Essential Oils, Perfume Materials
79. Perfumery, Cosmetics
80. Soaps, Cleansers
34. 81. Manufactured Fertilisers
35. 82. Explosives
36. 83. Chemicals N.E.S.
37. 84. Leather
85. Leather Manufactures
86. Tanned, Dressed Furs
38. 87. Rubber Materials
88. Rubber Articles N.E.S.

39. 89. Veneers, Plywoods
90. Wood Manufactures N.E.S.
91. Cork Manufactures
40. 92. Paper
93. Paper Articles
41. 94. Textile Yarn and Thread
95. Woven Cotton Fabrics
96. Woven Fabrics other than cotton
97. Tulle, Lace, Embroidery
98. Special Fabrics
99. Made-up Textile Articles
100. Floor Coverings, Tapestries
42. 101. Lime, Cement
102. Clay Construction Materials
103. Mineral Manufactures N.E.S.
104. Glass
105. Glassware
106. Pottery
107. Pearls
43. 108. Silver, Platinum
109. Copper
110. Nickel
111. Aluminium
112. Lead
113. Zinc
114. Tin
115. Uranium
116. Other Non-Ferrous Metals
44. 117. Metal Manufactures N.E.S.
45. 118. Power Generating Machinery
119. Agricultural Machinery
120. Office Machines
121. Metalworking Machinery
122. Textile and Leather Machinery
123. Special Industrial Machines
124. Machinery N.E.S.
46. 125. Electric Power Machinery

Index

207